FIVE STARS!

HOW TO BECOME A FILM CRITIC, THE WORLD'S GREATEST JOB

FIVE STARS!

HOW TO BECOME A FILM CRITIC, THE WORLD'S GREATEST JOB

by Christopher Null

sutro press

Also by Christopher Null

Half Mast: A Novel

Published by Sutro Press, San Francisco, California.
www.sutropress.com

Printed in the United States of America

Library of Congress Control Number: 2004097261

ISBN 0-9720981-1-9

10 9 8 7 6 5 4 3 2 1

First Edition

For the filmcritic.com gang

PREFACE

So you want to be a film critic?

Do you see every movie that hits your local multiplex? Are you the office gossip when it comes to celebrity weddings and breakups? Or maybe you just love to riff Monty Python lines with the guy in the cubicle next door.

Or maybe you just really love the movies.

While all of these traits are great, none of them are what being a film critic is really about.

To become a great critic, you need the following characteristics, in this order:

- You have seen a *ton* of movies and are able to separate them into good and bad. (If you love every movie you see or even most of them, you aren't cut out for this line of work.)
- You have the ability to write well.
- You have the time and inclination to watch and review five or more films a week. (I typically review one movie every day, at a minimum. In the past I've reviewed up to four in a day.)
- Finally, you need an outlet for publishing your work.

This book will help you develop all of these.

In Chapters 2 and 3, you'll learn a bit about filmmaking and film history. In the appendix, you'll find recommended homework to help get you up to speed on any classic and not-so-classic films you might have missed.

In Chapters 4 through 7, you'll learn how to construct a movie review and how to approach different styles of entertainment writing, including celebrity interviews.

Finally, Chapter 1 and Chapters 8 through 10 will help you find a place to publish your work (or create one of your own). Chapters 11 through 15 discuss how to get access to screenings, and etiquette once you are there. Also, these chapters provide other support materials for the aspiring critic. I'll even try to throw in some advice about finding time to see all these movies throughout the book.

I hope you enjoy the book, and I hope it aids you in your quest to become a feature film critic. I love to hear from readers and look forward to some of you even joining the ranks of filmcritic.com contributors. I've tried to create a book that answers every question you might have about becoming a film critic and mastering the trade. If I've overlooked something, or if you have any other comments about the text, please drop me a note.

Christopher Null
Editor in Chief, filmcritic.com
null@filmcritic.com

TABLE OF CONTENTS

CHAPTER 1:
THE MARKET FOR FILM CRITICISM

I am the first to admit there is something absurd about film criticism.

Here is a person who saw the same movie as everyone else, and just because he puts pen to paper, his thoughts are somehow more valid than yours? Familiar names like Roger Ebert and Pauline Kael somehow give an *opinion* about movies more weight. It's ridiculous. How does a critic know if you're going to like a movie or not?

So why do critics exist? Because they strive to entertain us and enlighten us with their commentary about the movies. When we find a critic we often agree with, we find someone who can help us connect with entertainment we would otherwise miss. We also avoid costly mistakes by skipping movies that look good on paper but which stink in reality.

Is film criticism art, as Kael liked to think? Depends on who you ask and what you read. There are critics who strive merely to entertain us with jokes, using a fictitious byline and broad humor in their writing, telling us little about the actual film. There are those that deeply analyze a movie, craft thoughtful prose, and place movies in a societal context, but without any entertainment value. And there are those rare critics who do both. This is when criticism becomes an art form on par with the movies themselves.

So does film criticism matter? That is, does the opinion of a film critic have any effect on the success or failure of a film?

Movie stars, directors, and producers are fond of bashing film critics, labeling them as trolls and bottom-feeders riding on their celebrity. When a badly-reviewed movie performs well in theaters, Hollywood laughs off film critics as powerless and ridiculous wastes of time, out of touch with the preferences of mainstream America. Fair enough: Many critics are elitists, sure, but most of us are just tired of seeing bad movies – we want to open people's eyes to the real gems of cinema.

But when a movie bombs at the box office, who takes the blame? Why, it's the press! The critics viciously assaulted the talent and didn't give it a fighting chance. They had it in for the film from the start. Jealous, malicious, whatever.

This, of course, is bollocks, but it brings forward a salient point: Do film critics have power in the business, and is there indeed a market for film criticism?

11

You better believe it.

Consider the story of Terry Gilliam's *Brazil*, which Universal Pictures refused to release due to its difficult themes and downer of an ending. When the Los Angeles Film Critics Circle declared it the best film of 1985 – without the film ever being released in theaters – Universal was shamed into putting the picture out. The movie now stands as one of the most highly-regarded films ever made, and Gilliam continues to acknowledge the L.A. critics as invaluable in helping *Brazil* get released.

SO WHAT ABOUT MY PROSPECTS?

How many people do you personally know who are actually employed as film critics?

Unless you're reading this book because you're a relative of mine (hi, Mom!), the answer is likely *zero*.

In the United States, there are about 200 major daily newspapers (out of 1,400 total dailies), plus an estimated 200 alternative weeklies which are big enough to have a critic on staff — not even a full-time movie reviewer, just someone who works there who occasionally reviews movies, too. Assuming each outlet employs three film critics, there are roughly 1,200 jobs in the newsprint market for movie reviewers.

Add in magazine critics (maybe 100, and that's optimistic) and broadcast and radio TV critics (probably another 300, and few of those are full-timers), and you've got a grand total of 1,600 jobs in the mainstream media.

The Census Bureau reports there are 280 million people in the U.S. Roughly half of them wish they could be a critic.

In other words: Competition is *intense*.

Now the good news: The internet has opened up the field dramatically. It's commonly said by both enthusiasts and naysayers that anyone can throw together a website and become a self-styled "film critic."

It's true. You've probably seen a lot of these sites yourselves. Many of them are heinously ugly, uninformed, rarely updated, or simply illiterate. Sadly, this is the norm and not the exception on the net. To be honest, there are perhaps a dozen film-oriented websites worth reading. At most.

For a critic starting today, chances are you'll hit the internet to publish your first reviews. If not for your own site, it'll be at an outlet like filmcritic.com (and even we would never take on a new critic without some sample reviews under their belts). You'll have to, because no newspaper or TV station on the planet will hire you without experience. Once you have a few years worth of clips written, this picture might change, but it's foolish to think you're going to replace Ebert simply because you send the *Chicago Sun-Times* a resume.

This is a long-winded way of saying this book is focused primarily on teaching newcomers how to break into internet criticism and grow a career from there. If you can't get a job from an existing net site, start your own. Seriously: It's easier than you think, and with a few hours of training you'll be able to put together a site that rivals many of the poorly-designed pages out there.

So, that's the good news. The bad news is that no one is exactly clamoring for more movie review websites. No offense to any of them, but following in the wake of filmcritic.com are sites like efilmcritic.com, entertainmentnutz. com, filmjerk.com, ecinemacenter.com, and countless, countless more. Who could possibly have time to visit all of these sites?

If you launch jimmysmithmoviereviews.com, don't expect a lot of traffic out of the gate. In the first month of filmcritic.com (that was 1995, when we were one of the first entertainment-oriented websites on the planet), we got about 100 visitors a day. I probably accounted for 10 of those visitors. Back then, there weren't that many websites, and there definitely weren't that many people with internet access, so those other 90 were probably just people who got there out of curiosity, random clicking, or sheer accident. The newcomer to the scene can expect a similar dearth of traffic while the site gets established. (I'll discuss how to build this up in later chapters.)

The nefarious flipside of the glut of review sites is the gossip site phenomenon. I loathe these websites. They (and they'll remain nameless) use anonymous writers who attend test screenings (where unfinished versions of films are screened for test audiences), read leaked scripts, and report on unfiltered rumors. There's not a lot of journalism going on here, and from what I've seen, the reporting is wrong more often than it's right. Sadly, Hollywood takes this junk seriously, believing it contributes to "buzz," thus feeding the monster until it grows bigger and bigger and bigger. Lately this power has waned, but the gossipmongers still hold Hollywood's ear: Much more so than the review sites, even the big ones.

This book won't tell you how to launch a gossip site or get your invective published on one. If that's what you're after, make up some stories and plaster them on the net. If you get sued for libel, don't come crying to me.

BREAKING IN - STEP BY STEP

Even if you're determined to ignore my advice (and who would blame you) and want to try getting a "Real Job" as a film critic at a newspaper or magazine, you need the same things in hand as you would to approach a website:

1. Clips
2. A resume
3. Professionalism

Clips are simple enough to obtain. Read this book. Rent a couple of videos or go to the movies. Write a few reviews. Three is a good number. Show them to your friends and demand honest feedback. Read Chapters 2 through 7 again. Write some more.

When you have three excellent reviews that you're not afraid to show the world (*not* the first three you wrote), work on your resume. Play up any writing experience and entertainment background you have. We get resumes all the time from people who tout their experience in retail sales or financial services. Doesn't really hurt, but it doesn't do a lot of good. If you're looking for a full-time writing gig (with a salary and benefits), you won't even get a return call.

Finally, there's professionalism. We get applications from young and old alike that are filled with typos and display the worst understanding of what filmcritic.com is all about. You need to research the outlet you're trying to get your foot into. Do the critics have a sarcastic style or a serious tone? How long are the reviews? Do they specialize in a certain genre? Do they have any nagging holes in their coverage (say, foreign films or independents) that you might be able to fill? Nothing gets my attention quicker than an applicant who has thoroughly searched our archives and submits a well-written review for a recent film that managed to slip by us. A candidate like this is a shoo-in every time, and we usually publish his sample review if it's decent.

FINDING OUTLETS

So you know about filmcritic.com, obviously. But where else can you find media outlets willing to publish your reviews?

For a budding film critic, the internet is far and away your best bet. Chapter 8 provides ideas on where you might look to sell your work as an amateur film critic, along with advice on how to approach those editors.

You might also consider your local newspapers. If you live in a small community, you might be able to parlay some basic experience in film writing into a regular job at your local daily.

If you live in a larger city, there's not a lot of point in trying to get a job at the major newspaper in town unless you have substantial experience in film and publishing, and even then these jobs are extremely hard to come by. If an opening does occur, it is typically awarded to a staff writer transferring from another department (for example, A.O. Scott, film critic for *The New York Times*, was the paper's former book critic). Same goes for television and radio. These are jobs where your experience and, more to the point, your contacts will dictate your success in the field. If you are reading this book, you really needn't bother wasting a lot of time, energy, postage, and angst applying for work at outlets like these. When you've long outgrown the information here and sold this book at a secondhand shop, *then* you should try to make the move to the big time.

Don't feel, however, that internet film criticism is a second-class occupation. Just because it's comparably easy to get into doesn't mean it's easier to *do*. Many internet outlets have standards just as high as a newspaper, though they operate on budgets a fraction of their size. You'd also be surprised at how many people rely on internet reviews as their primary source of entertainment news. Filmcritic.com has a readership on par with some of the largest newspapers in America. When you consider that only a small fraction of newspaper readers actually read them for movie reviews while *everyone* who comes to filmcritic.com is there for the reviews, the real power and reach of internet criticism becomes obvious.

Unfortunately, equally many internet outlets are terribly low-budget affairs with no real resources and even less interest in quality journalism. Movie fans slap together pages and scribble down the first thoughts out of their heads, then brand their prose as a movie review. Some people review movies based on the previews alone! Since the costs are so low and the intellectual capital required to do this even lower, sites like these plague the internet, though they are often abandoned and can be found in various stages of neglect.

The fallout is that Hollywood's publicity machine sees makeshift movie review sites and gossip sites (as discussed above) as the norm, and they're right. Publicists know that no one can start a magazine without a whole lot of money, and that presupposes that quality and readership will necessarily follow. They are also trained by years of dealing with the print medium; the internet is barely 10 years old, but it pales in comparison to well over a century of newspapers being with us. So print gets publicists' attention by default. An internet site, by contrast, is assumed to be a juvenile hobby until it is proven otherwise.

This effect makes getting access to advance movie screenings in your particular market difficult, even for respectable critics. You're guilty until proven innocent, so plan for this in advance by starting out as a professional and remaining that way.

I'll further discuss the tricks and tactics of getting access to screenings and press material in Chapter 10. But before you do that, you need to write a few reviews. And before *that*, you need to understand a bit about what you're writing about. I'll get to that in Chapter 2.

CHAPTER 2:
UNDERSTANDING FILM HISTORY

There's nothing worse than a film critic who doesn't know what he's talking about.

As with any career, if you intend to write about movies, you have to understand a little of the history of your field in order to make sense of it. The reason for this is not so you can look erudite and show off your knowledge of obscure cinema. It's because your reader really wants to know how *Gladiator* stacks up against *Ben-Hur*. Or how *Star Wars: Episode I - Attack of the Clones* looks in comparison to *The Empire Strikes Back*. Or if *Daredevil* is a rip-off of *Spider-Man*. Or how any gangster movie measures up to *The Godfather*. None of this should sound elitist. They are just common sense comparisons that deserve to be made.

The same goes for cast and crew. When Sandra Bullock inevitably makes a transition away from the dippy, somewhat pathetic character she plays in every film she's in, it will be important to have an understanding of the highlights (and lowlights) of her career in order to say something intelligent about the switch. Same goes for directors. The careers of Martin Scorsese and Steven Spielberg, among others, are defined by the way they have grown over time – including both the smash hits and the flops. Spielberg, in particular, surprises us with the way he combines crowd-pleasing action and humor with art-house thoughtfulness and the occasional misfire. Just watching his progression of films alone (in chronological order) is an excellent primer for understanding films and filmmaking.

On the other hand, I often use throwaway tripe cinema to illustrate the point that you don't have to spend a decade watching thousands of obscure foreign films to build a comfortable language for talking about movies. Take a movie like *A Night at the Roxbury*. No one is referring to the work of Douglas Sirk or Francois Truffaut in their "analysis" of this bomb. Get real. This is a pop culture movie based on a *Saturday Night Live* skit which aspires not to be art but raw entertainment. Deconstructing it as anything else makes you look foolish.

At the same time, even junk movies have to be analyzed legitimately on some level, and there are perfectly good "brainless" movies as well as the understood "bad" ones. Just because Adam Sandler's in it, a movie can't merely be dismissed as tripe without further comment. You have to understand *why* the movie is bad, and that's best done by drawing comparisons between similar films – think *Wayne's World*, another based-on-

SNL film that, of course, became a classic comedy.

Even if you intend never to delve into art house fare (which categorically requires a higher level of knowledge of the classics and cult films of the past), you need a working vocabulary of past and present films in order to properly interpret what you're seeing on screen. Try to think back to some of the first films you ever saw: You probably thought they were outstanding, simply because the spectacle was so new to you. This is the problem with many infrequent moviegoers, who will often write hasty hate mail when you pan a film they claim to love. Why did they enjoy *The Hot Chick* so much? Without drawing a conclusion about their general level of intelligence, it's often because they simply don't see many movies and don't have a serious frame of reference of what's good and what's bad. They are like those children you see in the theaters, staring ga-ga at the screen, enraptured by the colors, the loud soundtrack, and the tasty popcorn. You just don't get that experience watching *Wheel of Fortune* at home, no matter how much you turn up the volume. The more movies you see, the more you'll naturally come to understand what separates the good from the bad.

There's also the obvious reason to dig into the past: Can you review *The Empire Strikes Back* without seeing *Star Wars*? Absolutely not. Can you review the 2003 version of *The In-Laws* without seeing the 1979 original? That's debatable, but you should check out the original if you have time and can find it. What about less obvious connections: Can you review Todd Haynes's *Far From Heaven* (2002) without seeing Douglas Sirk's *All That Heaven Allows* (1955), which inspired Haynes's work? Yes, but your review will be far more informed if you've seen Sirk's film. Sirk, in turn, was inspired by other filmmakers before him, so you might also feel compelled to check out his predecessors.

Do you need to go overboard, spending $10,000 and five years of your life as you run through the entire inventory of your avant garde video store before writing your first review? No. You need to use your judgment to find a comfort level where you're happy with your depth of knowledge of cinematic history but still have time to see new releases (which, by far, represent the reviews people want to read).

Some critics feel that I'm wrong on this. In 1999, the venerable *New York Times* replaced retiring film critic Janet Maslin with its second-string critic, Elvis Mitchell (who has since resigned), and a former *book critic*, A.O. Scott. The venerable Roger Ebert inexplicably lambasted the choice of Scott, asking "Has he seen six films by Bresson? Ozu?" Jesus, has *anyone* besides Ebert? Personally, I've seen five Ozu films, and they are interesting in the abstract. However, I've almost never made a written reference to any of them in a review. I'd be happy to see that sixth film, but little of Ozu's work is available on video, and I can't (and won't) sit idle until I see Ebert's six magic movies. What's the point?

At the same time, I *have* seen virtually the entire bodies of work of Kubrick, Hitchcock, Woody Allen, Spielberg, and many more modern Western filmmakers, whose work tends to inspire far more contemporaries than Bresson and Ozu. (*Armageddon* and *Bad Boys* director Michael Bay probably is more inspired by his dog than any director who worked pre-1980.) But I've also seen my share of works by more obscure foreign directors, having reviewed 16 films by Werner Fassbinder and eight by Dusan Makavejev. Does this qualify me in any particularly special way to critique films? Not really. But it does build a certain confidence when facing a daunting art house movie, one where its merits as "art" might completely live in the mind of the viewer.

The bottom line: See all the films you can, current films and classics, too. The more movies you can see, the more rewarding you'll find your experience as a film critic.

BUILDING YOUR KNOWLEDGE OF FILM HISTORY

So where do you draw the line between building a comprehensive knowledge of cinema history with balancing the time commitment it takes to build it? By choosing your battles carefully and by prioritizing the most important works of cinema up front. The Appendix offers the filmcritic.com viewing guide, with 300 "must-see" films for any aspiring critic. By no means is this list meant to represent the *best* films ever made; rather it is designed to offer a mix of great films, highly influential films (whether great or not), classic missteps, and obscurities that will make you seem incredibly wise when writing your reviews. Naturally I'm sure I've forgotten many worthy entries; I encourage you to write me with your suggestions on revising the list for the next edition of this book.

Chances are you've seen many of these films already, either theatrically or on video. If you've seen half of the 300, and you can rent just three of the remainder each week, you'll have knocked out the entire list within a year. Armed with a basic knowledge of cinema essentials, I promise your reviews will be better than if you'd skipped these flicks. Your readers will thank you, and best of all you'll be able to start writing informed reviews almost immediately while continuing to perfect your craft as you practice writing.

Don't stop with the list in Appendix A, though. Make a list of movies you'd like to see. If you hear good things about a movie you haven't caught, add it to the list. Check your TV listings every week to see if any of the films are showing soon on network or cable TV (Turner Classic Movies is a must!) and save yourself the price of the rental. Another good way to dispatch a lot of films is to sign up for a DVDs-by-mail rental service like Netflix, Blockbuster, or Walmart.com. For as little as $18 a month, you can easily knock out three discs a week, if not more. I rent up to 20 movies a month through Netflix and have about 400 movies in my rental queue (the list of films I'm waiting to see – or see again). You'll find that the deeper your knowledge of cinema gets, the further you will explore into old, obscure, and offbeat films.

Another good idea for the novice is to buy or rent anything that Criterion releases. For those unfamiliar with the label, Criterion reissues classic films, often with extras you won't find anywhere else. Virtually all of their selections are "important" movies for one reason or another, so simply looking for the Criterion label is a way to ensure that you'll be investing your time in something that will teach you a little nugget of wisdom about cinema, something you didn't already know. Even better, these films often come packaged with commentary tracks from film critics and historians, with in-depth analyses you won't find in other reviews. What do the nuns walking across the plaza in *L'Avventura* (1960) signify? Check out the commentary track on the Criterion edition of the film and your experience will be substantially enriched.

On the other hand, listening to a bunch of commentary tracks is a massive time commitment, and you can be forgiven if you don't want to sit through hundreds of them. Therefore, it's much more important that aspiring film critics *read* a ton of movie reviews, preferably from those writers you'd like to emulate. (I'd humbly suggest filmcritic.com as the perfect place to start.) Get a sense for structure and style, and how different critics approach the same film in a different fashion. It's an invaluable part of the learning experience.

WHERE THE MOVIES CAME FROM

Many of you undoubtedly will skip over this section, and I can't blame you. History was my worst subject in school, and I simply have no aptitude for places and dates.

But the cliché is true: Ignore history and you're doomed to repeat it. This explains why so many bad movies are released today: Filmmakers, in their quest to earn the almighty dollar, have ignored the lessons of their forebears.

As a critic, if you ignore those lessons as well, you are doomed to write bad reviews until you take film history seriously.

By common consensus, the first movies began with Louis Lumiere's invention of the motion picture camera in 1895. The Lumiere camera (often just called "the Lumiere") could not only shoot continuous photographs, it could develop film and project it, too. Not until the advent of videotape would such simplicity again be part of filmmaking. The Lumiere, it should go without saying, shot in black and white (and poorly at that), and without sound. For decades, audiences had only short films to enjoy. Title cards told the story when expressions and reactions could not, and live music played by an organist in the theater punctuated who was good and who was bad.

Feature-length filmmaking took off in the early 1900s. D.W. Griffith's *Birth of a Nation* (1915) remains the seminal work of its time and the first "important" film ever made. Unfortunately, it is about the Ku Klux Klan (and not in a bad way), but the film deserves note if for no other reason than that Griffith got people to sit in the same seat for more than three hours in order to witness, as the poster proclaimed, "The birth of a new art!"

Other films of the era, including *The Cabinet of Dr. Caligari* (1920), *Nosferatu* (1922), and the acclaimed *Battleship Potemkin* (1925), would also endure for decades and remain classics. The work of Charlie Chaplin – including *The Gold Rush* (1925) and *Modern Times* (1936, in the waning days of the silent film) – was at its height in this era.

Potemkin would be a landmark film in its introduction of sophisticated editing techniques – intercutting between multiple characters and angles to show an event from different perspectives. This is commonplace now, and in fact, if an editor failed to do this, his picture would be laughed into oblivion by a bored audience. Today's action movies and even mainstream fare like Rob Marshall's *Chicago* (2002) are composed almost entirely of rapid-fire cuts, all originally inspired by the work of *Potemkin* director Sergei Eisenstein.

How much exploring you want to do in the world of silent films is up to you. Aside from a few classics like those mentioned above, I haven't gotten much enrichment out of the silent era, and many of the films have decayed so badly that they're hard to sit through. You certainly won't find yourself drawing comparisons with 80-year-old films very often in your writing. But make sure you check out at least one Chaplin movie, if only so you can see how comedy can be telegraphed without a rim shot and a laugh track – or even without any dialogue at all.

THE TALKIES

Alan Crosland's *The Jazz Singer* (1927), with Al Jolson, was the first film to feature synchronized sound, produced in an era during which Harry Warner (one of the Warner Brothers) famously asked, "Who the hell wants to hear actors talk?"

As it turns out, everyone wanted to hear actors talk. Within a decade, the silent film was dead and talkies were all the rage.

Filmmaking was also improving, with better storylines, more sophisticated camerawork, bigger budgets, and more advanced raw materials. You'll notice a giant leap in the quality of the image alone between *Nosferatu* and *It Happened One Night* (1934), thanks to improving cameras and film stock.

And those voices make all the difference. What would *Citizen Kane* (1941) be without the immortal line, "Rosebud...."? What would *Casablanca* (1942) be without, "...all the gin joints in all the towns in all the world..."? Reading title cards that contained the classic movie lines from the 1930s and 1940s just wouldn't have inspired the same reaction that has made the films of this era some of the greatest of all time.

Other recognized greats of this era include *The Maltese Falcon* (1941), *Notorious* (1946), and *It's a Wonderful Life* (1945). Just thinking about these films probably brings certain movie stars to mind: Bogart, Bergman, Grant, Stewart. These actors appeared in all the big movies of the era. Why is that?

Welcome to the "studio system," which put writers, directors, and actors under contract to make multiple films for designated film companies. Under contract, an artist would be obligated to make a certain number of films for that studio on an exclusive basis. Some of Hollywood's greatest power struggles occurred during this era, and while an in-depth discussion of the politics of the "Golden Age of Hollywood" is outside the scope of this book, it makes for fascinating research.

EARLY COLOR

Technicolor – the first color printing process and still the standard today – actually predates sound. First formed in 1915, the Technicolor Motion Picture Corporation would grow to prominence through the 1930s.

As with sound, color film was resisted by the establishment. It was deemed to be expensive, complicated, and simply unnecessary. But while sound in film would quickly overtake the scene, black and white projects would compete mercilessly with color films for decades. Case in point: The Academy of Motion Picture Arts & Sciences had two cinematography awards – one for black and white and one for color – from 1939 all the way to 1966.

Early color films often look dazzling because of the processes used to enrich the experience. For example, today's filmmakers focus on making skies look *real*, but in the 1930s and 1940s, the focus was more on making them look *alive*. Movies like *The Wizard of Oz* (1939) and *Gone with the Wind* (1939) aren't memorable because they look realistic, but rather because they are *larger* than life. Directors like David Lynch (*Blue Velvet*, 1986) still toy with color expectations today, but this is far from the commonplace practice it was in the early days of color.

ITALIAN NEO-REALISM

What, they make films outside America? You better believe it, and even if you're not a fan of foreign flicks (yes, subtitles are painful and dubbing is worse, but suck it up), the effect that European and Asian filmmakers have had on modern American storytelling makes studying them an absolute must for any serious critic.

Europe saw several film "movements" – informal schools of filmmaking which spoke to common themes and evoked similar images and stories – the first of which was Italy's Neo-Realism (literally "The New Reality") movement, born in the country's dark days following World War II (which, I needn't remind you, saw Italy on the losing side).

Crawling out of the depths of Mussolini's fascist state, Italian filmmakers began experimenting with the dark themes which gripped their country: depression, unemployment, death, and worse. Vittorio De Sica's *The Bicycle Thief* (1949) would be the pinnacle film from this time period, a sad story about a stolen bicycle which was shot using regular people instead of actors.

Federico Fellini would pick up on these ideas with masterworks like *La Strada* (1954), with Anthony Quinn's dim strongman resisting the love of a girl, and *Nights of Cabiria* (1957), about a prostitute who loses her money and is nearly drowned, all in the pursuit of love.

Fellini would grow more sentimental (while damning modern society outright) in later works like *8 1/2* (1963) and *La Dolce Vita* (1960), both of which cast dispersions on the film business – Fellini's chosen profession – as cutthroat and hateful. To understand why Hollywood works the way it does (despite the fact that these films were shot overseas), these two movies are required viewing. Fellini broke from Neo-Realism later in his career, as his films became stylized and surreal pageants – watching the tone of his films change as the '50s transitioned into the '60s is an excellent exercise for the aspiring critic.

Fellini's sentiments about Hollywood and the general vibe of Neo-Realism are still present in many of today's movies, especially independent films which bear a darker tone and offer a bleaker outlook on life. Unfortunately, what is lost in many of these later films is a social context in which they make sense. The Italians were reacting to their surroundings: a dreary and depressed society after World War II. When a snotty rich kid from Ann Arbor makes a movie about the decay of society, it makes a very weak point. At the same time, directors who really have pulled themselves out of the gutter, like California native Harmony Korine, often turn in movies so inexplicably bad it's difficult to find anything in them to enjoy. Ultimately though, while social context can enhance or detract from a film, in the end a great movie should be able to stand on its own (and for a long time), regardless of the state of current events.

THE FRENCH NEW WAVE

No film snob term gets thrown around more than the "New Wave," and rarely does anyone who mentions it have a real understanding of what it was all about.

The French New Wave (or La Nouvelle Vague) refers to a very short period of French filmmaking from 1958 to the early 1960s, populated by a group of filmmakers who were former film critics, believe it or not, for a magazine of the era called *Cahiers du Cinéma*. (When an angry reader asks you why film critics don't just make their own movies if they think they can do better, refer them to these guys.) Other filmmakers became associated with the group in later years, and filmmakers in other countries spawned their own versions of this type of filmmaking around the same time. In Britain this was called Free Cinema or the British New Wave. But it's the French New Wave that had the most profound and lasting effect on cinema.

The New Wave directors fancied themselves as *auteurs* (another commonly bandied-about film concept), which says that the director – above all others – is the "author" of the film and that he alone is responsible for every aspect of its success. This may feel like an insult to the writers, actors, cinematographers, and costumers of the world, and in many ways it's rubbish. But the so-called "auteur theory" is what propagated the New Wave. The films of this era are some of the best in history. But just as many are unwatchably conceited, pretentious, and bad, proving that movies can sometimes be best designed by committee (that is, by including a larger crew than just one person).

New Wave films have a common look: hurried, full of motion, and authentic. As with the Italians, films were shot quickly and on location instead of on sets. But in sharp contrast to Neo-Realism, editing tends to be jerky and jumps around from location to location. On the other hand, New Wave films can also be fluid, as in Agnés Varda's *Cleo from 5 to 7* (1962), which simply follows an actress for the two hours that elapse before she is to learn whether or not she has cancer.

Among the classic films of the era are Truffaut's *The 400 Blows* (1959) and *Jules and Jim* (1961), Godard's *Breathless* (1960), and Chabrol's *This Man Must Die* (1969 – Chabrol got a late start). None of these films are exactly uplifting, but their realism and gritty sensibilities have made them all classics.

As with Neo-Realism, the films of the New Wave find analogues today, though on an arguably smaller scale than the Italians. Most notably, realistic and naturalistic acting and directing styles are best seen in the Dogme 95 movement, discussed later in this chapter.

AMERICA IN THE 1950S AND EARLY 1960S

Beginning around 1950, the movies exploded into a cacophony of genres: musicals, film noir, high dramas, big budget westerns, romantic comedies, war movies, and more. The number of productions released by studios went through the roof, and movies grew more intelligent than ever. *All About Eve* and *Sunset Boulevard* both hit in 1950. *Rear Window* (1954) would follow *Shane* (1953). In 1960, audiences were treated to both *The Apartment* and *Psycho*.

Alfred Hitchcock, Billy Wilder, John Ford, George Cukor – these are just a handful of the titans of cinema that did their best work in the 1950s.

Drawing blanket observations about this era gets tricky from this point on. Film "movements" wouldn't really come back until 1995, with the Danish "Dogme 95" theory of filmmaking (more on this later). But film *artistry* would continue to develop as a craft. Consider Hitchcock's *Vertigo* (1957), with its acid-washed greens, psychedelic shots, and a mind game of a story that must have impressed even Orson Welles. If any film has proven itself to be "art" instead of "just a movie," it's *Vertigo*.

Movies would also take on a sense of grandeur missing from the eras immediately preceding and following. *Ben-Hur* (1959), *Lawrence of Arabia* (1962), and *Doctor Zhivago* (1965) were epic stories that actually had intermissions, unthinkable in today's world where studios would rather split a long movie into two halves to get you to pay for it twice than put a three minute break in the middle (as Miramax did with Quentin Tarantino's bloated *Kill Bill* films).

Epics are a critical piece of film history, because they provide a sense of the grandeur that filmmaking once commanded. Movies like *Cleopatra* (1963) took over the lot at 20th Century Fox, but the money-sucking production nearly bankrupted the company. On the other hand, *Lawrence of Arabia* stands as one of the greatest living testaments man has ever put on celluloid.

Sure, sheer length is a strange way to categorize films, but in this case it makes sense. These films are long because they have something to say (or at least they think they do). Putting this into perspective with the modern era, many films have become needlessly long because powerful directors are allowed final cut without studio tampering. Why *The Green Mile* (1999) needed to be three hours long, I'll never know. I enjoyed it at the time, but in my mind it's faded into a story that could be told in half an hour. The point is that compared to the *real* epics, a film like this comes up short, simply because it doesn't have nearly as much to say.

EXPLOITATION

A small sub-genre of offbeat films enjoyed a period of semi-popularity from the 1950s to the 1970s (though exploitation movies date back to at least 1937, when *Reefer Madness* memorably demonized marijuana). These movies are typically known as exploitation films, referring to the then-taboo subjects of sex, drugs, and ethnicity, all of which were invariably played for shock value and cheap thrills. Sometimes, as with *Reefer Madness*, they were meant as cautionary tales, warning kids not to engage in premarital sex or pick up hitchhikers. The term "exploitation" doesn't necessarily refer to exploitation of the actors, but rather exploitation of so-called "easy" subject matter and, indirectly, the audience's pocketbooks.

Exploitation films aren't nearly as scandalous today as they once were, but their influence is still palpable. Case in point: *Shaft* (1971), a classic "blaxploitation" film about a jive-talking detective. While the 2000 remake starring Samuel L. Jackson in the title role was hardly a success, the original *Shaft* was massively popular. It prompted a boom in black filmmaking, and even won an Academy Award for its memorable theme song. (In fairness, director Gordon Parks disputes whether *Shaft* is an exploitation film, indicative of how loaded the term can be.)

It's hard to peg many exploitation films as "classics," and few (*Shaft* excluded) are even enjoyable for more than a few kitschy minutes. Before you dismiss the latest horror movie to hit town as "the worst ever," though, you should spend some time with a film like the horror "sexploitation" film *I Spit on Your Grave* (1978), or the Nazi sexploitation flick *Ilsa, She Wolf of the SS* (1974). These cult classics pushed hot buttons then and continue to do so today.

While not precisely an exploitation director – he's more of the school of shock cinema – the work of John Waters is probably about as close to modern exploitation as you're likely to find. His *Pink Flamingos* (1972) has sent thousands of viewers running for the bathroom in disgust. Even his later films like *Serial Mom* (1994) played with expectations of wholesomeness and fed our hopes for gore by casting Kathleen Turner (then a goody-goody starlet) as a murderous neighborhood mother.

Simply tour your video store's cult section to find films like *The Rocky Horror Picture Show* (1975), *Faster Pussycat! Kill! Kill!* (1965), and *Big Bad Mama* (1974). None of these are great movies, but you should see a few of them, if for no other reason than to broaden your film experience outside of the usual Hollywood fare and to see some of today's bigger movie stars slumming it in low-rent productions.

LOVE AND PSYCHOS IN THE 1960S AND 1970S

The '60s were a time of both earnest experimentalism and severe disenchantment. Consider *The Graduate* (1967), ostensibly a movie about love but ultimately a sad and often cruel look at infidelity, ennui, and obsession. It's one of the great films of our time.

Catch-22 (1970), *A Clockwork Orange* (1971), *Deliverance* (1972) – these films gave us heroes that were hard to root for, yet we inexplicably wanted them to win. *The Godfather* (1972) is probably the penultimate example of this: Its protagonists are all ruthless crooks and killers, mobsters who wouldn't think twice before putting a bullet in your head. Yet we are trained to feel sorry for them and hope for their success.

The idea of sympathetic anti-heroes extends to films like *One Flew Over the Cuckoo's Nest* (1975) and *Dog Day Afternoon* (1975), but it's Martin Scorsese's *Taxi Driver* (1976) that created one of the most enduringly lovable psychopaths in cinema history. Or consider one of the most beloved romances of all time, *Breakfast at Tiffany's* (1961), which features a pair of leads who are best described as prostitutes. The influence of these and other films on modern cinema (consider the gangster heroes of *Pulp Fiction* (1994) and the lovable hooker of *Pretty Woman* (1990)) is impossible to overstate. Bad guys have never looked so good.

Moviemaking during this time often became a *journey* as well. Road movies became a popular way to tell the story of a character's growth by putting him on a physical trip. *Easy Rider* (1969) and *2001: A Space Odyssey* (1968) are both road movies of sorts, though the former is a far more obvious one. Road movies have since become a bit of a crutch, as the only way some directors seem able to craft a plot is by getting characters in a car and sending them into the desert. Sometimes it works (*Y Tu Mamá También* (2001)). Usually it is an awful mess (and goes straight to cable).

THE EVENT MOVIE - 1975 TO PRESENT

It's hard to peg precisely when the event movie became the norm, especially for summer moviegoers. But the film that immediately springs to mind is *Jaws* (1975), Steven Spielberg's low-budget ($12 million) shark movie that blasted onto movie screens in June and tore up the summer with $260 million in American gross. Shark paranoia became all the rage. Women (and men) feared the water. The quickie sequel was born. The film was referenced or spoofed in several hundred films that followed.

Suddenly, modest expectations went out the window as Hollywood became obsessed with creating blockbusters that would appeal to as broad an audience as possible – why double your money when you can get back 10 times as much? As budgets went up, so did actors' and directors' paydays, along with the hopes for endless streams of people rushing to the movie theater. Plots would be dumbed-down or pared of risk in order to make them more palatable to broad audiences. Marketing budgets would climb ever higher in order to guarantee heavy traffic on opening day. This spiral of increasing expectations continues today.

Spielberg's big success would launch the event movie in earnest, as films like *Star Wars* (1977), *Raiders of the Lost Ark* (1981), and *E.T. the Extra-Terrestrial* (1982) would follow in *Jaws's* wake. (All are in the top 30 grossing films of all time despite being released in the days of $4 movie tickets; *Star Wars* is number two, after *Titanic* (1997).)

Event films would quickly move out of the realm of just Spielberg and his filmmaking friend George Lucas and into the mainstream. Even films with seemingly small audiences would prove to have mass appeal thanks to uncanny casting and extraordinary marketing: *Grease* (1978) made $181 million at the box office. *Top Gun* (1986) made $176 million. Eventually, even animated movies would start breaking box office records as studios found the formula that kept kids engaged and adults interested enough to bring them back for repeat viewings, with *Toy Story* (1995), *Shrek* (2001), and *Finding Nemo* (2003) approaching or breaking the $200 million mark.

But many event movies, being more about the event than the movie, would suffer cruel backlashes from film critics, and often audiences as well. When attempting to make a movie that appeals to everyone, it's all too easy to make one that appeals to no one at all. The biggest flops in history – including *Cutthroat Island* (1995), *Ishtar* (1987), and *Hudson Hawk* (1991) – were all big budget extravaganzas that lost tens of millions of dollars at the box office and have entered the realm of infamy as some of the worst films ever made. Careers have ended and studios have gone bankrupt because of films like these.

Reviewing event films is surprisingly difficult, whether they're big-budget, straight-on action movies like *Bad Boys* (1995) or genre films like installments of *Star Trek*, *The Matrix,* or *Lord of the Rings*. Do you review the film or the spectacle surrounding it? Most of the time, these aren't movies made for the cognoscenti. You can eke a theme out of *Jurassic Park* (1993) if you really try, but fundamentally the movie is about watching giant CGI dinosaurs stomp around for two hours. Special effects and loud soundtracks don't stand on their own, but sometimes they really can carry a film. I'll discuss the "turning off your brain" issue in Chapter 4, but in a nutshell, consider event movies as a genre when you watch them. Does *The Phantom Menace* match the original *Star Wars*? Does the horror-comedy *Eight-Legged Freaks* rival *Jaws*? When you see the big summer blockbusters, ask yourself how they compare to the true greats of the genre, and you'll be on your way toward forming a critical opinion that will stand up better than the usual, "Wow, it was cool" commentary that the masses will invariably spout.

INDEPENDENT AND DIGITAL FILMMAKING

While Hollywood hasn't fundamentally changed much in the last two decades, those working on the periphery of the industry certainly have. In fact, virtually all of the innovation in cinema (outside of digital manipulation of imagery) has come from the independent film scene.

What is independent film? Even the definition provokes questions and arguments, but independent movies are widely defined as those funded outside the Hollywood studio system. We typically think of movies like *The Blair Witch Project* (1999) or *Swingers* (1996) as successful independents, but George Lucas's self-funded *The Phantom Menace* is actually an indie flick, too – of sorts – even though a $115 million budget is hard to consider in the same league as the $7,000 Robert Rodriguez spent on *El Mariachi* (1992).

sex, lies, and videotape (1989) is often considered the first modern indie, as the film's surprise success at the box office launched a boom in independent production. As videotape (and later, digital video) became an inexpensive alternative to film, many more low-budget and no-budget filmmakers began hitting the scene. Many of their films are unwatchable. Most never see the light of day. But some have endured as truly great works of art. Consider *Memento* (2000) and *Amelie* (2001), both financed by small companies and regarded as two of the greatest films in the last ten years. How do financially-strapped indies outplay the big guys? The theory is that a lack of cash forces filmmakers to innovate in ways they wouldn't ordinarily do, and that in turn breeds originality, excitement, uniqueness, and (hopefully) quality. Getting rid of the executive oversight committees can give a filmmaker even greater freedom.

In 1995, a collection of Scandinavian filmmakers took the low-budget ethic and fiercely independent ideology of the indie flick and immortalized it with a manifesto calling for filmmakers to abandon the trappings of Hollywood. The so-called Dogme 95 movement asked its adherents to follow a set of rules called the "vow of chastity," which included regulations such as:

- All shooting must be done on location instead of in a studio.
- No sound dubbing is permitted (even music).
- No camera tricks (or even black and white film) are allowed.
- No "superficial action," like explosions and murder, is permitted.
- The film must take place in the present and in the location where it is shot.

Heavy stuff, and for a few years the movement launched considerable discussion from adherents and detractors alike. The look of Dogme films like *The Celebration* (1998) is striking and different, and the stories are gritty, with a look and feel evoking the private movies of a close (but strange) relative.

Dogme filmmaking has become a minor phenomenon, to the point where even non-Dogme films (especially those shot on video, the preferred format of Dogme 95) are often lumped in with the movement or described as "Dogme style." Whether a director is intentionally trying to rid his film of the trappings of Hollywood, as formal Dogme criteria requires, or whether he's just low on cash and can't afford fancy lights and big stunt scenes is up to you, the critic, to determine.

DRAWING COMPARISONS

In many ways, drawing insightful and clever comparisons about movies is one of the easiest and most informative parts of film criticism. It almost goes without saying that you should make the obvious connections: to earlier films in a series (*Star Trek*), films which were remade (*The Italian Job*), or clear take-offs of other works (*Scream*). But how do you compare a film to a lesser-known movie or make a connection to an indirectly related film made 50 years earlier? In Chapter 6, I'll look more deeply at how comparative analysis can become a useful part of your critic's toolkit.

CHAPTER 3:
UNDERSTANDING FILMMAKING

You just walked out of the theater having seen the worst film of your life. But *why* was it so bad? Was it the acting? The story? Bad editing? Simply saying "it's awful" or "it's great" doesn't mean anything unless you can break a film down into its component parts. By doing this, you'll often find that a movie you'd first found unredeemable has some worthwhile aspects. As well, you may find that an otherwise excellent film is flawed in some way or another. The point here isn't to homogenize all your reviews into the realm of three stars (and I'll discuss avoiding this common trap in Chapter 7), but rather to give you a framework for analysis which you'll build out further as you begin writing your first reviews.

You can better understand the components of a film by better understanding how a movie actually gets made. The process described here is simplified, and movies can come about through wildly different methods, but for 98 percent of films that get released, this is how they come into being.

IN THE BEGINNING: HOW A MOVIE IS CONCEIVED

Someone has an idea. Maybe it's a writer with a brand new idea about a buddy cop film that stars Mel Gibson and an orangutan. Maybe it's a director who has become fascinated with the story of *The Odyssey*. Maybe it's a name-brand actor who wants to delve into direction with a pet project he's had for decades. Maybe it's a producer who reads a historical book about a race horse and decides it would make an excellent movie, too. Somewhere in Hollywood (and yes, most of the time it's in Hollywood), the wheels of creativity start churning.

If a writer or director has enough clout, he or she can take an idea to a studio or production company to *pitch* it. (Production companies are small, independent companies run by producers and A-list directors and actors; they typically have exclusive deals with the big studios like Warner Brothers, Disney, and so on, which will later finance and distribute the finished film. But studios may produce their own films on occasion, too).

Based on the strength of the pitch – a short, oral synopsis of the idea – an idea can be *optioned* (an exclusive arrangement in which rights to make a film are owned by a company or person for a limited time), and/or a film can be put into *development*. A writer may also be able to sell an option on a *spec script*, a full screenplay based on an original idea, in order to get his film into development. (When someone tells you they're "working on a script," they're actually writing a spec script. This is a nearly impossible way to break into Hollywood, since spec scripts are rarely bought, especially from industry outsiders. But since anyone can do it in their spare time, and without moving to Los Angeles, everybody tries.)

Development entails paying someone to write a real script – 100 or so pages of action and dialogue – while a producer (the boss of the movie who is ultimately responsible for everything from money to hiring cast and crew) recruits the talent. Movies in development might be given a few thousand to a few million dollars in order to see if a workable script can be delivered and if the necessary talent will sign on to the project.

If all goes well, a movie gets a budget from its financial backers (either the studio or multiple studios, if the budget requirements are too big and risky for one studio alone). An Oscar-winner like Steven Spielberg might even invest his own money, or a director who can't find studio backing may look to private investment (often from overseas financiers) instead. For a low-budget independent film, a filmmaker may raise money from friends and family, or simply max out his credit cards to pay for the film. When you see *executive producers* credited on a film, these are typically people critical to funding the movie. Rarely are they ever materially involved in day-to-day production.

It costs a lot of money to make a big Hollywood movie these days. Figures vary wildly, but if you hire an A-list actor ($20 million) or a big director ($10 million), include a few special effects ($5 million), and launch a TV-and-print ad campaign ($25 million), it's easy to see why the budget for the average production is pushing $80 million from start to finish. Indies obviously cost much less. As discussed earlier, *El Mariachi* cost only $7,000 to shoot (plus a bit more spent to finish up the film for theatrical release).

Budget considerations are important because they set expectations for you when writing a review. While I don't automatically forgive independents for every mistake in their film, I do give a little leeway for lighting and sound issues (these, along with set design, costumes, editing, and so on, are known as *production values*). For big-budget Hollywood movies, there's rarely an excuse for bad production values.

THE GUTS OF THE MOVIE

Once a budget has been set and the critical cast and crew are hired, a movie goes into *pre-production*. This entails building sets, casting the supporting roles, and hiring production crew, which includes these guys:

- Art director: Oversees set building and dressing; a production designer is an art director on a larger scale, responsible for the look of the entire film.
- Cinematographer: Works with the director on lighting, setting up shots, choosing film stocks and cameras, and overseeing the operation of the camera. Typically an army of lighting crew members (composed of gaffers (electricians) and grips (guys that carry stuff)) work under him. Also known as the director of photography or DP.
- Sound: A department responsible for recording sound on the set – from running the tape recorder (sound is recorded separately from the images) to holding the microphone. Sound recorded after the movie is shot is known as *ADR* (additional dialogue recording) or *foley* work (imitating sound effects on a stage).
- Other crew, like line producers, script supervisors, and assistant directors: These are support crew who assist in various facets of the day-to-day production of the film and are invaluable in making a film set run smoothly.

During pre-production, a director may rehearse with his cast – or not. Depending on the working style of the director and lead performers, rehearsal can last for months or may never occur at all.

Eventually, shooting dates are set, locations are finalized, and filming begins.

Day one of photography is the beginning of *production*. A typical film that doesn't require traveling to exotic locations or a dramatic change in the appearance of a character (such as Tom Hanks in *Cast Away* (2000)) can be shot in 28 days or so, the equivalent of 4 to 5 minutes of the finished film being photographed each day. Some films work fast, some work slow. Epics like *The Lord of the Rings* trilogy may be shot over the course of a year or two. Indie directors may work only on weekends, grabbing shots when they can and hoping their actors don't gain too much weight or cut their hair during the week.

Production is always a harrowing process, and anyone who has shot even a short film knows how grueling a shoot can be. Finally, though, the film must *wrap*, or come to a close, and the producer (and director) has no choice but to pray that everything has come out well.

The film then moves to *post-production*, which primarily involves the editing of the film. Since most movies are shot out of chronological sequence, and each scene is shot from various angles multiple times (these are called *takes*), an editor has a massive job in constructing a 100-minute-long finished

34

product from what can amount to hundreds of hours of raw material. The director usually works hand-in-hand with the editor in cutting the film, and at this point any special effects (like digital enhancements), additional sound effects, voice dubbing, or reshoots are ordered. The editing process typically can take four months or more.

A rough draft of the finished product (usually much longer than the final film) is shown to the producer and the studio backing the project after the editing process. Suggestions are offered, further cuts are made, and the final film begins to take shape. Test audiences usually will watch the film in order to gauge if the ending works, if the laughs are big enough, and if the pacing is right.

The final product rarely looks exactly like the original script. As an exercise, you should definitely read the scripts to some of your favorite movies (these are often packaged as books, and many are available online), especially if you can find early drafts of the screenplays. The first draft for *Groundhog Day* (1993) is atrocious; it's a miracle the final film became such a work of genius.

The legendary studio battles – *Brazil, Citizen Kane, American History X* (1998) – typically take place in the editing room, after the movie has been shot. Directors are sometimes fired and new editors are brought in to clean up what is perceived as a disaster. Usually the director's instincts are right and the studio is wrong, but that's another story for another book.

In the end, the movie is cleaned up with color mastering and sound enhancements, the picture is *locked*, a release date is set, and prints are ordered (one for each screen it will appear on – up to 3,500 or so).

INTO THE WORLD IT GOES

Once a movie is finished, the marketing onslaught begins. Trailers are produced from early footage (which is why you often see scenes in a preview that don't exist in the final product) and *buzz* for the film starts to build. Hopefully. Based on early previews and test screenings, a movie may be shelved or re-edited if it looks like it won't get people in the seats. The studio may already be out $60 million on production costs, but if there's no hope of earning that back *plus* the $20 million or more required to promote the movie, a film may instead be abandoned or released directly to video, DVD, or cable TV, where promotional costs are lower (or nonexistent), and some revenue can easily be salvaged.

Today, success largely hinges on a big opening weekend. If a movie doesn't earn back its production costs in the first three weeks of release, it probably never will. Studios ultimately use box office numbers to promote their films later to video retailers and renters, so having big numbers to show off is critical. ($100 million is the magic number to earn premium prices for subsidiary rights like network TV broadcasting.)

This, of course, is where you, the film critic, come in. Studios will claim until they're blue in the face that critics are meaningless to the ultimate success or failure of a film, but this just isn't true. Sure, many films are critic-proof (*Star Wars* movies, for example), but many rely completely on critical acclaim to build an audience (*Almost Famous* (2000), for example). Then again, this rule is hardly set in stone. *Star Trek* is widely perceived to be critic-proof, but the most recent *Star Trek* movie, *Nemesis* (2002), bombed at the box office after critics (including me) ravaged it. Some say the series is now dead, and die-hard fans sent me hundreds of e-mails, personally blaming me for killing the film. If that doesn't say something about the power of film criticism, what does?

CHAPTER 4:
WRITING YOUR FIRST REVIEWS

Now you understand film history and the basics of how a film is made. You're ready to write your first full-fledged movie review.

THE POINT OF A MOVIE REVIEW

Before you start to write, you need to understand the reason a movie review should exist. At its most fundamental level, the goal is simple:

You are helping the reader decide whether to invest his time and money in watching a movie.

Now the *Film Comment* crowd has a different goal, and that's to analyze film as an art form and to interpret its social significance. This type of writing is meant to be consumed after the reader has seen the film, not before, often exploring plot in detail (spoiling every plot point and even the ending), discussing in depth a writer and/or director's prior works, and most importantly explaining what the movie says about feminism, terrorism, politics, and so on. *Deconstruction* like this is often applied to books, of course, so why not extend it to motion pictures?

If you're reading this book, chances are deconstructing movies for their social context isn't your primary goal. Film school is all about this kind of analysis, but typical readers in mass media have little patience for this type of writing.

Does this mean you shouldn't be looking for themes and offering your perspective on what a film says about life, society, or philosophy? Of course you should. But when it comes to answering the question of whether a film is worth the money, these issues are often secondary.

The best way to do this is to just jump right in and start writing, but first you'll want a framework for structuring your review so it's not just a jumble of random thoughts.

THE SECRET OF A GOOD REVIEW

There is one simple, fundamental rule to writing a good movie review:

BE HONEST

That's it! Whether you are writing your first review or your 3,000th review, if you aren't honest with yourself, with the film, and with your readers, your review is useless. You can "be nice" about your criticism or you can get really detailed with your complaints, but all of this is meaningless if you don't tell the truth and provide an analysis that comes from your heart.

Keep this one golden rule in mind as you read the lessons in the rest of this chapter, for all of your analyses must absolutely be presided over by honesty.

HOW TO ANALYZE A MOVIE

For starters, rent or attend a movie that you haven't seen before. As you watch it – or after you finish – think about the following questions. If you can write in the dark, jot down the answers on a notepad as they occur to you during the film. Also, scribble any other tidbits (a line of dialogue, a quirky supporting character, a clever plot twist) that strike you as particularly noteworthy. As well, write down anything that strikes you as awkward, hackneyed, or a hallmark of bad filmmaking. Together, all of these notes will form the comments in your review. I'll analyze each of these aspects of critiquing in more detail later in the chapter.

A FRAMEWORK FOR MOVIE REVIEWS: BASIC QUESTIONS TO ASK YOURSELF

- Did the movie achieve its goal? In other words, did you laugh, cry, or scream in terror like you were supposed to? Compared to other movies in this genre, did you laugh/cry/scream more or less? Why?
- Is the story interesting? Here we're evaluating the script. Are the jokes stale or have you heard the dialogue in a hundred other movies? Is the plot stolen from another film? Can you figure out the ending after 20 minutes? Is the pacing too slow, or is the plot confusing? These are all problems to note. Typically they point to bad screenwriting.
- How are the performances? Is the acting believable? Could you really see these movie stars in these roles in life? Are the performances natural or stilted? Is one a standout above the others or does the entire cast shine? Is one actor miscast – or is the actor successfully exploring new ground? Is an actor being lazy by regurgitating an old character in a new role?
- How's the direction? Directing is difficult to judge, especially for a novice, because directors have a lot of help from supporting crew. Good acting is one sign of good directing, but when actors work well *together*, it's a clearer indication of a good director at the helm. Good directing also comprises the technical side of filmmaking: good shot selection, inventive photography, and

unobtrusive camera movements. Pacing is a critical part of direction, though this often is also a function of the editing and writing of the film: Do scenes begin only when necessary and end before they become boring? Does the movie develop a sense of quickening pace leading up to a climax or is the pace jerky?

- What about the support crew? Do the costumes and sets look authentic? Does the music gel with the rest of the movie? (There is nothing worse than a period piece that is saddled with awful synthesizer tunes.) Do the special effects look good, and is the sound at the right volume level? If you can't hear when you leave the theater, it's too loud. Consider the little details. These may not make or break the movie, but they'll help shade your review when appropriate.

- Was there a worthwhile point to the movie? A message? Anything that you'll remember in a week? Not every film will have a message, but the best movies – even if they're comedies or action films – should be memorable for more than just the laughs and the blood splattering.

- Is it too long? Too short? More importantly, does the length of the film match the importance of the film?

- Finally, how well does all of this come together? This plays back to the first question above: Did the movie achieve its goal? If you answered yes to that question you'll probably give high marks to most or all of the above queries. Did you enjoy the whole movie, not just a few scenes here and there? Does the finished product feel like one movie or a collection of little vignettes? Does it tell one grand story or a few amusing anecdotes?

It's important not to look at this as if it's a checklist, or as if you're grading a test. A film is a collection of elements both good and bad, but ultimately it is a single entity that should be considered as a whole instead of just a bunch of parts. For the most part, you will be able to answer most of these questions rather quickly as you think about the film minutes after you've seen it.

Chances are this is how you look at movies already, even if you don't realize it. When you leave a film, you either liked it or you didn't, pure and simple. If you're pressed, you will come up with certain things that stood out as good or bad, and you'll be able to riff on a good performance or a terrible plot point. Hey, you've got the beginnings of a movie review right there! Add a plot synopsis and a little structure and you'll find you can write a few hundred words of review off the top of your head. Once you go through the steps a few times, you'll find it easier and easier to apply critical thinking to an entertainment form.

The real challenge comes in extending off the cuff remarks with more detail, critical commentary, and your own personal writing style. I'll explore these issues in full in the remainder of this chapter and the next two. First, though, I need to discuss in more detail some of the basic criteria that you should use when preparing to write your first reviews.

ART VS. ENTERTAINMENT

The biggest mistake a film critic can make (aside from being illiterate or just plain boring) is putting all films on the same playing field. To look at two recent films, is it possible to compare *Meet the Parents* (2000) with *The Hours* (2002)? Both are great – even classic – movies, but trying to compare them head-to-head is foolhardy at best and irresponsible at worst.

This is not to say that you shouldn't consider an "art film" using the same level of objectivity – ultimately *all* movies should be weighed on a scale that asks if they are worth your investment of time and money. *Meet the Parents* and *The Hours* are both worth it – just for different reasons. Interpreting and explaining those reasons is your job.

While films are created for different purposes and with different goals in mind, fundamentally (and whether this is sad or not is debatable), most movies are primarily made to entertain teenage males and, hopefully, their dates. Careers are built on catering to this audience, from Adam Sandler and his antics to Jerry Bruckheimer's explosive extravaganzas. If there's a message to be found in a movie like *Billy Madison* or *Armageddon*, it's a pretty shallow one.

There are movies, as well, that are all about artistry. Ismail Merchant and James Ivory have worked for decades making art films that have little hope of earning more than a few million dollars at the box office. Instead, they are content to cater to smaller audiences with their richly-crafted morality plays set in exotic locales and with every actress cinched up in a corset. These movies are about looks, but that's not what makes them "art movies." Rather, the "art" in question is the rich themes found in the subtext. In the case of these costume dramas, it's typically found in the repressed emotions of the era (consider *The Remains of the Day* (1993), a film all about love lost because of indecision and over-cautiousness). Enjoyment is found not by onscreen spectacle and belly laughs, but by forcing you to reflect about how your own life may be mirrored on the screen.

So, is *Howards End* "fun" to watch, like a *Terminator* movie? Hardly (though a certain segment of the audience would argue with me on that point).

40

But is it a good movie? Absolutely, but for reasons that are entirely different than with *Meet the Parents.*

There are, of course, movies that transcend art and entertainment and prove themselves to be both. For my money, Steven Spielberg's one-two punch from 2002 is a case in point. His two films from that year, *Minority Report* and *Catch Me If You Can,* were not just two of the best movies released, they both also worked as pure entertainment while still being imbued with interesting messages and prescient themes. *Minority Report* was not just the best special effects movie of the year, it also featured great performances and a subtle warning about the dangers of government privacy invasion and technology abuse. *Catch Me If You Can* also featured excellent dialogue, acting, and terrific period sets from the 1960s and 1970s. But its story about Frank Abagnale's quest for fulfillment – driven by his divorced parents and his deep-seeded desire to reconcile them – is as touching as anything to come out of Hollywood in a decade.

Finding these gems and writing about them is what makes film criticism worthwhile. Unfortunately, the bulk of your time will likely be spent reviewing movies for their sheer entertainment value. Most Hollywood productions today aren't interested in building the movie around an artistic theme at all, as young audiences will be bored, confused, or put-off by it (or so the studios believe).

And then there are the films that neither entertain nor enlighten, with which you're probably all too familiar already.

FILM CRITIC VS. MOVIE REVIEWER

Much fuss has been made about the semantic differences between a "film critic" and a "movie reviewer." Pedants define the two quite differently: Movie reviewers write reviews of new releases for the masses in a fun and lively style, while film critics discuss films as art forms, in academic language, and typically in longer form.

I use the terms interchangeably, and while this book is definitely devoted to the "movie reviewer" side of the fence, it should also be usable by those interested in a more academic style of film reviewing. Ultimately, while the journalist film critic is helping the reader decide whether or not to see a movie, he's also responsible for increasing the reader's understanding of film as an art form, which is the goal of the academic film critic.

Why define these roles differently when the goals are so similar? That's a job, I guess, for the "film critics."

GENRE CONSIDERATIONS

Related to the art vs. entertainment question is the issue of genre. Horror movies, comedies, and dramas all need to be considered separately. I find it particularly difficult to review horror films, since the die-hard horror audience has a much different expectation than the "typical" moviegoer. A proper review should take that audience into account without pandering to it.

Consider also the problem of a man reviewing a film like *The Divine Secrets of the Ya-Ya Sisterhood* (2002), an unabashed "chick flick." I've yet to meet a male who enjoyed this film (though in fairness, all the women I know disliked it as well), but should the gender of the critic play into the review of the film? Isn't this unfair?

In some people's view of an ideal world, a critic could somehow remove himself from his race, gender, and preconceptions, but that's frankly impossible. And if this genderless, mindless blank was able to do that, what on earth could it possibly have to say worth reading? The reality is that you can't change your sex (not on a whim, anyway), and you shouldn't have to apologize for who you are when you sit down to watch a movie.

My solution? Embrace your differences and let the world know about it in your review. You're a woman reviewing a Schwarzenegger movie and you hate the action genre? Let the reader know up front. You're the whitest, most rhythm-free guy on the block and you're heading in to see *You Got Served*? Say so! Accept that the movie may not have been made for you, but try to put yourself in the mindset of the intended audience. Even if you hate frou-frou girl movies, there are still classics – like *Love Story* (1970), *When Harry Met Sally...* (1989), and *The Hours* (2002) – that stand out as benchmarks for the genre. As with any movie review, compare films to the way they can be made at their best, especially if you aren't normally a fan of the genre. Not everyone likes this solution – and many readers will foolishly tell you that you should only have genre fans review genre movies – but it is truly the most workable and sustainable solution.

I'll discuss more of the unique challenges of reviewing genre movies for niche audiences in other parts of the book. See also Chapter 6, and the section on subjectivity vs. objectivity, for more thoughts on this topic.

JUDGING AN ACTOR'S PERFORMANCE

One of the most visceral and obvious parts of a film is the acting, so let's start there.

You probably have favorite actors and actresses, but try to think of a film they were in that you didn't like. I'll make it easier: Robert De Niro in *Showtime*, *Analyze That*, or *The Adventures of Rocky & Bullwinkle*. Just because an actor is a perceived legend doesn't mean he can't turn in a rotten performance from time to time. The need for a paycheck can do that to any talent. As an exercise, think about another prolific actor who has starred in many good and bad movies (nearly all actors have: Look at the career of Marlon Brando, if you need convincing). This will help you separate a performer from the part, with the goal of helping you see past your natural bias for or against certain performers.

So, what makes a performance good or bad?

At its core is memorability. Why did Cuba Gooding Jr. win an Oscar for *Jerry Maguire*? Not because of any nuance he put into his role, but rather because he was so vocal, in-your-face, and, thus, memorable. He got in our heads. You couldn't help but have a good time when he was on screen. "Show me the money!" became a rallying cry for years. Gooding has tried to recreate this energy in subsequent performances, but none have packed the same kind of punch; his work has simply become derivative. This isn't to say that Gooding should be dismissed – his work in *As Good As It Gets* (1997) was a fine return to form, though the part was too small to merit much notice – but it does set a kind of baseline for evaluating his future work.

Consider some other truly memorable roles from classic and recent cinema: Malcolm McDowell in *A Clockwork Orange* (1971). Jack Nicholson in *One Flew Over the Cuckoo's Nest* (1975). Al Pacino in *The Godfather* (1972). Meryl Streep in just about anything, but *Sophie's Choice* (1982), in particular. These are roles that define an actor's career, roles that an actor can never escape from because he owned the character so fully. Consider Sean Connery as James Bond. For many purists, after seeing Connery in the role, no man who followed could do the series justice. Connery was just too good.

As with almost any criteria, the quality of a performance is subjective: Is Arnold Schwarzenegger in a *Conan* movie over the top or is it dead-on for the role? Is Jim Carrey *acting* or is he simply hamming it up? Or is he drunk? Is this good or bad? It depends on the movie and on your state of mind.

Broad acting occurs when an actor simply goes too far and overwhelms a character with an outrageous accent or excessive physical humor. When he upstages his costars, it is often known as *chewing the scenery*. In other words, the actor is a wood chipper, a paper shredder destroying the set as all attention is drawn to his performance.

This can be a good thing if a movie has no other redeeming qualities. Many a David Spade movie has been rescued (well, sort of) by the scenery chewing of the late Chris Farley. Think about Charlton Heston in any number of films, including *Soylent Green* (1973). Without his over-the-top performance, the movie wouldn't be worth watching.

In a better project, a hammy actor can be the kiss of death. One overzealous performance can ruin a good ensemble by making the rest of the cast look out of key. Tom Cruise's work in *Magnolia* borders on being too aggressive, but he pulls it back just enough to sell us the character and complement the overall tone of the movie. Cruise ultimately earned an Oscar nomination for the performance.

A more common problem with acting is that a performance will be *stilted*. This can be a function of poor training and preparation (watch a few student films and you'll see what I mean), bad casting, or badly written dialogue that just doesn't sound natural. Usually this is a problem with an actor who doesn't properly embody a role. Given stilted dialogue in a script, a professional actor will change it to suit his character appropriately. You'll never see this translation on the screen, because you won't notice the actor is reading scripted lines. He's just another person, and hopefully one that's engaging to watch.

It doesn't take a lot of effort to tell whether dialogue is stilted. Your ear will tell you if the words ring false – all you need to do is make note of the offense.

It's often unfair to blame just the actor for a bad performance: Consider the muscle-bound Vin Diesel delivering his erudite lines in *XXX*, philosophizing about politics while careening down the road in a stolen car. This is bad directing, bad writing, *and* bad acting. Diesel shouldn't be stuck with all the blame.

Much of a performance comes down to the little things that make or break it. If an accent is required, does it sound off? Are lines flubbed but left in the final cut? Is the actor improvising badly, or has the director lost control of his performer? Normally these problems should severely knock down your rating of a film ... but then again, Marilyn Monroe was probably the worst offender of all of these crimes, yet she somehow managed to make it all look good. Check out *Some Like It Hot* (1959), where she was reportedly drunk throughout the shoot and had to have her lines written on props because she couldn't remember them. Her loopy behavior nonetheless comes off as charming, as it served her lightweight role. Sometimes these flaws turn into quirky plusses instead of blatant minuses. Recognizing when that happens will elevate your review above the rest of the crowd.

Finally, a word should be said about *character actors*, people like Joe Don Baker, Michael Richards, and Philip Seymour Hoffman, who always seem to play a variation of the same strange character. Character actors serve a valuable purpose – we know what to expect the moment we see them because they've been typecast in a similar role in the past. Or, in the case of actors like Stephen Tobolowsky, they just look the part. A movie may only have 90 minutes to introduce a half-dozen major and semi-major characters, so taking a few shortcuts can make perfect sense in launching us into a film more quickly. These small and seemingly unimportant roles often can make or break an iffy movie. Consider how the scant few appearances of Jack Black elevate *High Fidelity* (2000) above its lackluster story.

A rich performance by a character actor – anything Hoffman or J.T Walsh does – can also prove to be a critical and truly masterful part of a particular film. In recent memory, Burt Reynolds in *Boogie Nights* (1997), Jack Palance in *City Slickers* (1991), and Robert Forster in *Jackie Brown* (1997) all created uniquely memorable characters from tiny tweaks of standby roles they'd been playing for years. Palance even won an Oscar for it, and dragged that character with him through the Oscar ceremony the following year. Don't let the fact that the performance is a variation on a familiar theme allow you to discount it.

In the end, weighing the performance of an actor is probably the least "scientific" part of reviewing a movie. You'll recognize most of the truly good performances when you think about the film in retrospect, but the bad ones will leap right out at you.

SCHOOLS OF ACTING

There are several formal schools (or styles) of acting – method acting being by far the most popular. It's worthwhile to familiarize yourself with them in order to be more conversant with the training and background that actors go through. Alone, these schools of acting mean nothing to the typical movie review, but they are useful in aiding the quality and detail of a critique's analysis.

Method acting is a style in which the actor attempts to recreate the emotions his character would be experiencing, drawing on "emotional memory" or a "sense memory," the events and experiences from the actor's own past that have an analogy to the events the character experiences. An actor may recall his own father's death when his character appears at a funeral – the goal often being to summon real sorrow and real tears in a tragic scene. When an actor asks, "What's my motivation?" he is looking for a cue to help draw out an emotional or sense memory. Method actors researching roles will often go to outrageous lengths to embody their characters, especially if they are playing real people. Robert De Niro is said to have insisted on the same style of silk underwear as Al Capone wore for his work in *The Untouchables* (1987). Method acting was

45

developed by Konstantin Stanislavski, and his book *An Actor Prepares* remains the quintessential work on the subject of method acting. (Sanford Meisner and Lee Strasberg are other popular names associated with the training and refinement of this technique.) For a quick primer, check out a few episodes of Bravo's *Inside the Actor's Studio*, which trains its students in the method system and frequently discusses it on the show. Marlon Brando, a die-hard method actor, brought the method to the forefront of cinema with his performance in *A Streetcar Named Desire* (1951). Watch and learn.

Brechtian acting is far less popular but can be a curious approach to an otherwise traditional movie or role. German playwright Bertolt Brecht thought that a performance would excel if it drew attention to itself. In other words, he wanted the audience to *know* someone was acting and to *know* that they were watching a play or a movie instead of real life. Today, this often leads to ham-fisted approaches to a performance, since most of the other performers will be method actors and the Brechtian performance will stand out. There are, of course, exceptions: The great Bill Murray was trained in improvisation (see below) but his style is extremely Brechtian. When Murray appears onscreen, there's never any doubt that you're watching a character created by Murray and a grandiose performance. Yet in films like *Caddyshack* and even *Charlie's Angels*, Murray steals the show with his outrageous dramatizations, even though they may be to the detriment of the other actors.

Improvisation is an extension of method acting, where an actor develops his character based on motivation and memory, then simply reacts "in the moment" to the other characters and the general situation of the film. Few films are improvised in whole or in part. Usually they are comedies. Check out Christopher Guest's *Best in Show* (2000) or Rob Reiner's *This is Spinal Tap* (1984) for two excellent and successful examples.

JUDGING SCREENWRITING

So much has been written about the craft of screenwriting that this section of the book could easily fill its own volume on how to critique it. But boil down a script to the essential elements and you can develop a shorthand for analyzing a screenplay.

Of course, you won't actually be reading a script when you review the movie. You'll be hearing a version of the script through the dialogue of the actors and the actions of their characters. Keep in mind some caveats: Actors may change lines or even improvise entire roles; directors may change scripts on the fly; editors may restructure stories after the fact; and scripts may be ruthlessly cut to shorten a film that's running too long. All of these are commonplace, actually. So judge writing in a slightly more abstract sense than you would acting or directing, since you never really know where to place the credit or the blame.

The key word, though, is *slightly*! Remember that without a script, a movie would never exist. Writing is easily the most critical part of a film, because there's nothing that can salvage a bad script. Bad acting, bad lighting, bad direction – all of these things can be transcended by a funny or touching story. Imagine seeing your favorite band in an echo-filled arena. You'll forgive a terrible sound setup if you really like the music anyway. This is somewhat less true for actors you may have an affinity for: I find that when my favorite actors appear in bad movies, it simply amplifies my dislike for the film, since their potential has been wasted. But if an actor I don't care for appears in a film with great dialogue and a clever story, I'm overcome by the quality of the script every time.

The most important aspect of any script is that it successfully creates a *suspension of disbelief.* Movies don't often emulate everyday life. If they did, no one would watch them. Instead they take us to riotous parties after high school graduation, to last-minute appeals for prisoners on death row, to epic space battles between rival planets. All of these require the suspension of disbelief in our minds, since we know Susan Sarandon is not a nun and Sean Penn was not executed by lethal injection in *Dead Man Walking* (1995). But does that film convince us to the contrary, even if it's just for the two hours we're sitting in the theater? Yes, and quite successfully. This is a testament to the actors, but it's also thanks to an understated and very realistic script. Imagine if a guard had accidentally dropped his keys in the death chamber and the power went out at just the right time, letting the nun and the convict escape to a happy ending together. This would be absurd, and it would ruin the film. Yet Hollywood makes terrible movies like this all the time, their major flaw being that we can't possibly believe that the events we're seeing could be true under any circumstances.

Now, it would seem that science fiction and fantasy movies like the *Star Wars* series or *Lord of the Rings* would suffer unilaterally, but actually the bar for suspension of disbelief is lower for these types of films. Why? Because the audience goes in willing to accept that the rules of present-day Earth don't apply to other galaxies or a distant/alternate future. Because the audience is also generally more willing to believe in The Force or the power of a magic ring, these films often serve as a unique form of escapism that traditional movies don't provide.

What films have the highest bar when it comes to suspension of disbelief? Ironically, it's the very films that get made the most: Action movies, especially those with a high-tech bent. All too often, the Schwarzeneggers, Van Dammes, and Jet Lis of the world appear invincible in fist, knife, and gun battles, taking out enemies by the truckload and never receiving a scratch. Yet when movies like Arnold's *Collateral Damage* (2002) take place in a terrorism-riddled present, we're supposed to believe these are potentially real events that would require a real hero to save us.

But we stop rooting for the hero whenever he has no genuine obstacles to overcome or when he has no other avenue left but to succeed at whatever mission he's been tasked with. Throw in the introduction of impossible (or extremely unlikely) technology, and the film gets that much worse. Schwarzenegger, in fact, spoofed these very problems in 1993's *The Last Action Hero* (though not very successfully).

One of the golden rules of screenwriting is that nothing in a film – the story, a plot point, a line of dialogue – has to actually *be* true, it just has to *seem* like it's true. What would a minister *really* say when he's eulogizing the deceased? It doesn't matter, as long as the audience doesn't say, "Oh, he'd never say *that*!" Many independent film directors seem to have a problem creating overly erudite characters – a garbage man who speaks with Shakespearean-class grammar, children who are too smart to know the words they're saying, and so on. This can occasionally be a clever way to create an unexpected supporting character where a rote cliché would otherwise appear, but too often *all* of a movie's characters speak with the same cadence and use the same turns of phrase, making the dialogue ring untrue. The TV show *Dawson's Creek* was often ridiculed for its too-intellectual teenagers – not that one of them was too smart for his own good, but that all of them were.

The rule also goes for characters with an uncanny sixth sense who immediately know where to find that crucial piece of evidence in mystery films. As well, when that evidence is conveniently forgotten until the final 15 minutes (consider the fateful 911 call unearthed at the end of Clint Eastwood's 2003 *Mystic River*), it smacks of lazy writing. If you find yourself saying (or hearing), "That would *never* happen," then you've been kicked out of the world of the movie and back into reality. This is never good.

STORY STRUCTURE

The heart of any screenplay is *structure*, and by far the most common story structure is the *three act structure*. It was popularized by Syd Field in various screenwriting books, the most popular being *Screenplay: The Foundations of Screenwriting*. I'll cover the basics here, but you are highly encouraged to check out Field's book (along with works by Robert McKee, Linda Seger, and William Goldman, if you're so inclined) for a more in-depth discussion about the art of screenwriting.

The three act structure suggests that great films of past and present adhere to a format with three acts separated by turning points. In its simplest form: boy meets girl, boy loses girl, boy gets girl back. These statements comprise three acts, with two *inciting incidents* or *turning points* between the three acts, each designed to spin the plot in a different direction. It's not hard to overlay a three act structure on any popular movie.

In *The Matrix* (1999), for example, Keanu Reeves' character Anderson/Neo discovers that he's living inside a computer generated simulation during act one. In act two, he breaks free of the Matrix, learns about the resistance, trains extensively, and learns he may be a prophesied superhero called The One (and is finally told that he is *not*). In act three, Neo goes into the Matrix to save his mentor, Morpheus, and comes to realize that he really *is* The One after all. Neo saves Morpheus and defeats his nemesis, Agent Smith (at least until the sequels). It's a perfect example of the three act structure working, and working well.

Moulin Rouge! (2001) is an unconventional film that still fits the mold. Act one follows Christian's (Ewan McGregor) introduction to the Bohemians as he falls for dancer/prostitute Satine (Nicole Kidman). In act two, he finds that Satine has been given to another, wealthier man, and he and the Bohemians craft a play that will save the club where she works. In act three, Christian and Satine's secret affair is discovered, and a plot to kill Christian must be stopped, all on the eve of the play's debut performance. The musical numbers and spectacle of the movie mask the underlying structure considerably, but a little thought reveals a straightforward plot structure that works very well in the context of this film. As with all well-structured stories, it works so well you don't actually think about structure and plotting as you watch it; you just go with the flow.

The school of counter-thought, of course, says that the three act structure is tired and boring. In other words, if you are expecting a turning point at the 30-minute mark and another one at the 90-minute mark, where's the surprise? Don't all movies become cookie-cutter versions of one another? It's worth thinking about.

Sure enough, five act and seven act structures have been floated, to minimal reception. Some movies – *Magnolia, Forrest Gump, The Wizard of Oz* – have so many plot twists or changes of direction that it's almost impossible to force them into just three acts. In the end it doesn't really matter how many acts a movie has, as long as it maintains energy throughout the film, builds to an exciting climax, and keeps you interested. In other words, a good story is more important than an artificial set of rules into which a script is shoehorned.

An analogue to these meticulous structure systems are what I call *no act* movies. These are either improvised or intentionally bizarre films that throw structure out the window. Sometimes these films can be incredibly successful. *The Blair Witch Project* (1999) is probably the best recent example of this; the story works because we never know where it's going to take us, while the film drags us deeper and deeper into the campers' nightmare. Robert Altman's *Short Cuts* (1993) is almost impossible to fit into any number of acts. Most of David Lynch's movies are intentionally unstructured, which has earned him a legion of fans which prefer oddball stories (not to mention the opposing legion, which do not).

It's usually not worth mentioning structure explicitly in a review, unless it deviates greatly from the mold. Often critics will say that a film drags in act two or has a weak third act, but you don't need to spend time outlining the acts of a film in full. Your plot synopsis will get the gist of the acts across well enough so the reader understands the basic plot structure without giving too much away. I'll discuss synopsis writing in Chapter 5.

Another effective technique is to discuss the general flow of a plot in broad strokes. Typically this is referred to as a *story arc*, the rise and fall of action, emotion, character growth, and other components that lend excitement and interest to a plot. Story arcs are commonly applied to specific characters, another facet of screenwriting theory.

Character arcs are essentially the same concept as story arcs, just on a character-by-character basis. A good script is always told through its characters and their dialogue instead of through simple action. This isn't just a rule that applies to dramas; *Die Hard* (1988) is probably the greatest action film of its era, but not because of any special action sequences – it's because of Bruce Willis' interesting character, John McClane, and the way he grows throughout the course of the film. His wisecracks don't hurt, either.

Considering the growth of each character individually through analysis of character arc can help identify strong and weak areas of a story. Again, this doesn't have to be a rundown of every character in the film, but offering a sentence or two on the growth of the protagonist (or a noticeable lack of growth) is almost always appropriate in a review.

Finally, *plot resolution* is a fancy way of saying that loose ends in the story are tied up by the end. Think of the plot resolution as the end of the story arc: Do the film's plot and subplots wrap up neatly without too many loose ends? A movie doesn't have to tidy up every single story – that can come off as a little too pat or convenient – but it's important that the audience isn't left scratching its head about, say, what happened to the villain left dangling off a cliff by his fingernails. Unresolved plotlines can be a sign of bad writing, editing, directing, or even acting (as scenes may have been cut for time or because they just didn't turn out well in front of the camera). Regardless of whose fault it is, this problem is always annoying.

COMMON SCRIPT PROBLEMS

In no particular order, here are some common problems to consider when evaluating a story. These can be minor flaws or major ones, but these problems tend to follow mediocre movies like a plague.

Poor pacing – Even good movies can have pacing problems, and typically these fall in the lengthy second act of the film. Movies are designed to have exciting opening acts and exciting finales – often leaving "the middle" with nowhere to go. The second act is also the longest portion of the film, and it takes real talent to design a scenario where characters experience growth, where the story arc builds, and where the audience doesn't get bored silly. You'll know poor pacing when you see it, because that's when you're checking your watch.

Voice-over – This is contentious, and you may feel differently, but conventional wisdom holds that voice-over is a weak way to tell a story. In other words: Don't talk about what you are going to see (or would have seen in the past), show it on the screen, and use a flashback if you have to. Most of the time, voice-over is added after a bad movie has been through extensive editing and still doesn't make sense. Often, voice-over is used to bridge plot holes or fill in plot gaps. I tend to agree that voice-over weakens a film, though numerous films have made excellent use of it (*Apocalypse Now*, *A Christmas Story*, *American Beauty*, and *Fight Club* come to mind). At the same time, voice-over is often a huge nuisance and takes you out of the action; most of us don't often hear otherworldly voices narrating important events in our lives or providing commentary on what we're seeing. The archetypal voice-over debate invariably centers around *Blade Runner* (1982); the original cut had it, the director's cut (available on DVD) does not. If you can check them out side by side, it's an excellent exercise. I'm in the minority: Personally I prefer the voice-over version.

Telling, Not Showing – Screenwriting books harp on this constantly, but filmmakers still make this cardinal error all the time. The problem stems from the idea that film is a *visual* medium, but writers are accustomed to the printed page and many have trouble thinking in pictures. It's the director's job to massage this material into something for the eye to see – but this doesn't happen in many cases, possibly because you are dealing with an inexperienced filmmaker, a small budget, or – most commonly – laziness in the storytelling process. It's an easy shortcut to take: Character A says to character B that he's feeling sad because he's in love with the girl across the hall and she doesn't know he exists. The "right" way to tell this story is to show character A pining for the girl, the girl snubbing him in the hallway, and A threatening to jump off a bridge in his despondency. Shooting all of that is a lot of work and requires genuine acting skill. It's easy – but makes for a terrible movie – to just shoot two characters *talking* about their problems in a bar.

Coincidence As Plot Driver – How many times have you rolled your eyes when a movie's action hero rounds a corner in a giant metropolis, only to come face to face with his nemesis? Why do romantic leads tend to cross paths at random? Simply to drive the plot, because the screenwriter couldn't come up with a better way to get the characters in the same room together.

Recycling Storylines – Stop me if you've heard this one before: Teens on a road trip break down in the middle of nowhere, then they're attacked by a gang of crazies. They've been making this movie since at least 1974, when the original *Texas Chainsaw Massacre* pioneered the idea. It's recycled every year or so, and it gets worse every time. While horror movies suffer most from this problem (after all, how many ways are there to get kids and killers together?), it commonly extends to action films and romantic comedies starring Meg Ryan, as well. Astute critics keep a watchful eye for less-obvious recycling. Remember that this doesn't necessarily mean a movie is *bad*, it's just something that should be noted in a review and which might point to a less-than-original script.

Cheap Shots – You know how an otherwise sophisticated comedy will often end a scene with a character tripping or falling down? Or a character will take a kick to the privates? This is a cheap shot designed to get a quick laugh out of you and hide the fact that the script didn't have any better way to transition to the next scene. Don't be fooled.

Lousy Endings – I can't count how many so-so or good movies have been ruined by terrible endings. Sometimes they just *stop*, as if the screenwriter's printer ran out of paper or the movie just ran out of money. But more often you'll see the *deus ex machina*, the "god from the machine," where a surprising plot twist comes out of nowhere to end the film. Based on the old Greek plays, which often ended with a god coming down from the sky, in modern times this refers to any overly convenient and unexpected ending to a film. For example, a helpful reserve battalion turns the tide of war, or a plane conveniently arrives to pick up an island castaway, just in time for the credits. The *deus ex machina* can be one of the most frustrating facets of a film and always merits harsh criticism.

Plot Holes – These are the little things that keep bugging you as you talk about a movie with your friends. In *Sneakers* (1992), Robert Redford and his crew go to outrageous lengths to beat a voice identification system, but at the end of the film we find that someone could simply crawl through the ductwork to bypass the system altogether. It's an annoying mistake that doesn't ruin the movie but does irritate you and points to problems with the script. In *Spider-Man 2* (2004), why does Dr. Octopus hurl a car at the only guy (Peter Parker) who could tell him where Spider-Man is? Octopus doesn't know Peter will be able to escape it since he isn't aware of his dual identity. The scene is simply an opportunity to provide an incredible action scene. You aren't supposed to worry about the plot problem. Fans who go to the movie "just to have a good time" probably won't care, but if it bugs you, it merits mentioning. Also of note, internet industries have sprung up around spotting plot holes. Visit www.movie-mistakes.com to see its encyclopedia of movie errors and discover what mistakes have been found in your favorite films!

JUDGING CINEMATOGRAPHY

It isn't absolutely necessary to understand the various schools of cinematography in order to review a movie (namely since most "schools" have faded away in favor of the constantly moving cameras and quick cutting that has become popular in the MTV era), but it doesn't hurt to know your history, especially if you're reviewing an older film. Italian Neo-Realism and the French New Wave (as discussed previously) are associated with their own visual styles, but these are both considered larger than their cinematographic components. The following schools comprise mainly photographic techniques, but the terms can also be applied to a film as a whole.

GERMAN EXPRESSIONISM

German Expressionism is probably the oldest major school of cinematography. Originating (obviously) in Germany in the 1920s, Expressionism sought to express characters' states of mind through lighting, camera angles, and even sets and costumes. (Since this was the silent era, directors and cinematographers had to do everything they could to get across the mood of an actor whose voice could not be heard.) Look no further than the deep shadows of *Nosferatu* (1922) to see the archetypal example of this cinematography style.

Expressionism still impacts filmmakers today, particularly in the use of shadow and mood lighting to convey the ominousness of a situation. Think about the prototypical horror movie taking place in a haunted insane asylum and you'll find the absolute terminus of Expressionism today. The works of Tim Burton (*Batman, Edward Scissorhands*) are also tremendously influenced by the moodiness of Expressionism.

SURREALISM

The art world commingled with cinema more closely in the realm of surrealism than any other. Salvador Dali, the king of the surrealist movement, even worked with Disney on an animated film in 1946 called *Destino*. (It has only recently been released theatrically.) Dali also collaborated with Alfred Hitchcock on the dream sequences in the film *Spellbound*. His touches are unmistakable.

Aside from Dali's dabbling, surrealism is most evident in the works of Luis Buñuel and David Lynch, whose works are almost entirely surrealistic from start to finish. Dreams blend with reality, shapes and forms shift, and characters change identities. You'll probably be more familiar with the works of Lynch (*Blue Velvet, Twin Peaks, Mulholland Drive*), who plays with surrealism in most of his works, with film running backwards and sequences that push the boundaries of what we expect from reality. Some of this is directorial style, but a lot of it has to do with cinematography.

Thanks to modern computer graphics, today's directors can tinker more freely with surrealist elements in their films. Many a drug sequence has put the viewer into an affected state of blurred vision with weird pans and zooms designed to disorient the audience. These don't amount to much more than camera trickery and needn't be considered as part of the surrealist movement (which is pretty minimal to begin with), but understanding the origins of such effects can be helpful in select reviews.

HYPER-REALISM

Not so much a movement as a style, hyper-realism has been practiced by countless and diverse directors over the years and across the continents. Douglas Sirk is best known for this style. His films are famous for their ultra-crisp colors and too-perfect set designs, which make you feel like you're in a strange alternative universe that very closely – but not precisely – resembles our own. The result is strangely disconcerting and alienating, but hard to put a finger on, exactly.

To see hyper-realism in action, check out Sirk's 1956 drama *All That Heaven Allows* and then watch Todd Haynes' 2002 homage, *Far From Heaven*. Sirk was probably only vaguely aware of the disorienting effect of the style, but Haynes's approach to mind-scrambling color and design is intentional. These are films that can generate substantial conversation and analysis for their production designs alone.

Japan has long been steeped in hyper-realism (or simple realism, at the very least), dating back to the works of Yasujiro Ozu and earlier. Ozu's 1959 film *Good Morning* looks like it could have been made by Sirk. Today's Japanese directors, obsessed with blood-splattered violence and long shots of decaying cityscapes, use color in ways that American directors never dream of. Watch a watershed film like Takashi Miike's *Audition* (2000) and see how he alternates between surrealist and hyper-realist approaches to create a truly disturbing end product. Be warned: You will have nightmares.

MODERN ADVANCES

Fundamentally, cinematography hasn't changed in the last 40 years. Cameras are a bit better, lighting is more sophisticated, and directors have learned a few new tricks with pulling focus and using dollies. But in the end, film stock and lenses are pretty much the same as they've been for years.

Today's real advances – or changes, really – in cinematography have been products of the digital revolution. Digital effects make it easy to warp time, space, color, and just about anything else you see on the screen. Whole armies are created on computer, and battles are fought with the push of a button.

Is this good or bad? It depends. Movies like *The Lord of the Rings* trilogy are eye-catching spectacles, but I find them cinematically cold and obviously fake. Consider the ridiculously overrated *Gladiator* (2000), which was deeply tweaked with CGI. The battle scenes are great to look at, but are enhanced to the point where they look unreal. Especially those tigers. Compare these scenes to the all-too-realistic chariot race of *Ben-Hur* (1959). *Gladiator* can't hold a candle.

MAJOR CINEMATOGRAPHIC CONSIDERATIONS

Aside from an overall school or style, general cinematographic techniques will inform your opinion of a film greatly, whether you choose to write about cinematography explicitly or not at all in your review. I'll discuss the major cinematographic elements of a film here.

Camera Movement – It is possible that Robert Rodriguez's micro-budgeted *El Mariachi* (1992) is singularly responsible for getting filmmakers to pick up their camera and move it around in a scene. (Though he's now a big shot, Rodriguez still holds and operates the camera himself on most of his films, virtually unheard of in the movie business.) On the flipside, it is probably *The Blair Witch Project* (1999) that finally took camera movement beyond the terminal limits of nausea; anyone prone to motion sickness was forced out of the theater during that film.

With too little movement, the eye becomes bored and the film requires more cutting between various angles. It can be visually dull and lazy. If you find your mind wandering during a film, and it's not because of the lackluster script, then it's often the camerawork. With too much camera movement, a film becomes too showy and too apparent to the audience that they're "in a movie." See the sequel *The Bourne Supremacy* (2004) for a perfect example. Directors who never stop moving the camera, like Lars von Trier, not-so-subtly want you to know that they are personally involved with the production of the movie. They want that directorial stamp to be felt, regardless of what it does to their film. Unfortunately, it can take you out of the story and into the moviemaking process, which is almost always a terrible idea. (That motion sickness issue is nothing to sneeze at, either.)

Somewhere between the "plant the camera on a tripod and leave it there" approach (check out Ozu's *Tokyo Story* (1953)) and the "never put the camera down" conceit of *Blair Witch* is a happy medium where the viewer is integrated into the scene and yet the movement of the camera doesn't draw attention to itself. You'll learn to find that balance as you critique more and more movies.

Lighting – Is the picture too dark? Or is it too dark *on purpose*? Horror movies and film noirs often make excellent use of light and shadow, but many mainstream films do, too. Consider the film *Road to Perdition* (2002), which used rain-soaked night shots to perfectly set the film's mood. But for an inexperienced cinematographer, shadows can wreak havoc with a film, as harsh lines are created across actors' faces or as backlighting washes out the shot, leaving the foreground indiscernible. Bad lighting is often the product of a low budget or an amateur crew. You rarely see problems with it in films today. Most often you'll see bad lighting in movies that are shot directly on video, which is very unforgiving when it comes to lighting problems. If a movie has a lighting problem, you'll notice it immediately, and it will almost invariably impact your

56

ability to enjoy a film.

Framing – Amateur filmmakers rarely know how to position all the elements on the screen properly, which is known as *mise en scene* and includes other elements of *art direction*, *set design* and *decoration*. Properly defined, *mise en scene* is the arrangement of performers and properties for production before a camera. Look at the way a movie like *Fail-Safe* (1964, itself a low-budget production) contrasts wide shots of its war rooms with close-ups of its tense and sweaty heroes. Intelligent framing (placement of people and objects within the boundaries of the screen) and blocking (sometimes synonymous with framing, but often specifically referring to movement of people and objects on the screen) help a film look its best.

Bad framing is mostly noticeable during scene transitions. A common example among low-budget films occurs during dialogue: One character is shown in close-up, then the scene cuts to the person he's addressing, only he's shown from the waist up. This disconnect pulls us out of the film. Good cinematography should, at best, awe us, and at worst, not be noticed at all.

Another related problem includes something called "crossing the line": Characters in a conversation should appear on opposite sides of the screen, facing the center (and thus, each other) across an invisible line running up and down through the screen. This helps the viewer when the camera cuts between characters, as we expect to see the person on the right facing the person on the left, and vice versa. If both characters are shown on the right side of the screen facing inward, this becomes confusing and unintuitive. Fortunately, professional directors and cinematographers rarely make framing errors.

Use of Angles – The Dutch angle (where a scene is shot from a titled diagonal orientation) is at once one of the most interesting and most annoying camera tricks around. Directors like Quentin Tarantino and Oliver Stone always find clever ways to place the camera in unexpected locations to get that perfect shot. This can also be emulated with CGI: Consider the opening sequence of *Fight Club* (1999), which begins inside the main character's brain and ends up on the outside of his head.

Overuse of kooky angles is a common problem – a crutch used by lazy directors to hide a weak script or other flaws. The most notorious example is *Battlefield Earth* (2000), which features few shots *not* taken at a Dutch angle. Unfortunately, director Roger Christian was not able to use them to mask the fact that he was shooting one of the worst movies of all time.

Depth of Field – This refers to the placement of people or objects in the foreground and the background, and the interplay between them. In simplified terms, "depth of field" refers to the fact that a camera can only focus on objects at or around a certain distance – and objects closer or further away will both be out of focus. But camera trickery can allow both near and far objects to be in focus at the same time.

Some of cinema's most masterful shots make use of depth of field tricks. Orson Welles was a genius at this. The opening scenes of *Citizen Kane* (1941) provide the best primer on depth of field you'll find. John Frankenheimer's *The Manchurian Candidate* (1962) has a few great examples, too. I can't think of a *bad* example of a director playing with depth of field; it isn't a common trick these days because it requires careful blocking that most directors don't have time to muck around with.

Location Shooting – Most of today's films are shot, in part at least, on location. Contrast this with Hollywood's Golden Age, when everything from *Cleopatra* to *Who's Afraid of Virginia Woolf?* was shot on a stage or on the back lot (an outdoor set owned by the studio). Location shooting adds a degree of realism you simply can't get in your backyard. Contrast the *Lord of the Rings* series with films like *Ben-Hur* or the aforementioned *Cleopatra*: *Rings'* landscapes look real because they are real, *Cleopatra*'s are obviously staged. (What you think about the CGI effects in *Lord of the Rings* is another matter, to be discussed below.)

Don't let phony sets ruin your impression of older films, though. This was simply "the way it was done" for decades, as travel to far-flung locations with gigantic crews and heavy equipment was difficult or impossible. Today, more portable equipment, easier access to travel, and guerrilla-style shooting has made location shooting the norm.

CGI – CGI stands for computer generated imagery, and it's undoubtedly the most powerful – and abused – advancement to hit filmmaking in the last 20 years. CGI has opened the door to a new era of special effects. Films like the *Lord of the Rings* trilogy couldn't have been made at all without them. Entire characters are crafted in CGI, from *Star Wars'* Jar-Jar Binks to *Rings'* Gollum. These two examples show how CGI can make or break a film: Viewers lobbied for Andy Serkis, who voiced and provided the body movements for Gollum, to receive an Oscar, while *Star Wars* fans created a version of *The Phantom Menace* with Jar-Jar edited out.

CGI is simply a tool, but any good critic will analyze its use carefully. CGI isn't always attached to science fiction. Films like *Cast Away* (2000) use CGI to make environments look more realistic and cinematic, or to make weather look exactly the way the director wants. The waves crashing around Tom Hanks' island are a good example – they aren't there in the original footage. CGI also can save money, as buildings can be virtually constructed by computer, and later burned down or destroyed by virtual armies.

In a review, a good critic will consider the *quality* of the CGI instead of the mere fact that it was used. CGI objects and characters often have a not-quite-real feeling, a problem generated by the fact that the technology isn't quite as perfect as filmmakers would like. CGI buildings and other static objects tend to look great, but when CGI objects move, they defy gravity a bit – like in a Wile E. Coyote cartoon – and don't cast shadows and reflect light in quite the right way. Skin and hair is particularly difficult to replicate with CGI.

Ultimately, how much of this you forgive (due to immature technology) vs. how much you count against a film's rating (after all, the director decided to use CGI instead of hiring extras, building sets, using miniatures, or creating animatronic monsters) is completely up to you. Film critics rarely agree on the effectiveness of CGI, so if it becomes a focal point of your reviews, make sure you apply your rules consistently across other films that use the technology.

Color – Once in awhile, a filmmaker has the bright idea to shoot in black and white instead of color. *Schindler's List* (1993) is the most notable example, as Spielberg sought to harken back to the days of WWII, when few films (and virtually no war films) were shot in color.

Color is also easily tweaked during the development process, and it's common for the director and/or cinematographer to run through the film and ask for more yellow here, less blue there. This is known as "color timing." Color timing is typically used to give a movie a uniform color tone, but other filmmakers intentionally wash color out of their movies, leaving only hints of blue and red on the palette. The recent American remake of *The Ring* (2002) is a good example: The bleak tone of the film is aided by muting the otherwise lush greens of the Pacific Northwest, as the bright colors of the foliage would have made the movie seem cheery instead of ominous. In *Panic Room* (2002), director David Fincher casts everything with a strong green tint, making us feel sick to our stomachs – setting both the tone of the claustrophobic situation and symbolizing the diabetic daughter's medical condition. In *Traffic* (2000), Steven Soderbergh contrasts his various stories through different film stocks and color treatments, effectively pitting the U.S. lush life against the gritty reality of the south-of-the-border drug cartels.

Sometimes washed-out color is used rather blatantly to attempt to manipulate a weak film into feeling darker or moodier than it otherwise would be. This crutch can help a bit, but it usually makes little difference in the end.

Joe Carnahan's *Narc* (2002) is largely a run-of-the-mill cop drama, but he toys with color to give the movie a more gritty, urban cachet than it otherwise would have achieved.

Use of color (or lack thereof) is easy to spot. Be sure to mention how effective such film treatments are when you see them.

Miscellaneous Camera Trickery – A whole grab bag of other tricks merit mention in this section, from Sam Raimi mounting a camera on a motorcycle and riding it through a forest and a building in *The Evil Dead* (1981) to the "bullet time" effect in *The Matrix* (and its endless imitators). These are stunts that can range from mere curiosities to industry-shattering effects (as with the bullet time process). It isn't hard to notice such effects – that's why the directors put them in the films to begin with – and they always bear mention in your reviews.

JUDGING DIRECTION

No offense to the cast, crew, and other creative components of a movie, but the director is the soul of the film. Ultimately, he is responsible for the success or failure of the movie. Everything from the script to the actors to the wardrobe choices are affected by the director, and thus as a critic, you can feel comfortable blaming him for *anything* that goes wrong.

Sure, you'll want to lay blame and give credit where it's due. A great Jack Nicholson performance is going to be due to Jack. *Fight Club* (1999) is a great movie due to Jim Uhls' excellent adaptation of Chuck Palahniuk's book. But David Fincher takes that raw material and turns it into something grandiose and unique. Ridley Scott and Steven Spielberg invariably leave thumbprints on movies that make them special and identifiable as part of their oeuvre.

Some directors are completely inseparable from their work. David Lynch is the ultimate test case here. It's hard to tell where the script ends and his psychosis begins.

The director's thumbprint – whether it's subtle, like Spielberg's *Schindler's List* (1993), or over-the-top, like Lynch's *Lost Highway* (1997) – is what makes film criticism impossible to approach with any kind of scientific regularity. It's also the trickiest part of a critic's job. Whether you're a fan of *Lost Highway* or not completely depends on how you respond to the visual imagery of Lynch.

Almost as a proof that there are no reliable "rules" in film direction, Lynch is also responsible for *The Straight Story*, one of the sweetest and most straightforward films in recent memory. Critics have tried, and invariably failed, to explain this departure from his earlier work. Ultimately it's a lesson that you can't approach a movie review with preconceived notions, and that every film must stand on its own. Go into a movie with your preconceptions intact and you invariably set yourself up for disappointment. (In general, most critics agree that the less you know about a film before you see it, the better. More on this later in the book.)

DIRECTORS AND ACTORS

What does it mean to "direct" a film? It means a lot of things, but the most important element is directing the actors. You'll often hear certain directors referred to as "an actors' director." Robert Altman earns this title, as does James L. Brooks. This is often a subtly disparaging remark about an actor who's taking a stab at directing (meaning, obviously, that he's foremost an actor that doesn't really know anything about the technicalities of filmmaking). But many legitimate directors are genuine "actors' directors" – because they care most (or appear to care most) about the performances in their movies.

Woody Allen is an actors' director, and by all accounts he *hates* actors. But he has their complete respect because of his understanding of the craft of acting and the psyche of the actors' minds. Allen treats actors like cattle or small children. His approach seems to work: Say what you will about Allen's movies, but you can't seriously claim that they feature bad performances. For Allen, his stories don't always work, and his directorial approach can be misguided, but he really brings out the best in his stars.

Oddly, Alfred Hitchcock pioneered the "actors as cattle" approach – in fact, he is personally credited with coining that analogy. But Hitch's success with actors is generally limited. He worked with some greats, but in many of his films, Hitchcock is clearly more concerned with the intricacies of developing his plot and getting the perfect shot. Who is the better director? Allen and Hitchcock represent the pinnacle of the field; how can you pick between them? The point is not to get overly caught up in the process of direction but to understand how that process affects the end product.

STORYTELLING, PACING, AND REVELATIONS

Film direction is a game of show and tell. A typical film can be completely described in one paragraph of succinct text. How a director uses a full 100 minutes to lead us through that text is what makes him a real storyteller. I touched on these issues in the section on screenwriting, but the director is also responsible for properly pacing the film and merits some repetition.

Pacing is an essential element of great films. You'll know bad pacing when you see it: You'll find yourself bored, confused, or both. Some critics use the number of times they check their watch as a benchmark for the film as a whole. If you're too involved to think about the time, chances are you're watching a very good movie. The script and the direction work together here, but deciding what scenes could move more quickly and what scenes need time to develop is what makes or breaks a great director.

One of the most critical tools in the directors' toolbox is deciding how and when to reveal information to the audience. Few thrillers begin by telling us the identity of the bad guy. The point of the movie is to figure it out: Where and how that revelation is made is part of what separates good thrillers from bad. (That said, some great thrillers, such as *American Psycho* (2000), tell you right up front who the villain is.)

Alfred Hitchcock isn't called "the master of suspense" for nothing. He knew perfectly well when to reveal information on screen, often keeping it hidden from the characters until the last second. The archetypal example is this: If two characters sit at a table and talk for five minutes and then a bomb goes off, there's no suspense. But if you show the bomb under the table to the audience – but not the characters – with a five-minute countdown timer, and then have the characters talking obliviously while the bomb ticks down, that's suspense. Will they discover it? Will they try to defuse it? What will happen next? The audience will be on the edge of its seat. These two vignettes might otherwise look very similar on film, but the end result is much, much different. Since few movies are as simple as the "hidden bomb" example, it takes a great director to understand how differences in pacing affect the final product, and it takes a seasoned critic to comment on it.

Another related trick in the director's toolkit is having certain actions take place off camera. Great directors know that *not* showing a key event – a murder, a love scene, or even a pratfall down a flight of stairs – can be more effective than showing it in its full glory. Very little of Lawrence's torture in *Lawrence of Arabia* is shown on camera. Most of it takes place off camera. In the end, the movie cuts to a long shot of the Turkish commander, coughing as he peeks out from behind his office door. It's a powerful moment that requires nothing graphic to be photographed.

EDITING

I lump editing in with direction because most films are edited in conjunction with the director. Can you imagine writing a 1,000-page novel and handing it off to another person, then having him deliver you a finished, 200-page manuscript, all without comment from yourself? Of course not, and most directors couldn't either, which is why most are critically involved in the editing process.

Editing rarely is understood fully by either the audience or the critics, because great editing goes unnoticed. As with bad sound and bad makeup, editing is something that tends to be visible only when it's done poorly. Do scenes run on too long? Do cuts within a scene happen too often – or not enough? Are characters with lines confusingly not shown on camera? Does the film feel jumpy, uneven, or otherwise cobbled together? It's impossible to know whether the fault lies with a bad editor or a director who didn't get the right shots to start with, so it's best not to go off half-cocked, assigning "blame" to one or the other. You'll know bad editing when you see it. Leave it at that.

The use of editing trickery is a frequent crutch – much like camera trickery – used to mask problems with the script or the direction. As with cheap special effects, editing tricks aim to distract you from what's actually going on. Fades and wipes (where one scene slides in over another) are generally regarded as unnecessary and invasive, taking the audience out of the mood a film has set. There are always exceptions – comic book-style movies often make great use of the wipe – but you should always consider such trickery with a critical eye.

DIRECTORIAL ECONOMY

Great directors know how to do a lot with a little. Budgets are hard to come by, and you can't always get every shot you want when you're under the pressure of the set. Creative directors make the best of this by taking the tendrils of a botched or merely so-so shoot and creating something worthwhile – even great.

Consider a couple of popular techniques.

Montages can get across a great amount of information in a limited time by compressing a story into vignettes set to music. *Voice-over* can be used to hide sound problems and move the story along by showing one series of events while explaining another. *Repetition* can show us a scene several times but from different angles (popular with high-dollar action sequences).

All of these tricks can be used masterfully, but they can also backfire severely. Voice-over (as discussed earlier) is widely considered the worst of all crutches, but films like *Young Sherlock Holmes* (1985) prove that some directors can work wonders with it. *GoodFellas* (1990) is another example of how voice-over can enrich a film.

Too bad, then, that most attempts to spruce up a movie with these techniques fail, hence the poor reputation they have with film critics. But don't automatically assume voice-over equals hack filmmaking. Ask yourself whether it serves a legitimate purpose, fits the style of the film, and makes the movie better than it would otherwise be. A good critic will distinguish himself by not overusing clichéd criticisms ("voice-over is bad") just as a good director will distinguish himself by not overusing the clichés to begin with – and both will understand when a cliché can be a good thing.

Even if a director has copious resources, how best to utilize those resources can be a major stylistic decision. Lars von Trier economizes in many of his films, though he could easily do something more lavish. In his recent *Dogville* (2003), he didn't build sets. Crude chalk outlines stood in for the walls of the set's structures, and the director used minimalism like the play *Our Town*. This alone doesn't make the film good or bad, but it says something about the director's approach to the material, as well as something about the themes of the film.

PRETENTIOUSNESS

Here's a thorny issue. You know pretentious movies: They're staples of art-house cinema, loved by "film snobs," shunned by the general public, and impossible to spot unless you sit through them. The bigger issue is that one man's pretentiousness is another man's art. The best example I can think of is John Sayles' *Limbo* (1999), a little movie about three people stranded on an island who undergo the usual chatty-character developments for two hours. At the end, a plane is seen approaching: We know that it carries either their rescuers or a man sent to murder them. Sayles ends the picture right there. The plane never arrives. Roll credits.

Now to a few people, Sayles was making a statement about – well, about what I have no idea. Perhaps about the unpredictability of the future? Who knows? To me, the film absolutely *reeks* of pretentiousness. You can almost hear Sayles' smug voice, "I called the film *Limbo*, didn't I? That's how I left you at the end? Aren't I clever!?"

That isn't clever, it's lazy. My theory is that Sayles didn't have an ending, so he just quit, slapped a non-sequitur title on the movie, and left it at that. There's no statement there, and there's no art at all in quitting your movie before you get to the end. This is the absolute heart of pretentious filmmaking, and Sayles should have been banished from the industry for it. Again, that's just one man's opinion.

Still, I recognize this is the murkiest of issues. Some people loved *Limbo*. I find them mentally questionable, but remember, to each his own. *L'Avventura*,

Citizen Kane, 2001: A Space Odyssey – these are all great, five-star movies. But there are people who think *Kane* is clichéd and obvious, a pretentious attempt at "greatness" with an obvious "secret" at its end. How can they possibly feel this way about one of the best movies ever produced? There's no accounting for taste.

Pretentiousness – just like subjective enjoyment – is a matter of personal opinion. You like it or you don't. You "get" it or you don't. Did I not "get" *Limbo*? Perhaps – but it's just as likely there was nothing to "get" in the first place. Even Sayles can't shed any light on the subject. If he were to say he had a salient point in mind with the film, that doesn't excuse its holier-than-thou execution. Remember, the road to hell is paved with good intentions.

Analyze every movie with a glance toward pretentiousness – especially independent darlings like *Kill Bill* (which spawned a firestorm of debate over whether Quentin Tarantino was spoofing kung fu cinema or whether he'd completely lost his marbles and finally swallowed his own ego) and *Memento* (was the backwards storytelling the most clever plot device of all time or the biggest cop-out in history?). Is this movie trying to be *too* clever? *Too* minimalist? Is there too much of the stamp of "the director" on the film? You'll know it when you see it, but rarely will you be able to put it into words. If a movie leaves a bitter taste in your mouth and makes you blatantly aware that someone's God-like hand was involved in its production, chances are you've uncovered at least a little pretentiousness. Call it out, but be prepared for some backlash – this is where more hate mail is generated than in any other aspect of film criticism.

ANALYZING THEME

Without getting too sappy and pedantic, remember that movies generally *are* art. And because they have two hours to explain themselves, they almost always have a thematic message. (The works of Rob Schneider are excluded from this statement.)

Unless you're reviewing a blatant popcorn movie (most horror films are notoriously theme-free), always include an analysis of theme in your reviews. Not only does it enrich your writing and the minds of your readers, it enriches *your mind* by forcing you to push beyond mere judgment of the actors and a discussion of the lighting. Some movies, like *Citizen Kane*, are easy to figure out. They all but come out and say so in the dialogue: *Kane*'s theme is that all the wealth in the world can't make you happy, and nothing you do can regain the joy of youth. Consider *It's a Wonderful Life* (1946): It's even more blatantly obvious. *Life* says that no matter how bad things get, they could probably be a lot worse! It also tells us suicide is wrong, big corporations are evil, and angels exist, but that's another story.

Consider instead Kubrick's *2001*. It's a gorgeous movie, with the last 40 minutes of the movie dialogue-free. But what is its message? Interpreting this film is one of film criticism's little joys. Sure, we can draw thematic interpretations from the disassembly of HAL – something about man vs. machine, the loss of innocence, the dangers of artificial intelligence – but what to make of the end of the film, with the old man, the star child, the journey through the infinite? No one interpretation is right or wrong – *but it is important to try to come up with one!*

BUT DID YOU LIKE IT?

Finally, we come full circle. Among all the analyses of acting, screenwriting, direction, theme, and other nitpicking, you might forget to mention: *Did you like the movie?*

This is the most important question of all, yet many critics dance around this issue. Think about how you discuss film with your friends. What's the first thing you say? Either "It was great" or "It sucked!" And most people leave it at that! They don't go into great depths about characters or discuss which school of cinematography it belonged to. Our movie-going culture, for better or worse, has become conditioned by the "thumbs up/thumbs down" mentality pioneered by Siskel and Ebert. So for a moment at least, turn off your brain and go with your gut: Is it a good movie or a bad one? Did you have fun? Did you laugh or were you scared? It doesn't take an expert to make a judgment like this. Either you liked it or you didn't. Say so.

There's real value to this, as it's irrational to expect the average person to have to wade through thousands of words of jargon to make what amounts to a simple buying decision: Which movie should I go see tonight? As film critics, our primary job is to help people spend their money wisely. After that, we can jabber on and on about character development and Dutch angles. For some movies (Sandler, Van Damme, you know the ones), there's no other way to evaluate the film except on a gut level. Don't feel bad about doing so.

CHAPTER 5:
PUTTING THE PIECES TOGETHER

Now that you've analyzed the various components of the film, it's time to add in the supporting pieces of the review and put the entire review together. The first thing I'll analyze is the plot synopsis.

THE PLOT SYNOPSIS

For veteran critics, the plot synopsis is the easiest part of a review, but for novice critics it's a make or break proposition. Write too little about the plot and your readers won't know enough about the movie's story (an especially big problem when the movie in question is not a mega-advertised Hollywood blockbuster). Write too much and you'll not only bore the audience to tears, you'll give away key plot points that "spoil" the movie for readers.

The latter problem is far more common. Novice critics who aren't comfortable writing their analysis fall back on plot summaries just to fill space. A long review *looks* like it carries gravitas. But all too often I read novice reviews that are filled with 500 words regurgitating the plot, followed by 100 words of tepid analysis. It's probably the worst kind of review there is.

A good plot synopsis forms the core of the review. For some readers, that's all they'll want to read, no matter how great your analysis is. (It's a sad fact of life, but it merits consideration: A lot of people just want to know what the movie is about and couldn't care less what you think.) This is why many critics – even the big names – spend so much time droning on and on about the plot points: They know many readers just don't want to hear how good the lighting and editing are. Plus, it's *really* easy to write like this. This, sadly, is lazy film criticism.

The perfect plot synopsis is a taut three to 12 sentences, depending on the complexity of the movie. Your goal is to establish the critical elements of the film without spoiling key plot points or giving away so much detail that the reader will feel like he's seen the movie already. The key elements to set up for the reader include:

- **The setting**. If it's important, where is the action occurring? If it's a period piece, what year are we talking about? Will the action be confined to a haunted house or is this a globetrotting *Indiana Jones* style adventure? With movies like *The Lord of the Rings* series, you'll need to spend extra time setting up the fantasy world we're about to visit: When you have otherworldly settings, nonhuman sentient creatures, and magical powers, expect to burn a few extra sentences on the setting.

- **The main characters and the stars**. Sometimes you'll want to save the identity of the actors for later in your review, for variety or whatever reason, but you'll always want to identify the key characters in the film in your synopsis. With large ensemble casts like *Gosford Park*, try to focus on the five or six most important characters. You can always drop in supporting players later in your review. The idea isn't to dissect the entire cast list but to paint, with broad strokes, who the movie is about.

- **The plot points in the first act**. As a general rule of thumb, don't synopsize more than the first act (about the first 30 minutes, see Chapter 4) of the movie. In general, the first inciting incident or "twist" is OK to mention (in *The Sixth Sense*, it's OK to say that Cole sees dead people, but I wouldn't go beyond that). Go beyond this point you'll start to *spoil* the film – one of the biggest mistakes you can make in a movie review. Exceptions may be made depending on the film and the importance of surprises in the plot: It doesn't exactly ruin the movie to say that the end of *Short Cuts* involves an earthquake. But it doesn't really make your review better to write about the ending of a film anyway. When in doubt, *less* plot discussion is the best route.

- **The genre of the film**. Is it funny? Is it horror? Is it a funny horror movie? Don't assume that your audience has memorized the trailer. But it isn't necessary to use the words "*Annie Hall* is a romantic comedy" if the tone of your review gets that across.

Once you've gotten these out of the way, you've covered plot. Let's look at a few actual examples to see how a good plot synopsis should look.

Here's an excerpt from filmcritic.com's review of *The Others* (2001), which has a tricky setup.

> *The Others* brings us to the British Isles of 1945, where the repressed, icy Grace, played by Nicole Kidman, cares for her kids Ann and Nicholas (Alakina Mann and James Bentley) in a colossal house, where things are in turmoil. Grace has been told that her husband (Christopher Eccleston), who's fighting in World

War II, is missing and unlikely to return. The house's staff has simply vanished. And to top it all off, Ann repeatedly sees visions of another family who she says used to live in the house.

Ann tries to explain what she sees to her dubious mother, who drums Christian doctrine into her children's heads and has an impatient streak. At first, Grace doubts her daughter. But when doors fly open and unknown screams are unleashed, Grace strives (unsuccessfully) to gain control of the situation. Meanwhile, the new housekeeping staff, led by the friendly Mrs. Mills (Fionnula Flanagan), acts peculiar. Mrs. Mills tells Ann that she has seen the same visions, and that their presence will lead to some changes in the house.

That's nine sentences that give you the basics of *The Others* and vivid detail but without even approaching the plot twists in the film.

Here's the synopsis from my review of *Fight Club*.

Fight Club is the story of Jack (Edward Norton), a mild-mannered day-job schlub/insomniac. To combat his lack of sleep, Jack takes comfort in various support groups for ailments he doesn't have, where he finds a sudden freedom from life's pressures, surrounded by people on the verge of recovery or the verge of death. Soon enough, Jack becomes "addicted" to the support groups, but things get worse when the freakish Marla (Helena Bonham Carter) tries to take over his space – obviously getting off on the same thrill as Jack.

Soon, Jack is back where he started, and on a flight home from yet another business trip, he encounters Tyler (Brad Pitt), a nutty character reminiscent of The Mad Hatter, William S. Burroughs, and The Unabomber all rolled up into one. When Jack arrives at home, he finds his condo mysteriously blown up, and he ends up moving in with Tyler in a craphole of a house. Tyler takes Jack down a road of self-discovery, mainly through violence, and together they found Fight Club, an underground bareknuckled boxing society – a big step beyond "self-help."

As the movie progresses, so does the darkness of Fight Club. Its membership skyrockets, and its extracurricular activities turn subversive.

That's eight (longish) sentences, but the concepts of *Fight Club* are tricky to get across succinctly. Still, had I wanted to write a shorter review, I could have left out the back story about the support groups and Marla altogether, leaving that part of the movie for the audience to discover. At the same time, *Fight Club* is also a twist-driven movie, and again, this synopsis goes to pains not to give it away.

Here's a shorter synopsis that's just as effective of covering *The Ring* (2002).

> Following a number of false starts that establish the film's unbalanced mood, *The Ring* rehashes an urban legend about a videotape. Very few people know its contents, though it's believed that the images found on the tape recap one person's nightmare. Initially I thought that tape was *Police Academy 5: Assignment Miami Beach*, but I was wrong. Once you watch the video, the phone rings and a child's voice on the other end of the line whispers, "Seven days." You now have one week to live.
>
> When a close friend of the family dies following a viewing, Seattle newspaper reporter Rachel Keller (Naomi Watts) promises the victim's mother she'll ask around about the tape. Rachel watches the tape, receives the phone call, and her personal seven-day countdown to destruction begins. Her only hope of survival is to solve the mystery of the images on screen before her departure time arrives.

The writer spends almost as much time making jokes as he does discussing the plot of the movie. Only one character is introduced, and the rainy Pacific Northwest setting of the film is saved for a more in-depth discussion later in the review.

Some movies (you know the ones I mean) can be easily synopsized in one sentence. Great example from the filmcritic.com archives: "*Scary Movie* is a parody of *Scream*." There's no real "plot" to *Scary Movie*. It exists simply to make jokes about the horror genre. That's all that needs to be said about the plot for the reader to understand fully what the movie is "about." What additional movies the film parodied and whether *Scary Movie* is funny or scary at all is what the bulk of the review covers.

For more examples of good story summaries, pay attention to the plot synopses in the example reviews that continue through the remainder of the next few chapters.

COMBINING THE PLOT SYNOPSIS WITH ANALYSIS

You've analyzed the components of the film and have a solid grasp on the mechanics of the plot. Now it's time to put the two together into a review.

As you get started, you should try to follow a simple template for structuring your reviews. The best reviews don't follow a template, of course, but for a beginner, you should start simple and work your way toward more complicated review structures. (I'll cover some of these in more detail in Chapter 6.)

Here's how a solid, but basic, 600-word review ought to look.

- "The lead" – Also known as a "lede," you want to grab the reader's attention with a powerful statement, a witty remark, a joke, or an obscure fact. Many, many reviewers start off their reviews by jumping right into the plot. This is not only lazy, it's boring. Some critics spend far more time on the lead than they should. (Roger Ebert is notorious for boring us with hundreds of words of personal anecdotes that have little to do with the movie he's reviewing.) Keep it to one paragraph; 75 words is about perfect. Leads are covered in the following section.

- The plot synopsis – As discussed earlier, 150 to 200 words of plot synopsis is just about right, split into two paragraphs.

- The analysis – The guts of the review. Spend about 300 words (in three or four paragraphs) discussing your thoughts on the direction, the script, the acting, and the supporting components of the film, as relevant. If you analyze every single bit of a movie, your analysis could easily run to 1,000 words or more, which is certain to bore your audience into oblivion. (Once I read a 3,000-word review of *Final Fantasy: The Enemy Within*, possibly the biggest waste of both the author's and the reader's time I can imagine.)

    So what do you omit? When in doubt, talk about the high points and the low points, erring toward those that support your overall rating. A five-star review might mention six to eight highlights: a key actor, outstanding dialogue (with examples), direction, editing, the score, cinematography, and set decoration. That should be plenty to support your rating. A mediocre or bad movie might merit only four points of analysis: A great actor's work is marred by an inferior script, the editing is too choppy, and the special effects are questionable.

    No matter how much you write in this section, the most important thing to remember is that you communicate your overall impressions of the film through the tone of your analysis. Nothing smacks of amateurism worse than writing about nothing but high points, then slapping the film with a low rating.

- The conclusion – It doesn't have to start with "In conclusion…" but you should come up with some way to wrap up your thoughts quickly and coherently, leading to your overall opinion of the film. Remember that your reader wants to know whether he should spend $10 on the movie, wait for DVD, or skip it altogether. It's important to understand that's why you're writing this thing in the first place. I'll cover conclusions in greater depth later in the chapter.

THE LEAD

You want to start your review with a bang, not a whimper or a whine. Challenge the reader to sit up and take notice of what you have to say. Online, you can easily find 200 reviews of a movie on opening day. What's going to make yours stand out?

You need to grab the reader immediately with your writing but still stay on topic. Rambling about what you did earlier in the day isn't going to make any sense in the context of a movie review. Leads are impossible to turn into templates, but with practice, they'll come to you. As you watch a film for your review, think about how you'll create a clever intro for the review. Most of the time, it will come to you out of thin air. Sometimes, you'll know exactly how to start your review months before a movie ever comes out. And sometimes you'll dump that idea for something you think of the minute you sit down to start writing.

How about some samples of leads that work?

Here's one that's funny:

> A soldier's life has been famously characterized by hours of boredom punctuated by moments of stark terror. Well, *The Alamo* manages to capture half that story.

This lead offers some interesting or insider-ish trivia (albeit, trivia about an uninteresting movie):

> In case you've been wondering, *Feeling Minnesota* is a film

"inspired by a line in a Soundgarden song," according to the production notes.

This one delves deeper into a movie's background:

> No modern traveler has more notoriety than Merhan Karimi
> Nasseri, who has been stranded in Terminal One of Paris's
> Charles de Gaulle airport since 1988. Nasseri was expelled from
> Iran in 1977 and spent 10 years trying to gain political asylum
> in Europe. That all came to an end when his bag was stolen
> in Paris, essentially stranding him at CDG. In 1993, a movie
> was made about him (*Lost in Transit*), starring Jean Rochefort.
> Nasseri's life reappears on screen this year in *The Terminal*,
> courtesy of Steven Spielberg and Tom Hanks. And shamefully,
> Nasseri goes unmentioned in the movie's production notes.

Or you might begin with a witty observation about the title:

> With a title as curious as *13 Conversations About One Thing*,
> most moviegoers probably want to know what the "thing" is
> before plunking down their bucks to see the movie. Well, that
> "thing" appears to be happiness, and the search for it. But
> don't let that fact and the peppy title fool you – this film isn't
> filled with a bunch of inane chick chatter. Writer/director Jill
> Sprecher's follow-up to her debut *Clockwatchers* has an overall
> tone of despair and a faint hint of evil, much like that first film.
> It results in a surprising, bold, satisfying drama with a mildly
> depressing wave running through it.

Here are two different approaches to *Kill Bill: Volume 1*:

> Quentin Tarantino's fourth film, *Kill Bill*, reminds us why we,
> as a collective moviegoing society, wish he'd work more often
> than he does. The acclaimed director rocketed to cult stardom
> with *Reservoir Dogs* and *Pulp Fiction*, cranked out an overlong
> homage to film noir in *Jackie Brown*, and then slid off the
> filmmaking radar for the better part of six years.

And…

> The Miramax hype machine was working overtime on *Kill Bill*,
> breaking Quentin Tarantino's epic pastiche of revenge into two
> volumes. Rather than serve this quasi-retro samurai saga in
> one three-hour heap, *Kill Bill* serves itself out in portions. *Kill
> Bill* reveals Tarantino as a sham auteur ripping off Hong Kong
> action flicks and 1970s B-movies for their surface frills. He's the
> cinematic equivalent of karaoke or bad photocopies, mindlessly
> adopting style while forgetting the basic precepts of storytelling.

Note how the first lead sets up the generally positive tone of the review, right
from the first sentence. Likewise, it's clear from the start that the second lead
will be a pan, using words like "sham," "mindlessly," and "hype machine."
Without actually analyzing anything, both of these leads cue the reader into
what he should expect in the following paragraphs.

There's no good rule saying what makes a good lead or a bad one. Funny,
serious, wildly insane – you'll find the approach that works for your style,
the outlet you're writing for, and the individual movie you're reviewing. Sure
there are some general rules of thumb – don't lead your review of a Holocaust
documentary with a Nazi joke – but common sense will guide you.

THE CONCLUSION

I've covered how to get started with a review; here's how to wrap it all up.

The last paragraph of a review is where you want to wrap up your thoughts
about a movie, leaving the reader with a concise and memorable set of
thoughts about the film. If they take away one thing about the film, here's
where you want to say it.

Here's where all the criticism that comes before should come to bear upon
your final word and rating of a film. It's also where the intangibles come into
play. How often did you check your watch? When the end came around, did
you want to see more or were you ready to leave? What was the vibe in the
audience? If it's a kids' film, did they seem engaged in the movie, or were they
wandering around the theater? I don't often use audience response as a metric,
but if you're reviewing a film that's not exactly in your ideal genre, your
conclusion can add a minor caveat or small support for your comments.

Let's look at some examples: Does James Cameron's masterful direction
of *Titanic* overcome its rather poor script? Books could be written about the

cornball dialogue and contrived scenes in the movie, but Cameron works through these limitations so well that you almost forget they're there. *Titanic* has serious faults and delirious highs: Does one side overcome the other? It's up to you to connect the dots and make a complete picture of the movie that transcends the minutiae of what's good and what's bad. How does the movie make you *feel*? There's no science in this. It comes from the gut.

Let's look at a few solid conclusions

Note how Sean O'Connell comes full circle in this conclusion to *Troy* (2004), bringing events on screen back to the audience:

> In place of gods and goddesses, *Troy* plugs in the Hollywood equivalent – a golden-haired and Gold's Gym-defined Pitt. Looking very much like the lost Hanson brother, *Troy*'s leading man may be the film's weakest link. Labeled the greatest warrior of his age, Achilles shoulders an arrogance that borders on indifference. In a feeble attempt to create a traditional anti-hero, Pitt casually disrespects authority and wears his "death wish" mentality like a badge of honor. As *Troy* grows in stature and intrigue, Achilles gradually withdraws. The warrior couldn't look more disinterested, and as a result, the audience eventually begins to feel the same way.

Here's a good one that brings the movie together and puts a personal spin on the review:

> With *Super Size Me*, Spurlock puts a very human face on questions that concern the nation as a whole. That this face happens to be his own only makes the film more entertaining. I haven't touched a Big Mac since.

I didn't really have anything good or bad to wrap up my review of *American Wedding* (2003) with, so I threw the review into an entirely different direction in the end. Got nothing better to say? Why not jump into another pool?

> Finally, let's all speculate what has become of the no-shows at the wedding, including Mena Suvari, Tara Reid, Shannon Elizabeth, Natasha Lyonne, and Chris Klein. Are these kids' stars too big to appear in this film? With movies like *The*

Musketeer, *Van Wilder*, and *Rollerball* among them, all of these
actors could use a hit, badly. *American Wedding* may not be a
great comedy, but hey, it ain't no *Gigli*.

TONE AND VOICE

Tone and *voice* are essentially interchangeable terms, both referring to
the general approach you take to writing. You can have an irreverent tone,
a serious tone, a jokey tone, or just about anything else tonally. You can
organize a career around a certain tone: Chuck Schwartz is known as the
"cranky critic," for example. The idea is to find a voice that works for you, and
stick with it throughout your review and from one review to the next. The key
to tone in a movie review is *consistency*.

This means you shouldn't start off a review with a fawning, sycophantic
voice, then suddenly slam the movie in the end with a low rating and a
negative conclusion. Too often critics will rave about points in a movie that
ultimately add up to very minor plusses. In the end, they're forced to take
back those positive statements and qualify them with the serious negatives
about the film. The ultimate effect is very disorienting and reads badly.

You also want to be stylistically consistent from one review to another.
Obviously you don't want every review to read identically, but you do want
them to feel like they were all written by the same person. You'll have to
switch focuses constantly, as I discussed in Chapter 4 in the section on Art
vs. Entertainment, but you don't want to swing so wildly that one looks like
it's not even from your body of work. Even if you're getting intellectual in a
review, try to keep your general stylistic approach consistent.

Tone should also be appropriate for your audience. Even if your reviews are
targeted at an adult audience, if you're reviewing G-rated fare, your review
shouldn't be littered with profanity. A good rule of thumb is that your tone and
language should be on par with the MPAA rating: Feel free to pull out all the
stops for NC-17 stuff, but tone it down for the PGs and Gs.

THE LITTLE THINGS

The experience you gain over the course of writing hundreds of reviews will
teach you more than this book can, but here's a collection of general nuggets
of writing advice that will hopefully get you ahead of the game.

- **Write the way you talk.** Too many critics revert to stuffy, high school,
  English-class writing when it comes time to put pen to paper. This is the

worst mistake you can make. Use contractions, slang, and pop culture references. Write as if you're talking about the movie to your best friend, not a professor. He isn't reading your reviews, I promise. Even though you typically don't know the reader personally, you want to make him feel like you do. It builds rapport with the audience and keeps them coming back for more.

- **Go easy on the thesaurus.** A lovely turn of the phrase is appreciated, but don't go overboard with flowery language. The goal is to be conversational, not to impress your reader with your grasp of obscure words, especially when you aren't actually saying anything. Trust me: This will turn off more people than it dazzles. For example, don't write "Nicholson imbues his recital with the astuteness of a proficient actor who's countenance informs years of experienced acumen" when really you're just trying to say the acting is good. Better yet, tell us *why* it's good.

- **Avoid jargon.** Try not to use too many industry words like *mise en scene* unless you absolutely have to. Your reader shouldn't need a dictionary to understand your review.

- **Don't write too much about "me."** This is probably the biggest mistake that amateur critics make: Don't fill your review with comments that begin with "I thought" and "I felt." People are reading your review not to see what you think, but to see what you think *they'll* think. It's a subtle distinction and it doesn't demand you change much in your writing, except you need to refocus the subject of the review on "you" instead of "I." In other words: "You'll be bored after 10 minutes" is far preferable to "I was bored after 10 minutes." This isn't an engraved-in-stone rule, but try to keep it in mind; it greatly improves readability and your audience will identify better with the writing. In simplest terms, cut out the word "I" from your review and it will be far stronger.

- **Don't forget the supporting data.** At filmcritic.com, we include special areas for director, writer, producer, and cast list. We also add the MPAA rating, the website for the movie, and, of course, a star rating. Some reviewers add the running time of the film, more details about the MPAA rating (profanity, violence, nudity), the release date, and so on. Pick what you want to include, and standardize it every time.

- **Be funny.** The bulk of film criticism just doesn't work for the ultra-serious. Make jokes. Have fun. It's a movie, for God's sake.

- **No spoilers!** Do not spoil the plot of the movie by revealing more than the most basic of plot points. Ever!

- **Less is more.** Brevity is the soul of wit, as Shakespeare famously said. And he was right: The longer your review, the less likely people are to read it to the end. I've found that 600 words is just about perfect, but you'll find that the more movies you review, the longer your typical review will get, as you have more background in the field upon which to draw.

- **Read other people's reviews.** Find critics you like and read their work religiously. The more you read, the more you'll write like they do, and the more you'll like your own writing.

- **Ask for feedback.** Get others to comment on your early reviews and break bad habits before they set in.

- **Write every day.** Or as much as you can, really.

- **Be honest.** My number one rule. I'll keep hammering on this throughout the book.

STRUCTURING THE REVIEW

Now I'll give you some complete sample reviews of various types and formats. I'll start with a few simple ones that provide the components of a review in the expected order, then gradually delve into more complex structures in which the components become blended. Your first reviews should attempt to mimic these early examples. I have tried to use examples from recent films, as the movies are more likely to be fresh in your mind.

Sample #1: Dawn of the Dead (2004), ★ ★ ★*1/2, by Annette Cardwell*
Here's a very well-written review that is nonetheless straightforward in structure. In this review, Annette Cardwell starts with a fun intro sentence, then discusses the original movie and its updating. A quick three-paragraph plot summary follows (watch for the interesting language she uses and the shout-out to *The Breakfast Club*). The remainder of the review comments

on the action, the acting, and the photography – while staying within the confines of what we expect from horror movies. Her conclusion appeals to both genre fans and casual moviegoers alike. Annette gave the film 3.5 stars on our five-star scale.

When there's no room in Hell, the dead walk to the mall. That was the message of horror master George Romero's 1978 anti-consumerism flick *Dawn of the Dead*. This 2004 remake by first-time director Zack Snyder takes away a lot of the social message, and fills it instead with plenty of head-blasting zombie-killing mayhem and a surprisingly unpredictable storyline that – while far from perfect – is a lot of fun to watch.

The plot loosely follows the Romero original. This time around, the star of the survivors' crew is Ana (Sarah Polley), a nurse who wakes up from a romantic night with her boyfriend to a nightmarish world gone undead. Her neighbor's cute kid has turned into a flesh-eater, and has taken a big bite out of her sweetheart, turning him into one of her vicious kind. And, all over her idyllic suburban Wisconsin town, the dead are walking again; they're hungry, and they can run like the dickens.

Ana stumbles across some other "living": a cop (Ving Rhames), a recovering bad boy (Mekhi Phifer), his pregnant gal pal (can you see where this is headed?), and a level-headed everyman (Jack Weber). They make for the safety of a well-stocked shopping mall, holing up with three security guards and hoping to be rescued by the military. Not a bad way to spend a zombie crisis! Much like the original, Snyder's version shows our castaways indulging in the consumerist joys of the shopping mall and the company of each other – kind of like an apocalyptic *Breakfast Club*.

After more survivors make their way to the mall, it soon becomes clear to nurse Ana how the zombie disease spreads: by bite; and the only cure is a shotgun blast to the head or via a little taste of fire. So what do they do now? Wallow in their mall bounty until they're starved out? Or find a way to escape? And to where?

The new *Dawn* isn't short on fast-paced, extremely gory

action, especially in the several awe-inspiring scenes of zombie masses overrunning city, state, country, and possibly even world. But there are also an excellent handful of comic touches thrown in, helping to keep the movie from droning downward into cliché. For example, there's the rooftop conversation using dry-erase boards between Rhames and a gun-store owner islanded across a mall parking lot, followed by that same gun-store guy's sniper-style shooting game, picking off zombie celebrity look-alikes for points. In total, this update has all the brutality of such recent undead favorites as *28 Days Later*, but still maintains the humor that Romero worked into his *Dead* trilogy. Romero fans shouldn't be too let down by that mix.

The talented cast, which includes such proven performers as Polley (*The Sweet Hereafter*, *Go*) and Rhames (*Pulp Fiction*, *Out of Sight*), are only icing on the cake. Let's face it; zombie flicks don't pose a serious acting challenge for some of these folks. But in the end, they help build the suspense and sustain the humorous elements. Much of *Dawn* wouldn't have worked well without their efforts.

And finally, Snyder keeps the whole thing visually fresh with a range of shooting, from slick, commercial-like filming to *cinema verité*-style grainy DV. He even ventures to expand the movie into its closing credits (rather nastily, I might add), which further keeps this film from ever being dull.

The only warning I offer is that this is one gruesome blood-fest. Snyder establishes very early on, prior to the opening credits (set tidily to the musical stylings of Johnny Cash), that he's not afraid to let the blood packs splatter. But once you get used to the carnage, you may just find yourself on a rather terrifying yet thrilling little ride. And if you're already a die-hard zombie movie fan, you'll leave your memories of the Romero version behind, just to indulge in the delights of Snyder's wild, new, imaginary interpretation.

Sample #2: The Day After Tomorrow (2004), ★★, *by Sean O'Connell*
In this review, Sean O'Connell references another then-current release (*Shrek 2*), and pokes fun at a "serious" film for being unintentionally ridiculous. Note his reference of an obscure TV show (*Riptide*) for comic

effect, and he pokes fun at his own inability to comprehend the movie's plot. Use of quotes from the movie adds a unique touch to the review, and note the final paragraph, which earned us hate mail from a high school teacher, who sent a photo of the girls on his academic decathlon squad. Structurally, this review is a little more nebulous than the *Dawn of the Dead* review, but the components are still in the traditional order, by and large.

Move over, *Shrek 2*. DreamWorks' ode to ogres in love produced its fair share of guffaws, but it can't hold a candle to Roland Emmerich's latest world-in-peril thriller *The Day After Tomorrow*, clearly the funniest film you'll see this year.

Laughs may be unintentional, but they come at a fast and furious clip. A news chopper flies alongside multiple tornadoes marauding Los Angeles but remains airborne and unscathed. Survivors holed up inside of New York's public library are advised to "ride out" a pending ice age, which I thought typically lasted thousands of years. A Rhode Island-sized block of ice breaks off its glacial base, and the crack just happens to run through the middle of climatologist Jack Hall's (Dennis Quaid) Antarctic camp. And former *Riptide* star Perry King plays the President of the United States! C'mon people, that's funny.

These disastrous scenarios come courtesy of some abrupt climate shifts that Hall shouts about in his best Chicken Little voice. Global warming, it seems, is melting the Earth's ice caps, which in turn are affecting the temperatures of ocean currents that create our warmer climate regions. Resulting storms that resemble hurricanes are sitting squarely over the planet's northern hemispheres. Hall states that a series of recent climate shifts mirror prehistoric patterns that signaled the start of an earlier ice age, and he predicts that a similar freezing will occur in the next 7 to 10 days.

It didn't make much sense to me as I watched it, and it makes less sense as I type it out. But who cares, right? So long as major cities get some massive face lifts, summer movie junkies should be mighty pleased. Emmerich delivers plenty of gawk-worthy popcorn goodies in his Weather Channel upgrade. Snow falls in New Delhi. Hail the size of basketballs bombards

Tokyo. And in Manhattan the sewers back up, causing a debilitating stench ... so nothing new there.

Tomorrow should be a lot more amusing that it actually turns out to be. The already-slow-moving production pauses frequently for philosophical ramblings on our abuse of the environment. Emmerich stacks the odds against his characters in such a clumsy fashion that laughs build instead of tension. It's hard to get all worked up over rain, sleet, and snow. Doesn't the post office deal with this on a regular basis?

Sensing a potential dissatisfaction in his CGI situations, Emmerich oversteps the boundaries of credibility and makes potentially threatening scenarios seem silly. A thrilling race to retrieve penicillin from an ocean liner grows ridiculous when *Tomorrow* tosses escaped wolves into the mix. The "outrunning the ice" sequence defies all forms of logic, especially when you notice that certain characters aren't even wearing gloves in what's supposed to be subzero weather.

When it comes to developing credible human relationships, Emmerich as screenwriter proves he's all wet. Quaid gets credit for keeping a straight face while burping out phrases like "super cool air from the upper troposphere." His typically frigid performance, however, ices over any chemistry felt between he and his alienated wife (Sela Ward) and stranded son Sam (Jake Gyllenhaal).

Oceans rise and temperatures drop. Impressive set pieces are frozen over or totally submerged. In between each death-defying sequence, Sam puts the moves on Laura (Emmy Rossum), the hot chick on his academic decathlon team. Wait one second. I'm willing to believe an ocean liner floating down Fifth Avenue. But a gorgeous brunette like Laura participating on the academic decathlon squad? My imagination can only stretch so far.

Sample #3: The Terminal (2004), ★ ★ ★, by Christopher Null
The Terminal presents a mediocre film, which is tough to write about. Note in this review how good points are balanced with bad points, and how plot summary is occasionally blended with analysis on the fly. I discussed the lead of this review earlier in the chapter. Of special note is the paragraph

discussing theme (third from the end), and the commentary on Kumar Pallana's supporting performance, both of which would go unmentioned in a shorter review with less depth.

No modern traveler has more notoriety than Merhan Karimi Nasseri, who has been stranded in Terminal One of Paris's Charles de Gaulle airport since 1988. Nasseri was expelled from Iran in 1977 and spent 10 years trying to gain political asylum in Europe. That all came to an end when his bag was stolen in Paris, essentially stranding him at CDG. In 1993, a movie was made about him (*Lost in Transit*), starring Jean Rochefort. Nasseri's life reappears on screen this year in *The Terminal*, courtesy of Steven Spielberg and Tom Hanks. And shamefully, Nasseri goes unmentioned in the movie's production notes.

In *The Terminal*, Spielberg gives us Hanks as Viktor Navorski, a visitor from the fictitious country of Krakhozia in Eastern Europe. Hanks, made up to be pasty and lumpy, puts on a mush-mouthed accent reminiscent of Yakov Smirnoff, and finds himself landing at New York's JFK on a mission we won't discover until the end of the film. We know only that it involves a Planters peanut can.

Too bad for Viktor that his visa is denied once he lands in the U.S. – his country's government has been overthrown during the course of his flight. The U.S. no longer recognizes his passport, and his country no longer exists. Viktor can't come into the U.S., nor can he return home. Homeland Security agent Frank Dixon (Stanley Tucci) has no choice but to sequester him in the airport's international terminal, strictly forbidding Viktor from setting foot outside.

Viktor, who barely speaks English, quickly comes to understand his predicament, and soon enough he's taken up residence in part of the terminal under construction. He learns to read and subsist on quarters refunded from the Smarte Carte machine. He becomes friends with the local shopkeepers and airport staff, and he falls for a sexy but scattered flight attendant (Catherine Zeta-Jones) who happens through.

Months pass. Will Viktor ever get out of the terminal? Dixon, who's up for a big promotion, wants him out of the airport

83

by any means necessary, eventually goading him into trying to escape so he'll get arrested. In one of the more interesting character spins in the film, we learn that figuratively, Dixon is as much a prisoner of the terminal as Viktor. Their sparring leads to some of the movie's more memorable moments.

It's strange and unfortunate then that those memorable bits are so few and far between. Spielberg's ballyhooed terminal set, built from scratch and shiny as hell, is nothing more than a giant vehicle for product placement for some 35 real-life stores. (I was initially shocked to see a La Perla lingerie outlet in the terminal, but it turns out there really is one in Munich International. Amazing. But why couldn't they get the real CNN to appear on the airport TVs instead of the phony "GHN" network?)

Consumerism aside, the main problem is the coldness of Viktor's story. We don't feel *for* him, we simply pity him like someone with a severe speech impediment. Viktor's not really a hero. He's not fighting for anything aside from the contents of that peanut can (which turns into a thin subplot at best), and his romance with Zeta-Jones borders on the absurd. He's just going with the flow, doing what he's told. The result is an extremely hollow movie that goes on for far too long (two hours, feels like three) and chases about three too many, go-nowhere subplots. Blame it on a lackluster script if you will (Jeff Nathanson wrote *Catch Me If You Can* but also penned *Speed 2*); this story would have worked better as a broad comedy instead of a mopey think piece mixed with a romance.

Thankfully, flashes of humor in the film flirt with brilliance. Hanks delivers a few good belly laughs, but it's Kumar Pallana (*The Royal Tenenbaums*) who steals the show as a paranoid Indian baggage handler. He's both rude and hysterical in every scene. Pallana needs his own sitcom, stat.

Buried in *The Terminal* you'll find a theme or two. One is rather clever, about how The New America is obsessed with keeping foreigners out of the country while in reality they're running the infrastructure at our airports. The second is a little less successful, about how you can feel alienation and loneliness despite being surrounded by throngs of humanity. Unfortunately, there are probably no two people alive who have less business exploring a story about alienation than Hanks and Spielberg, who thrive on acceptance by people – and get it at every turn.

The film is very well made, and from Spielberg we'd expect nothing less. It unfortunately comes with all of his baggage and nothing groundbreaking to speak of. When we enter the terminal for the first time, a voice-over may as well boom out, "*Look at the masterful set I built!*" All of Spielberg's other hallmarks are in place too, right down to the intrusive John Williams score. After two outstanding flicks (*Catch Me* and *Minority Report*), I suppose he deserves a meatball.

Ultimately, two hours in *The Terminal* closely resembles two hours in a real airport terminal. It's also not unlike the experience of talking to a foreigner who barely speaks English: Strangely intriguing, but kind of sad and deeply frustrating.

Sample #4: Eternal Sunshine of the Spotless Mind (2004), ★★★★★, by Sean O'Connell
Sean O'Connell takes a more blended approach in this review, alternating regularly between synopsis and analysis throughout, painting a more abstract picture of the film. Interestingly, he doesn't even introduce the main characters until the fifth paragraph. This film earned the site's highest rating, so watch for how the review cues you to that consistently with positive language.

Jim Carrey fans who roll in the aisle and clutch their sides every time the lanky megawatt talks out of his rear will despise the first 30 minutes of *Eternal Sunshine of the Spotless Mind*. They shouldn't be able to form an opinion on the remainder of the film because most of them will have walked out by then.

Carrey traditionally makes silly comedies for his loyal supporters and risky pictures for his critics. His career path to date has alternated every bombastic *Bruce Almighty* with a tragic *The Truman Show*, and whatever Carrey camp you subscribe to will help you determine whether or not *Sunshine* is worth your time.

An opinion on screenwriter Charlie Kaufman also helps. Kaufman's complicated credits include head-scratchingly gifted gems like *Being John Malkovich* and the flawed yet intriguing

Adaptation. His latest is another trademark odyssey into the brain that makes an extended stop at the human heart, something we don't expect from this clinical and cynical scribe.

When couples split, they tend to focus on the negatives in their failing relationships. Typically a string of bad experiences led them to the break-up point, so those unpleasant memories remain fresh in the mind. Lacuna Inc. helps ease that pesky heartache. The Manhattan-based company specializes in a medical procedure that can erase specific memories from someone's brain. Miss your dead dog? Can't stand the thought of your ex-lover? Have any trace of those memories wiped clean.

He doesn't know it yet, but introverted Joel (Carrey) has been erased from the mind of his impulsive girlfriend, Clementine (Kate Winslet). The couple has been on the rocks as of late, and Clem's tired of dealing with Joel's "boring" ways. She just didn't let Joel in on her decision – he has to find out through mutual friends. Shocked by the notion, Joel reluctantly visits Lacuna head Dr. Howard Mierzwiak (a very vanilla yet God-like Tom Wilkinson) and signs himself up for the same operation.

After laying its rocky groundwork, *Sunshine* sets up shop in Joel's house-of-mirrors mind as two preoccupied lab technicians (Mark Ruffalo and Elijah Wood) erase his memories of Clementine. The operation simultaneously releases *Sunshine* from the confines of reality, encouraging Kaufman and director Michel Gondry (who previously worked with Kaufman on *Adaptation* and *Human Nature*) to be as creative as they wish without the burden of having to make excuses for wandering too far from the straight path. Kaufman cooks up a fascinating premise of mending broken hearts, but Gondry deserves extra credit for conjuring the right images to match the story's wickedly clever asides.

A logical plot progression adds an intriguing twist. The Lacuna techies work backwards on Joel, starting with his break-up and careening towards the day he first met Clem. Of course, Joel's memories of his lost love improve with each revelation, though we're never sure whether these are accurate interpretations of their early relationship or affectionate recreations Joel keeps in his head. Either way, the comatose Joel

86

changes his mind (literally) mid-session and wants to hold on to his fondest Clementine memories – which means he has to somehow outrun the scientific process. Here Kaufman is given the opportunity to address fate, explaining that Joel's efforts are unnecessary, for he and Clem are destined to meet again. But he chooses not to make things that simple, leaving it up to his audience to noodle through these concepts on our own.

The highest compliment I can pay *Sunshine* is that it makes complete sense from start to finish – high praise indeed for an idea this convoluted. We patiently wait for Kaufman's complex combination of raw emotions and forensic science to collapse in on itself, yet it never does. Kaufman's script and Gondry's cast maintain an amazing sense of continuity, even as the brilliant story dips and slides into surrealistic mental realms. Ultimately though, its Carrey and Winslet's spot-on tender performances that help solidify Joel and Clementine's bond, even as we realize that despite their penchant for meeting up, they have little hope of ever staying together.

Sample #5: Requiem for a Dream (2000), ★*1/2, by Jeremiah Kipp*
Finally, here's the text of Jeremiah Kipp's controversial 1.5-star review of *Requiem for a Dream*. Note how he doesn't offer a block of text about the plot anywhere; it's dribbled out piecemeal in paragraphs 2, 5, 6, 7, and 9. It doesn't even follow the narrative chronologically, and yet he manages to paint a picture of the film that not only provides a vivid picture of the plot, it makes a very strong case for why he didn't like the film. Whether you agree or not with Jeremiah's review, it's easy to see the picture he paints of the film through the combination of a plot synopsis with thoughtful analysis. The reference to Pasolini may be a bit much for amateur critics, but it's an excellent way of recalling classic cinema in a modern context.

Imagine *Trainspotting* without any trace of humor and you're on the right track. Picture Pasolini's *Salo: 120 Days of Sodom* shot by some MTV music video kid interested in the novelty of his new camera. Darren Aronofsky (*Pi*) stacks one degrading sight atop another without implicating the viewer, nor providing any framework or reference for his visual rape of his audience – all smoke and mirrors disguising a great, vapid emptiness.

For starters, I've never seen Coney Island junkies who look as pretty as Harry (Jared Leto) and Tyrone (Marlon Wayans), who bear a passing resemblance to the kids from Calvin Klein ads. They're drug dealers who have high aspirations, saving their earnings for a better tomorrow. Placing all their cash in a locker, they sit under the boardwalk smoking up and dreaming their grandiose dreams. Too bad they get high too often off their own supply. The good times can't last forever.

The drug use scenes are done in vivid smash cuts showing dilating pupils, squeezing needles, the sizzle of white powder cooked in a spoon. We never see these kids shoot up – rather, we see abstract images. Every time this technique appears, it's too flashy and aware of its own experimental filmmaking approach, a purely stylistic flourish.

Kronos Quartet wrote the driving, thumping, angry, brutal violin score which drums like a hammer and chain beating you into submission. Harry, Tyrone, and their ambitious if drug-addled friend Marion (a very good Jennifer Connelly), who could be a great designer were it not for her plunge into addiction, eventually become slaves to their own destructive destinies. They run out of money, and in the second half of the movie they move through a bleak winter, suffering the eternal torments of the damned.

Each situation is set up so neatly, we're certain where the path will lead. Harry sports a nasty welt on his arm which doesn't look so good. Tyrone discovers that maybe that trip to Florida to track down some fresh supply was a bad idea – since them southern boys don't like colored folk. Marion eventually telephones a sadistic pimp (Keith David) and sells her body for drugs.

The movie's first scene involves Harry stealing his mom's television set. She can always go right down the block in half an hour and buy it back. That's their adorable dog and pony show, and poor Sara Goldfarb (Ellen Burstyn) is too nice, too soft around the edges, so apathetic she won't do anything about it. Her husband is dead, and Harry is all she's got left.

Burstyn is so good, so unglamorous, and so believable as a Brighton Beach Jewish mama, that she shines through Aronofsky's bag of tricks and delivers a strong, sad, comic performance. At first, Sara seems to share the addiction of the film's other characters, endlessly watching her television, but when she gets a surprise phone call asking her to appear on a TV show she realizes she's too overweight to fit into the red dress her husband once admired her in. She goes on a diet.

Unfortunately for the audience, midway through we realize that Sara's in trouble. She's gone to a quack doctor for some diet pills, which turn out to be speed. She's gnashing her teeth in no time, and the worst is yet to come.

Sara's refrigerator starts roaring like a lion as the images become fuzzy and, well, straight out of Terry Gilliam's superior *Fear and Loathing in Las Vegas*. In short order, Sara wears the same junkie shoes as her younger co-stars. While it's painful to watch a harmless old woman descend into the circle of hell, she could easily have escaped it by going to *another* doctor for a second opinion.

Some critics are sure to fawn over *Requiem*. It goes further than most films into uncomfortable territory, and the spinning visuals are technically accomplished. I'm sure Aronofsky's courage will be extolled – yes, it's so bold to show human misery without sympathy or understanding.

I'm not against violence or torture onscreen. The best film to compare *Requiem* to is Pasolini's *Salo*. Wisely, Pasolini used restraint with his camera and simply filmed people being sexually abused and beaten without showy fanfare. *Salo* creates a hollow, disturbing feeling of helplessness.

Ultimately, Aronofsky lacks that crucial insight when showing the nature of horror. His gaze feels inexperienced. Perhaps young filmmakers should not attempt to tackle the bleak world before they have had a chance to go through it themselves. (*Salo* was Pasolini's final film; Mike Leigh's bleak *Naked* was made when he was middle-aged.)

Once we get past the notion that addiction is a horrible thing (which I don't believe is news to anyone who will watch *Requiem for a Dream*), the question remains: What purpose does this film serve? Let me know if you figure it out.

CHAPTER 6:
ADVANCED REVIEWING CONCEPTS AND TECHNIQUES

By now you should have written a handful of reviews and practiced the standard format I've discussed in earlier chapters. Hopefully you are already progressing into more complex writing structures and finding a style that you're comfortable with.

You're inevitably going to look back on your early reviews and cringe. You'll find the language to be trite, the writing simplistic, and the jokes juvenile. I feel the same way about my early writing, and it can be painful to read a decade later. Put it past you, and improve your craft. This happens to every writer, and the sooner you delve into more advanced concepts and techniques, the sooner you'll perfect your writing.

Remember: Your review will compete with hundreds of other reviews of the same movie. Why should anyone read yours? You have to make the writing the very best you can. Here's how to do it.

KEEPING LEADS FRESH

Writing clever and original leads is one of the most difficult parts of journalism. After 100, 1,000, or even 10,000 movie reviews, you're bound to start repeating yourself sooner or later. There are only so many references to the "Golden Age" of movies and observations that "this is the summer of sequels" a sane person can stand.

How do you keep leads fresh? It isn't easy, but here are a few ideas to help spur your creativity when it comes time to write those all-important first sentences. If you're stuck, give one of these a spin.

- **Trivia about the cast and crew.** Obscure facts about the star, the director, the script's origins, the making of the film, or any other aspect of the film can be great fodder for a lead. Budget overruns, production delays, massive publicity hype, and other making-of gossip is fun to play with as well. Referencing a director's previous films – particularly if there's a big gap in quality between then and now – also works.

- **The origins of the story.** Is the movie a remake or inspired by another film? Is there a true story somewhere in the origins of this movie? The less obvious this is, the better it makes for a lead (and if it doesn't fit the lead, you should incorporate it later in your review).

- **Pop culture references.** Celebrities in the news (think Paris Hilton), hot TV shows, music groups, and the like, are always ripe for the picking. These leads don't make for the best reviews, of course, but they can get you out of a jam if you're having trouble thinking of something better. They also tend to date your review, so don't rely on pop culture unless you're reviewing current releases and not classics.

- **Personal anecdotes.** Did something funny happen on the way to the theater? Overhear an interesting nugget on the way out? Keep your eyes and ears open for fresh lead material.

- **Jokes.** If all else fails, you can always make a joke about the movie, its stars, or even yourself. A play on words about the title can be funny, too.

- **The blunt approach.** Want to grab the attention of the reader? Say it outright and without fanfare: "This is the worst film of the year." Period.

- **Spinning the plot.** It is possible to get right into the plot of a movie without a traditional lead, as long as you do it in a creative way. With shorter reviews, a synopsis lead can work fairly well, especially if you make it funny. Imagine a plot synopsis lead for the book *Great Expectations*: "Pity poor Pip. Not only is his family a bore, his only friend is an ex-con on the run!" No need to play it serious and severe, even if the subject matter is humorless.

- **Anything else!** Non-sequiturs can work if you use them properly. Try not to stray too far from the movie at hand, but don't worry about delving into strange territory in the pursuit of originality.

Again, the point is to keep your creative gears spinning. You can turn just about anything into a lead, as long as you spin it the right way.

FIGHTING PRECONCEPTIONS AND MANAGING EXPECTATIONS

This is a tough one. How do you approach a movie you've been wanting to see for years? Films like *Lord of the Rings* and the *Star Wars* prequels show that critics aren't immune from hype: They want to see hot movies more than anyone, and of course they want them to be good.

Same goes for the movie that "looks awful." Or you know a movie's going to be bad because it's released in the February dumping ground, when nothing good comes out. And then there's "bad buzz," which is impossible to ignore. *Gigli* is a great, recent example of this, a movie tried, judged, and hanged in the court of public opinion before it was ever seen. In many cases, this is justified, but as a critic, you have to put this all aside in order to maintain some semblance of objectivity when you enter the theater (more on this in the next section).

How do you deal with this? The first step is to *avoid advance information*, good or bad. That means don't go to the gossip websites. Don't read a lot of movie magazines. Don't watch trailers. And most importantly, *don't read any other reviews before you write yours*! (This also helps you avoid any unintentional plagiarism.) Ignore as much gossip as you can. It's hard for a movie fiend to stay away from advance information about movies, but if you're serious about your career, you'll do it.

Foremost, these things are critical to keeping your writing original and unfiltered through other people's opinions – which you may completely disagree with. Whether it's major or minor and no matter how much you think you're immune to it, other people's opinions *will* color yours. This is called *groupthink*, and entire psychology books have been written about it. The more information you consume about a topic, the more likely you are to find yourself unconsciously agreeing with the common consensus.

If you find yourself colored by advance information (good or bad), try to put it aside. Consider the source: What does an anonymous web post *really* mean about the ultimate quality of a movie? Nothing. What does a 200-word review in *Variety* mean? You didn't go into film criticism to fall in line with everyone else, did you? Ignore it, and convince yourself that you can draw your own conclusions.

In the end, if you find you can't ignore a piece of information, disclose it in your review. Admit that you've read about the bad buzz, that you've heard other critics' reactions, or that you're obsessed with *Star Trek* and knew the entire plot before you set foot in the theater. There's nothing inherently wrong with this, as long as you fess up to it.

This all applies of course to new releases. If you're reviewing a film like *Heaven's Gate* (1980), it's impossible to separate the movie from the backlash it received. Again, there's nothing wrong with this. Recognize the critical consensus to date, and use it as a point of debate in your review. Hopefully you'll be able to offer some unique insight as to why a movie is better than its reputation suggests, or why a box office blockbuster is actually junk. That's what film criticism is all about.

Bottom line: Listen to what your mother told you and try not to worry too much about what other people think. You'll be a far better critic for it.

SUBJECTIVITY VS. OBJECTIVITY

Film critics receive a common complaint from readers annoyed that a review is "too subjective," complaining that a critic has brought his personal biases into a film and is unwilling to see the true merits of the movie.

What does it mean to be *subjective*? Merriam-Webster defines *subjective* as "characteristic of or belonging to reality as perceived rather than as independent of mind; peculiar to a particular individual." Contrasting with *objective*: "relating to or being experience or knowledge as conditioned by personal mental characteristics or states."

So in a nutshell: Subjectivity is personal; objectivity is plural – only *conditioned* by "personal mental characteristics." In a scientific analysis, subjectivity and objectivity are miles apart: There are laws of chemistry and physics, and by observing behaviors of materials in response to these laws, objective measurements can be made. A subjective analysis of a chemical reaction ("The explosion was cool!") would merit a failing grade, for obvious reasons.

But contrast this to the world of film: Do dry, clinical analyses of movies make for lively, interesting, or even remotely informative reading? The trade magazines *Variety* and *The Hollywood Reporter* publish capsule reviews that tick off the relevant players and make a watery judgment about the quality of the script, the lighting, the sound, etc. They are some of the least interesting reviews you can find, but they are designed with one goal in mind: To make an objective, educated guess about how well a film will do at the box office. Rarely do they give you any insight into whether the critic actually *liked* the movie.

Now let's contrast this with a gossip website, where an anonymous poster raves about a film being the best movie of all time. These comments are not informed by experience or backed up by example; they're off-the-cuff, subjective remarks. Talk show host Larry King called *Bringing Down the House* "one of the funniest movies of all time." This comment isn't backed up by logic; it's simply subjective (not to mention a shameless ploy to get some ink on the poster).

As you can see, neither pure objectivity nor subjectivity is the best approach to writing a well-reasoned, memorable review.

What's the right approach? I think of reviews as subjective, but backed up by solid arguments. The trick is to sound informed (*objective*) without coming off as pedantic. Also, you have to use lively language and offer personal opinions (*subjective*) that those 1,200 other critics aren't already spouting – but you have to provide evidence as to why your opinions are valid. Remember, your reviews are unique because the film was experienced through your eyes, not through some mythical lens of pure reason. There would be no differing opinions if your unique personality didn't inform your review.

This is admittedly tricky and difficult. It takes years of practice to find the right balance behind reason and instinct. And even when you do, people will still complain about your subjectivity. Ignore them all, and keep working at it.

INACCURACY IN MOVIES

Wait, War Admiral wasn't as big and Seabiscuit wasn't as cheap as they made it out to seem in the movie *Seabiscuit* (2003)?

When Hollywood makes a movie, they don't like to let the facts get in the way. History is painted in broad strokes, which is why movies about Pearl Harbor can last longer than the attack on Pearl Harbor, or why nonexistent people can take a ride aboard the *Titanic*.

How you decide to judge these issues is a personal choice, and one which you might consider on a case-by-case basis. I felt the tweaks made to the *Seabiscuit* story weren't distracting to the point where they weakened the movie. If anything, by making the horse more of an underdog, the story became more compelling. On the other hand, the liberties taken with Bob Crane's life story in *Auto Focus* (2002) were disturbing to me, unnecessarily pillorying a man who had been through a lot and was all but demonized and reinvented as a failure. But that's just me. Other critics saw the drama on its own, without overly worrying about how it jibed with history.

A related issue is faithfulness to fictional source material. Few critics had problems with Peter Jackson's liberties with *The Lord of the Rings*, which made man more susceptible to the power of the evil ring and turned the dwarf Gimli into a puppet used for comic relief. I didn't care for the changes, personally, but again that's just me, and I certainly received hate mail that accused me of being needlessly priggish, perhaps rightfully so. Then again, despite being a celebrated piece of literature, *The Bonfire of the Vanities* (1990) emerged as one of the worst films of its era, thanks in part to its attempt to turn a 700-page book into a two-hour movie. Trimming a long story down to its essentials is always a primary job of a screenwriter (witness *Adaptation*), but making sense of those essentials is even more critical. It's difficult to fault a screenwriter for changing "facts" in a case like this, not just because those facts are made up, but often because he's simply trying to get his point across in the most efficient way possible.

In other words, I tend to give a wide berth when fictional works are being adapted. Of course, if I really like the book, that's a whole other story.

In the end, it's up to you to draw conclusions about these issues: Ask yourself whether historical or source material liberties add to or impede the storytelling, whether they come off as true in spirit or blatantly hollow and wrong. Again, I treat issues like this as they arise and try not to set too many pat rules about this.

PERSONAL REFERENCES

I've mentioned this before, but it bears repeating: Try to write about yourself as little as you can. No one is reading a review to hear about your personal life. You want to inject your personality without injecting your entire person into the writing.

Some of the field's most engaging personalities do this just right. Joe Bob Briggs is unmistakable in his writing, and in audio and video appearances. But he doesn't bore us with vignettes about his childhood or talk about his personal distaste for the B-movies he reviews. He talks about what's on the screen and spins it with his unique brand of humor. He engages the audience into empathizing with him, with jokey phrases like, "Don't you think she'd see the killer by now?" Again, the focus is on the reader and the film, not on the writer.

The simplest way to avoid this common problem is simply to scrub the words "I," "me," and "my" from your reviews. This forces you to write in absolutes. Remember: It's understood that this is your opinion, so you don't need to qualify every sentence with an "I thought" or "In my opinion." Be blunt: "Harrison Ford's performance is wooden." "The direction is reminiscent of Fellini." The more you can get to the heart of the movie by scrubbing out unnecessary language that adds nothing to your write-up, the better your review will be.

AVOIDING ELITISM

What a hateful thing the hoity-toity movie review is. Caught up in deep discussions of symbolism, references to obscure Russian cinema, and unending commentary on the use of light and shadow, elitist writers alienate the audience into oblivion.

There is nothing wrong with writing about symbolism, film history, and lighting – I've talked about all of these earlier in the book, after all. But how much is too much? If you're writing for the *Film Comment* crowd, which is read by aspiring filmmakers, film students, and scholars, there's no such thing as too much analysis. But the average reader has a tolerance level for elitist or pretentious commentary. As this book presumes you are writing for a mass media audience, here are some guidelines about where to call it quits:

- Remember, most viewers just want to know if a movie is worth their time. For comedies, is it funny? For horror, is it scary? Make sure you answer the primary question before digging deeper.

- Don't make too many references to something no one's ever heard of. Sure, Fassbinder has made some great movies, but an oblique reference to an early work of his will confuse more people than it enlightens. If you're reviewing a classic film or a work that has direct parallels, feel free to ignore this advice. As well, if your goal is to get people watching more Fassbinder movies, then dig in!

- Don't be a prick. Comparing Adam Sandler to Buster Keaton doesn't make a lot of sense. Recognize that style and movies have changed in the last century. Constantly pining that "they just don't make 'em like they used to" gets tiresome, quickly, and makes you come across like a crazy old man.

- Just because something is new doesn't mean it stinks. This is a corollary to the previous rule. A handful of older critics denounce everything currently made as juvenile and obscene. That's often a fair critique: A lot of today's movies are juvenile and obscene. But if you can't regularly find something wonderful in today's cinema, you should consider retirement. If you no longer love the movies, why are you still reviewing them?

- Avoid pretentious language. Even if you're going to draw arcane comparisons, you don't have to drop pretentious words in the process.

96

For example: "The staircase gunfight in *The Untouchables* is directly inspired by *Battleship Potemkin*'s 'Odessa Steps' sequence." This is much preferred to: "*The Untouchables* draws its impassioned impetus from the paradigmatic 'Odessa Steps' sequence in *Battleship Potemkin*." No one talks like this. Don't write that way, even if you're trying to be deadly serious.

One counter-argument offers that the movies one typically associates with elitism – *The Rules of the Game, Battleship Potemkin, Grand Illusion* – weren't made for "elite" audiences. They were made for everyone, from the director's heart and soul. So why not use them as references? Again, the rule should be: Everything in moderation. A reference to one of these films is fine, but in-depth comparisons to a multitude of these movies are probably not in your best interest.

I don't mean to discourage writing for a sophisticated audience. But understand that if you do decide to go this route, that audience will be very demanding, very critical, and very small.

UNIQUE GENRE CONSIDERATIONS

So far I've discussed how to evaluate the most common types of films – mainstream comedy, drama, thrillers, and the like. But what about some of the less common genres, which can be trickier to review without some special consideration?

In this section of the book I'll explore several sub-genres that merit a little different treatment from the critic.

EVALUATING SLAPSTICK COMEDY

If critics are accused of misunderstanding one genre more than any other, it's slapstick comedy. The typical "adult" comedy (often a romantic comedy) is designed to have an interesting story to match its gags. But lately, more movies have been eschewing storyline in favor of simple gross-out humor, outrageous costumes, and stupid jokes. These movies are designed for a young and relatively oblivious audience which isn't really interested in plot resolution, character development, or simply good filmmaking. They want to laugh at Adam Sandler getting kicked in the crotch.

How do you approach a movie like this? Film critics fall into one of two camps: You can lambaste the movie for its stupidity and take it to task for appealing to the lowest common denominator, or you can go with the flow and try to appreciate it for what it is. Does every movie, even a silly slapstick comedy, need to have a fulfilling story line? I believe it does, and I take movies to task for failing to live up to that promise: After all, just because a movie features physical humor doesn't mean it can't offer something for the more cerebral moviegoer.

Sure, you are permitted to "shut your brain off" from time to time and enjoy a movie on its own terms. The problem with doing this is that you paint yourself into an inconsistent position. Why let one movie off the hook when you're going to blast everything else for being vapid?

It's a slippery slope, and there's no easy solution.

Bottom line: If you want to blow off the little critic in your head once in a while for a movie that really made you laugh, no problem. Just be sure that it truly is the knee-slapper that you say it is. There's nothing worse than giving a comedy a free pass so it doesn't have to have the basic characteristics of a real story... only to have it turn out not to be funny, either.

Here's an example of a review of a total throwaway movie that is nonetheless a pretty funny ride. The film didn't have any message (it's a sarcastic remake of an old buddy cop show, after all) and little in the way of story or character development. But even I laughed repeatedly when I saw it.

Starsky & Hutch (2004), ★★★★, *by Jesse Hassenger*

How gratifying to laugh at a movie starring Ben Stiller again. Not just occasional chuckles, as in *Duplex* or *Along Came Polly*, but big, genuine, generous laughs. A solid, well-timed comedy can be such a relief; *Starsky & Hutch* is no more than that, but that's part of its charm.

This charm may not be entirely expected. After all, it is (1) an adaptation of a 1970s cop show, (2) arriving maybe a decade after the peak of seventies nostalgia, (3) assembled by director-writer Todd Phillips (*Road Trip, Old School*), whose previous movies were only funny to the extent that the actors could overcome his aimless, slapdash staging (Will Ferrell, no problem; Breckin Meyer, less so).

To be sure, *Starsky & Hutch* doesn't have the flow or build of a truly great comedy. It is, as the credits put it, a Todd Phillips movie, so there isn't an intricate plot so much as a sure-fire concept. But the framework of a cheesy '70s cop show provides the minimal structure his movies have been lacking; Ben Stiller (Starsky, the uptight one) and Owen Wilson (Hutch, the laid-back one) do the rest.

The best decision Phillips has made is to allow the film, despite its cops and crooks, to proceed as a comedy, not an action picture with jokes; the few chases and shootouts aim squarely for humor, and pyrotechnics are at a strictly TV-ish level. It doesn't come off as yet another campy throwback so much as a subdued tribute.

Stiller and Wilson have appeared in several movies together, so even the fact that the screenplay, on its own, barely establishes their meeting, rivalry, and (of course) partnership doesn't much matter. In an early interrogation scene at a biker bar, the duo effortlessly switches from slapstick to verbal riffing. As they debate the aptness of underworld nicknames, you're not thinking about exactly why the interrogation is taking place (something about cocaine) but reminded, in the wake of disappointing films from both actors (*Along Came Polly*, *The Big Bounce*), just how funny this pair can be. Their dueling/dueting comic styles – Stiller's flummoxed rage and Wilson's amiable detachment – are perfect for the worn-out "buddy" formula. The actors are adept at striking both contrasts (most obviously in demeanor) and common ground, as they team up to discuss flirting strategy with some cheerleader chicks.

Those chicks, played by Amy Smart and Carmen Electra, highlight one of Phillips's remaining problems: His almost pathological refusal to let women be funny. There's a gaggle of terrific female performers on *Saturday Night Live* — Amy Poehler, Maya Rudolph, Rachel Dratch — who could've struck gold opposite Stiller and Wilson. Instead, we have Amy Smart with feathered hair, and the boys do all the work. Frat boy habits die hard.

But other supporting players like *Old School*ers Vince Vaughn and Will Ferrell, as lead and supporting bad guys, enliven the scenes that don't feature the central cops, and Snoop Dogg, as informant Huggy Bear, does his part to nudge the movie toward actual, non-winking cool. I smiled a lot, especially at Starsky's gung-ho running style, and a scene I will refer to only as "the part with the knives" made me laugh harder than I have at a movie in months.

Starsky & Hutch, then, is exactly the sum of its parts. It's less inspired on a conceptual level than *Zoolander*, the other major

Stiller-Wilson collaboration, but it isn't saddled with Jerry Stiller making prostate jokes, either. It isn't about anything more than several funny actors darting between mini-set pieces, but you won't go more than a minute or two without a laugh.

EVALUATING SATIRE

Very few good satires get made these days. Mel Brooks used to be the master – with spoofs like *Young Frankenstein* and *Blazing Saddles* deftly skewering horror and western genres. Today, Brooks is a shell of the past, with weak flicks like *Dracula: Dead and Loving It* pale imitations of his masterworks.

For a satire to work, a few extra criteria need to be met. First, it has to obviously be a satire. Second, as with slapstick, it has to be funny. These are two surprisingly difficult shoes to fill, which is why the genre has fallen out of favor in recent decades.

Consider the dismal failure *Hollywood Homicide* (2003), which attempted to spoof the *Lethal Weapon* series and its ilk, with Harrison Ford playing an L.A. cop who moonlights in real estate sales. Not only was the satire barely evident on first viewing, it wasn't funny either. The double blow was enough to make most people forget the movie ever existed, despite starring one of the world's most sought-after actors.

The *Scary Movie* films are more blatant parodies, spoofing a year's worth of movies at a time. Read how this review discusses the comic effect of *Scary Movie 3* (easily the best in the series) while referencing the movie's source material as well. You can't make a spoof, parody, or satire without doing both, and you can't review one without doing both, either.

Scary Movie 3 (2003), ★★★, *by Norm Schrager*

There are lots of ways to churn out sequels, particularly comedies. You can speed along like a runaway train to capitalize on a surprise hit – Miramax rushed *Scary Movie 2* into theaters one year after the original's release – or you can reset and go for broke. The latter approach seems to be the *Scary Movie 3* motive, with new writers and veteran parody director David Zucker (*Airplane!*, *The Naked Gun*) joining the fray. For its efforts, Miramax gets a perfectly average movie, with fresh moments, lame retreads, and more opportunity for big box office.

100

Scary Movie 3 sticks with the program: mind-bogglingly dumb characters hustle their way through spoofs of the industry's most popular recent films. It's no mistake that the roasted movies – in this case: *Signs*, *The Ring*, and *8 Mile* – all pull in huge money and attract a young audience.

That demographic gets plenty to laugh at during the film's winking intro. Jenny McCarthy and Pamela Anderson play two blond dimwits, mocking the open to *The Ring* while joking about their real-life infamy, and um, enormous boobs. In true *Airplane!* style, Zucker gives us a long look at Pam's ample set, giving Russ Meyer a run for his D-cup-per-minute money.

The goofy playfulness continues as Charlie Sheen and Simon Rex take a stab at *Signs*, playing a familiar pair of farmer brothers. When the pair admits that their dogs are "acting strange," Zucker gives us the single funniest visual of the movie, a throwback to some of the most absurd and creative moments of his memorable parodies. While *Scary Movie 3* has its amusing moments, the movie never nails it that well again.

Zucker and the writing team (including Kevin Smith and the prolific Pat Proft) do their best to balance the giggles between dialogue and slapstick, with both used to fine effect during a rap showdown sequence. Too often, though, the movie leans on the physical stuff too hard – so hard that fighting becomes the mode of humor. Queen Latifah gets into it with the spooky chick from the *The Ring*, as do a few other stars in the film's incredibly thin 78 minutes. It gets a little old. Zucker may be a semi-legend, but he hasn't directed a parody in 12 years, and he gave us *My Boss's Daughter*.

Scary Movie 3 does push through, and often succeeds, thanks to the silly energy of its cast. Anna Faris leads the charge (she's been in all three movies) as the perfectly ditzy know-nothing, Simon Rex is a charming numbskull, and dependable Leslie Nielsen shows up to play the President. Zucker even throws him a famous line from *Airplane!*, pleasing those of us that have seen that classic too many times.

Months (weeks?) from now, *Scary Movie 3* will make for great group viewing at home, but considering it worthy of a full-price ticket may be a stretch. You may, instead, want to bone up on other films in order to get all the jokes in *Scary Movie 4*. Or you can enjoy what you get, knowing that many of us laugh every time some poor idiot gets kicked in the nuts.

EVALUATING SEQUELS AND REMAKES

Sequels and remakes present a unique challenge in that they have source material that most of the audience will be familiar with. In most cases, it's impossible to review a sequel without discussing its predecessor. In some cases, like the *Lord of the Rings* movies or the two *Kill Bill* movies, each film is designed as part of a bigger experience. If you haven't seen *Kill Bill Volume 1*, you simply have no business reviewing the sequel. Check out the review of *Scary Movie 3* in the prior section for an example of how much weight to place on earlier films in a series.

Remakes can be a bit dicier. Not many people who saw *Ned Kelly* (2004) saw the 1971 movie of the same name. (Not many people saw the 2004 version either, but that's another story.) *Ned Kelly* was a generally faithful remake, but both movies are unremarkable, so does it add much to your review to discuss its predecessor?

Just getting access to an original film that's been remade can be tricky. *The Four Feathers* (2002) is actually a remake of a number of films (and an adaptation of a novel) made between 1915 and 1939. None of the original films are readily available for rental, so how is the modern critic supposed to consider them in his review?

In general, my rule of thumb is watch whatever source material you can, and read the book from which a script is adapted if you're so inclined. If you can't find the material or the time, don't sweat it. Draw comparisons to the original if you can. For remakes of classic movies, like *The Manchurian Candidate* (2004), reviewed below, try to set the bar higher. It's critical to see *Manchurian*'s watershed source material before you try to review the update, if for no other reason than to place it in a historical context.

Remakes and sequels are currently in vogue in Hollywood and will likely continue to be so for a long while, so this issue can be raised up to 20 times a year. Even old series (like *Star Wars*) are revived decades later. Franchises like James Bond and *Star Trek* seem eternal. There's simply no escaping sequels and remakes, so get used to dealing with them. Luckily, when a sequel or remake comes out in theaters, the studios typically have the good sense to release the original source material films on DVD beforehand. How much you choose to relate a review of a 2005 James Bond movie to 1962's *Dr. No* is up to you, but all things equal, context is a good thing.

My review of *The Manchurian Candidate* remake follows. Compare its context vs. the *Scary Movie 3* context above. One is a film of social and political importance. One is a stupid comedy that's easily forgotten. See for yourself if the reviews are clear enough in that distinction.

The Manchurian Candidate (2004), ★ ★ ★ ★*1/2, by Christopher Null*
   I'm a huge fan of the original *Manchurian Candidate*, so naturally I approached Jonathan Demme's redo with some amount of trepidation. In this, the year of the shoddy remake, we've already seen such hack jobs as *The Stepford Wives,* *The Big Bounce,* and *The Punisher*, among a half-dozen or so updates. The catch of course is that the original *Manchurian* is a classic. If Demme screwed it up, it wouldn't be the same as if he'd botched a Dolph Lundgren movie.
   With a heavy sigh of relief, I'm happy to report that Demme's done right by the original. Demme takes the best of the 1962 movie, updates it appropriately for the corporate power-trip of the 2000s, and puts some spin into the plot, so even if you watched the original on DVD last week, you still won't be able to guess how this one will end.
   For those unfortunates unfamiliar with the original, here's the story: Years after the Korean War, Bennett Marco (Frank Sinatra) finds himself haunted by strange nightmares about one of his army buddies, Raymond Shaw (Laurence Harvey). Meanwhile, Shaw's mother (Angela Lansbury) is masterminding his stepfather's vice-presidency bid, a simple homage to McCarthy's communist witch hunt. As the film develops, we learn that Shaw has been reprogrammed somehow – show him the queen of diamonds in a card deck and he'll do anything you say, even murder the presidential candidate so stepdad can take his spot.
   Heavy stuff. The new *Manchurian* does it just as well. Here's the new spin: In 2008, Gulf War veteran Ben Marco (Denzel Washington) is a nervous wreck, plagued by nightmares about his army buddy Raymond Shaw (Liev Schreiber). Shaw is an up-and-coming politician, just like his mother (Meryl Streep), who's pushing her son for the VP slot in the upcoming election. (So this time around Shaw actually *is* the titular "Manchurian"

candidate, not his father – a common misunderstanding about the first film.)

What's Manchuria got to do with it? In Demme's version, Manchurian Global is a conglomerate with hands in millions of pockets. It'll do whatever it takes to make more money – even if it means coming up with an elaborate brainwashing scheme to control a few key politicians ...

The movie spins and spins until evocations of Hitchcock become inevitable. As well, the updates make sense and work well. Instead of hypnosis, the villains use microchip implants. Instead of starting with a tea party, we see Shaw's "lost patrol" playing poker in the confines of their tank in the Kuwaiti desert (the film's sole homage to the original's cards). Instead of making politicians the villains, Demme puts the hurt on hotly topical multinational corporations. Demme doesn't just keep us guessing about how the plot will develop, he keeps us intrigued about how he'll spin society in 2008 and what clever symbol of greed he might drop in next.

Two days after seeing the film, I find myself going back to key questions and reinterpretations of the movie. Most intriguing, and I don't think this is a spoiler, is this: Does Shaw *know* he's been brainwashed all along? Think about it as you watch Schreiber's dead-on politico performance (inspired by RFK and a worthy successor to Laurence Harvey). If your head explodes, I disclaim liability.

Also excellent is Meryl Streep, who, like Lansbury before her, is due for an Oscar nomination here. She chews up the screen like Hillary Clinton on PCP. Hell, I'm ready to vote for her in the next election.

Washington, as the film's nominal star, is also very good, but the script takes a few too many pains to give him monologue opportunities and repetitive scenes, especially during his paranoid "investigations" into Shaw, which uses the "visit-the-old-army-buddy-oops-he's-dead" routine once too often. Some jerky editing creates a few scenes that are rough around the edges; more than one conversation makes a leap that doesn't quite make sense. Finally, some leaps of reality (a vice-presidential nomination convention?) just don't make a lot of sense.

These are minor flaws that are easily overlooked in the end. The new *Manchurian Candidate* isn't just a great remake – it may just be the greatest remake ever remade.

EVALUATING DOCUMENTARIES

If you're a typical reader, you probably aren't getting into this business to review documentaries, and that's a shame, because in the last 15 to 20 years, a number of outstanding documentaries have been released.

Films like *Crumb* (1995) and *Hoop Dreams* (1994) have just as much drama as fictional films. They may even have more, and why shouldn't they? The human experience is what dictates the creativity of writers and filmmakers, so isn't real life every bit as interesting as fake life?

Sometimes it is, sometimes it isn't. Many documentaries – if not most of them – get sidetracked by the filmmakers themselves, who often feel so passionate about their subject that they fail to let him or her do the storytelling. They start to insert themselves into the story to a degree where it becomes distracting and pointless. So many movies purport to tell the story of an obscure and ostensibly interesting individual, only to end up as the story of the filmmaker.

In *Crumb*, the only trace of director Terry Zwigoff is in the gothic mood the film establishes as it tells the story of noted cartoonist R. Crumb and his eccentric family. Still, Zwigoff has a thumbprint on the film, masterfully coaxing information out of Crumb, lighting and editing the film appropriately for his subject matter, and keeping the pace varied between depressing vignettes and upbeat oddities. It's as close to perfect as a documentary gets.

Just because a filmmaker appears in his own film doesn't mean it's automatically bad. To look at the flipside of documentaries, consider Michael Moore's career. His movies are as much about him as they are about current events. In fact, with each progressive movie, there's more Moore to be found on camera. Does this mean Moore's a bad documentarian? No, he's just got a different style, producing his films more in the vein of investigative journalist than casual observer. This turns off purists, but it engages audiences, which is part of the reason why *Fahrenheit 9/11* (2004) is the highest-grossing documentary of all time.

Reviewing documentaries can be dicey, and the experience is often much like reviewing an independent film. Budgets are typically miniscule, filmmakers have virtually no crew, and access to source material and interview subjects can be a problem. Most documentaries these days are shot on video because of the cost benefits and the large amount of footage that needs to be photographed. You'll have to consider, as you would with any film, whether this detracts from the experience or worsens the movie.

Another common problem with documentaries is "talking head" syndrome. This is caused by the overuse of static interviews with people sitting in chairs rather than relying on archival footage or scenes with action. The best documentaries get subjects off their butts.

Other than these concerns, documentaries should be weighed using the same criteria as fictional films. Next you'll find Jeremiah Kipp's review of *Genghis Blues*, a good documentary about a blind musician and his trip to Mongolia. Kipp doesn't really touch on the technical side of the film in his review, but rather focuses on how compelling the story became to him, despite his initial skepticism.

Genghis Blues (1999), ★★★★, *by Jeremiah Kipp*

Gosh, I had to be dragged kicking and screaming to see this film.

Here's the premise: Filmmakers accompany a blind blues musician to the small country of Tuva, just north of Mongolia, to participate in the 1995 throat-singing symposium in Kyzyl. My roommate passionately rhapsodized over it for days, yet nothing about this premise connected with me. "Lemme tell you something, pal – I'd rather watch mute nuns performing *The Sound of Music* than watch these guys do their... their... their crazy *throat-singing ritual*!"

Just goes to show, you can't judge a book by its cover. Boy, did I feel silly when I actually sat down to watch *Genghis Blues*, one of the more exhilarating and passionate documentaries about music and culture to appear in recent years. Who would have thought I'd actually love this music and want to learn more about it?

There are too many layers of *Genghis Blues* to discuss within the context of a review. And unfortunately, the act of describing the adventures of our filmmaking team and their companion, Paul Pena (blind, mouthy, and sharp as a whip) might strike readers as, well, *boring*.

Who would think that you could get excited about these characters packing for their long trip east, riding in planes, buses, and cars for thousands of miles through the desert? Or that the history of this small country would prove exciting?

You wouldn't expect the musical performers who gather at this event to cause the average viewer (me) to sit bolt upright on the couch, mouth agape in amazement, as they sang notes which seemed like the distant rumblings of an underground cave or an impossibly beautiful wood instrument. The experience was beautiful and strange.

This is no stodgy, academic *National Geographic* special. The people of Tuva are lively and buoyant, pleased, and excited that the American, Pena, would take such an interest in their art of throat singing, which allows them to voice more than one note at the same time. Pena is also familiar with their vivid, colorful garb and language, long banned by the Communists.

And he's blind. He learned it all by translating from Tuvan to Russian to English*, in Braille!* Rocky Balboa, you're a stinking chump. You ain't nothing!

The story is inherently dramatic. This is Pena's first time in this country, whose customs he has studied so passionately. As a participant in their competition, he's under enormous pressure created by his own fear. Right before he goes on, he's in the midst of paralyzing stage fright (which multiplies itself by a thousand when he's told that he cannot perform the song he had prepared, as some of the audience would be offended).

Paul and the filmmakers also journey through the land, meeting shamans and wrestlers. They take part in a goat slaughtering ceremony and bless themselves in the water of sacred rivers. While the filmmaking is rough, sometimes choppily cut together, you can't beat the beautiful landscapes or the appreciation that shines through Pena's face. This American has found his spiritual home.

Genghis Blues doesn't make Paul into a saint. As a blind man, he's often confused and disoriented, battling bouts of self-doubt and depression. It's heartbreaking to learn that in America the farthest he can walk alone is the corner store, that he often feels alienated or misunderstood as though he were some freak. And when some of his medication runs out, they may need to cut short their trip to Tuva, so *Genghis Blues*, for all its fascination with exploring new sights and sounds, is not without tears.

Saddest of all, an artist like Paul Pena can only find acceptance in a foreign land that doesn't look at his craft with confusion and misunderstanding. If *Genghis Blues* accomplishes anything, it makes Pena's world accessible to folks like me who might not give a damn, were they not led to the stream and asked to drink.

EVALUATING FOREIGN FILMS

Don't like subtitles? Neither do I. Nothing distracts more at the movies (aside from the guy kicking your chair) than having to read little text at the bottom of the screen rather than concentrate on the images.

But that doesn't mean I (and you) can't enjoy foreign films. Reviewing them requires more discipline and a more careful hand, but with the right approach you should find yourself comfortably evaluating movies in languages you've never heard before.

Fundamentally there's nothing about a foreign film that merits different treatment, but two things deserve special consideration.

First is the social context of the film — in relation to the country in which it was created. Many, if not most, foreign films that are released in the U.S. are skewed toward political and societal issues. Few Israeli romantic comedies make it to our shores: Most Israeli cinema that we see concerns in some way Israel-Palestine relations, or the experience of living in such a hotbed of violence. The film *Promises* (2001), is an excellent example of this, exploring the lives of Israeli children in a world filled with terrorism.

As well, I don't think I've seen a Croatian film from the last 10 years that wasn't deeply affected by the civil war and turmoil in Yugoslavia. The problem here is that most Americans have had minimal exposure to the crisis, so understanding a film placed in a modern Bosnian setting won't immediately make sense to the uninformed viewer. As such, you owe it to yourself to more fully understand the current events of a region before you attempt to critique its cinema.

The second consideration is the audience of the film. More than any other genre, foreign films attract a highly educated audience that is looking for more than sheer entertainment from a movie. As such, it's your duty to more fully analyze the issues and intellectual challenges posited by a foreign picture versus a mainstream American release. I'm not suggesting you abandon the careful approach of balancing art and entertainment concerns I discussed in Chapter 4, but when in doubt, err toward the side of art. Your review will look silly and juvenile if you don't.

A case in point is the Brazilian film *City of God* (2002). This movie is filled with violence and swirling action, but it's placed in the context of social upheaval in Rio de Janeiro over some 20 years. The moviegoer who wasn't interested in Brazilian history could be entertained by the movie as a drugs-and-action flick. The viewer looking for something deeper (along with the critic, one would hope), will find a powerful message about Brazilian poverty and the cycle of violence in the slums. You might even discuss both of these angles in your review.

A final issue worth noting is dubbing. You rarely see (or hear, rather) dubbed films today, but once in awhile one slips through. You're far more likely to encounter dubbed tracks if you review classic Asian cinema, which is notorious for its use of badly dubbed voices that would never match up with the lip movements of the actors. Regardless of whether you enjoy dubbing or not, it's important to note the quality of any dubbing in a review, if for no other reason than to prepare the reader for what to expect.

In this review of *Y Tu Mamá También*, the critic spends most of his time analyzing the film on its merits and establishing its place as an alternative to American sex comedies, then dips into social commentary at the end. You'll also see another example and more detailed approach at tackling a foreign film in the following section on classic films.

Y Tu Mamá También (2002), ★ ★ ★ ★ *1/2, by Norm Schrager*

When a film opens with a handheld shot of two teens humping under a *Harold and Maude* poster, one can assume the movie is different. *Y Tu Mamá También* is certainly that – an original, harsh, funny slant on the traditional road movie, as experienced by two Mexican teens and their gorgeous 28-year-old tagalong. Filmmaker Alfonso Cuarón (*Great Expectations*) strips the familiar genre to its core, exposing the trailblazing characters at their barest, figuratively and literally.

As go the minds of most 17-year-olds, Tenoch and Julio think about sex. A lot. They talk about sex a lot. They quickly screw their girlfriends before the girls depart for a European summer vacation, they simultaneously masturbate while hollering out their thoughts (*Salma Hayek!*), and they make fun of their respective, uh, members. Tenoch, the wealthy son of a politician, and Julio, living with his lower-class mother and activist sister, plan to spend the summer getting high and getting laid.

109

When the boys conjure up images of a fictitious beach to impress Luisa, the young wife of Tenoch's cousin, she buys it, and asks to go with them. Surprised, the guys make a couple of quick moves (like getting a car), and the trio is on the road. They cruise through Mexico, on a road to nowhere, unsure of their destination… especially because it doesn't really exist.

Cuarón and his co-screenwriter brother Carlos create the journey as a symbolic fantasy, a trip taken for the hell of it, representing the lack of direction for all three characters. The boys, unsure of their futures, and certainly over-confident in their sexual prowess, live an almost existential life. It doesn't really dawn on them that, at some point, they will have to end up somewhere. For Luisa, she feels that a new, foreign, uncharted path is just what she needs – her life has been consumed with caring for a sick relative and quickly marrying. She's never had the experiences of raging like an animal, playing games, controlling men.

Boy, does she get her chance on this road trip. If sex was front-and-center for the boys before they left, it's an all-encompassing phenomenon once on the open trail. Cuarón does a fantastic job of combining raw, unabashed desire with complex awkwardness, shooting many scenes with no-edit, single takes, allowing his incredible actors (Diego Luna, Gael Garcia Bernal from *Amores Perros*, and the astounding Maribel Verdu) to live the roles. The dialogue is graphic, and the performers are wonderfully shameless and boldly courageous. The whole package makes for enticing, sometimes eye-popping, excitement.

Cuarón does comment on the economic and class structure of Mexico – similarly and with sometimes as heavy a hand as Kurosawa in his modern-day Tokyo films – but they are topics worth thinking about, especially as the poor and displaced surround the three aimless characters.

An additional treat is Cuarón's use of an objective narrator – he fills in the blanks as the rest of the film's soundtrack disappears. In the film's opening, he provides the back story; toward the middle, he lets us know characters' thoughts and secrets; and at the end, he tells of a future that no one else in the film knows. It is a thoughtful, humorous tool, which Cuarón even uses to drive some anticipation, eliminating the film's sound each time, but then waiting a couple of breathless seconds before adding the narration.

There are coming-of-age movies out there nearly all the time, but very few with the heart and wild sexual soul of this one. But you can forget your bittersweet *Summer of '42* or your goofy-raunchy *American Pie*. It's brutal action and graphic discussion by way of a pre-adult road tale. And as for the title, it means "And Your Mother Too." You figure it out.

EVALUATING CLASSICS

Even if you are only reviewing theatrical releases, eventually you'll come up against a classic film to review when it's reissued. *Vertigo, Dr. Strangelove,* and *E.T.* have all seen revivals in theaters in recent years.

How do you review a movie that's been around for decades and which the audience has almost unilaterally already seen? Well, very carefully.

Classics are called classics for a reason: Because most people think they're very good. Does this mean you can't pan a movie like *Vertigo*? No, but if you do write a negative review, you better cover your bases and provide far more context for your criticism than you normally would.

Many novice critics err by holding older films to modern-day standards. As with foreign films, classics have to be placed in a context of the time they were made in order to make any sense in a reasonable review. In any film from the 1940s or 1950s, you'll find that morals were much tighter and censorship dictated what you could show and say (and even how long a kiss could be). It doesn't make sense to decry a cutaway from a love scene or a decapitation when this simply wasn't allowed during the era. At the same time, if modern sensibilities have caused a classic to lose its power (consider the once-shocking *Freaks* (1932) or X-rated *Midnight Cowboy* (1969), which were both deemed too scandalous for wide release in their respective eras and seem tame by today's standards), you should mention this as well. In other words, place a film in its historical context, but understand that it is being viewed by a modern audience.

Similarly, advances in filmmaking technology and technique have made many classic films look dated. Consider the original *Star Wars* and *Star Trek* movies. Both suffered from awful special effects and were cleaned up by the directors years later. In fact, your readership is more likely to want to know about this cleanup process than about your opinion on the film itself, with which they'll be all too familiar. Most reviews of the reissued *Star Wars* films (all featuring new effects) focused on the few minutes in which footage had been changed or enhanced.

For films that are presented as they were originally released, you have a little more leeway in how to approach a review. If you're reviewing DVDs, this is going to come up constantly, as classics are released on the new platform with far more regularity than recent releases. You could easily build a career on writing about movies no younger than 20 years old and never run out of new material to review.

For these films, I typically take a direct approach, almost as if I was reviewing a current release, but adding any notes about just how classic a film actually is. The vast majority of DVD reissues are not really *classic* classics but simply old movies that haven't previously been available on DVD. With 200 to 300 major releases every year, it's going to take a decade for the history of American film to reappear on DVD, and most readers will have long since forgotten what they thought of *Porky's II* or *Funny About Love*. With movies like these (not regarded as classic in any way), feel free to treat them as you would any other film, while still paying homage to the era in which they were produced. As always, the goal is to balance the needs of a modern reader with the understanding of the limitations and social setting of the era in which a work was created.

Here's another predicament: If you review *Citizen Kane* today, can you reveal the ending without catching heat? To spoil movies like *The Sixth Sense* or *The Crying Game* when they were released would get you drawn and quartered. Is it safe to spoil a movie that's 60 years old? I'd err on the side of *not* including spoilers, even for such well-known twists as the identity of Norman Bates' mother in *Psycho*. Why? Because younger readers may just be stumbling across a movie for the first time, and you don't want to ruin it for them. (Avoiding spoilers also helps make your reviews more palatable when syndicating to buyers like DVD merchants, who are appealing to a broad market that may potentially include novices. I'll discuss syndication in Chapter 9.)

Here's a classic movie review (which is also a foreign film) that does an excellent job at putting the movie in a historical and social context. It's clearly written in the present as a retrospective (and I've left intact the writer's discussion of the DVD special features, which is common in classic movie reviews), so you'll note how the author comments on this movie and its cast and crew in relation to films that came later – as opposed to doing it the other way around, as you would in a typical review.

Mamma Roma (1962), ★ ★ ★ ★, *by Jake Euker*

If you want to go along with me, I can explain to you the filmic considerations that make Pier Paolo Pasolini's *Mamma Roma* such an extraordinary work: its importance as a bridge between Neo-Realist and new Italian cinema, its formal quirks, its Marxist reckoning of the underside of Italy's post-war "economic miracle." And, indeed, viewers who wish to pursue these elements can find discussion of all of this and more on the generous extras included in the new Criterion release of the film.

But a substantial part of the beauty of *Mamma Roma* is that you don't have to go deep to emerge from it satisfied. The premise of the film is universal: The title character (played by Anna Magnani) is reunited with her 16-year-old son Ettore (Ettore Garofolo), who was raised by others (just who remains unclear). Hoping for a better life for him than she had, she aspires to better herself and to provide her son with opportunities in a post-war Italy that still struggles with the consequences of its defeat. The details with which Pasolini fills in this sketch are what made it the cause of a furor in its day: Mamma Roma is a prostitute, and her plans for bettering her son's life include such schemes as blackmailing a restaurant owner into hiring him. Mamma Roma is committed to her son like any mother, but, being a streetwise woman, her care extends to arranging for his deflowering in the bed of a fellow whore. She works hard to shed her streetwalking past – she even buys a stall from which to sell vegetables – but a love from her past (Ettore's father?) disrupts her life with some regularity, demanding money from her and sending her back into the night. And, most tragically, the gains she manages can be hard to discern amid the barren legacy of Fascism in which she lives – her new, "better" home looks much like her previous one – and Ettore himself begins to reject her, still stinging from her absence during his youth. Before long, he begins to decipher the clues offered him about his mother's livelihood, and he turns to crime.

Central to the film's success is Magnani's Mamma Roma. Both she and Pasolini were, for different reasons, dissatisfied with her performance, and explanations are offered in the interviews included in the two-disc set. But watching the film today it's impossible to understand what's not to like. Magnani (best known to American audiences for her Oscar-winning performance in 1955's *The Rose Tattoo*) is magnificent in the title role, developing utterly convincingly from a hilariously earthy bon vivant to a harried mother with aspirations to the bourgeoisie. Magnani wears her feelings nakedly; everything she feels is present in her face, voice, and boisterous, contagious laugh. As her son, Garofolo is a Neo-Realist gamble that pays off: The director wrote the piece around the handsome young man after spying him waiting tables, and his natural screen presence trumps his untrained performance.

At its heart, *Mamma Roma* is compelling melodrama told in a singular cinematic style. (The highlight of the film is a pair of long takes in which Magnani walks the nighttime streets of Rome, ranting about her condition in life and fabricating stories about her youth, while companions join her, keep stride for awhile, then fall away as others replaces them. These are exhilarating, free-wheeling cinematic moments without close parallels anywhere.) The film is successful on this level, but for those interested there's much more here to explore. The Criterion edition includes, for instance, the short film *La ricotta*, a minor masterpiece released the year after *Mamma Roma* as part of the omnibus film *RoGoPaG*. In it, Orson Welles stars as a director helming a Technicolor costume piece about Christ's passion (the film is in black and white except when depicting the film-within-the-film), and the work proved so effective an attack on Italian society that Pasolini was actually sentenced to prison for having made it. A feature-length documentary by Ivo Barnabò Micheli details the director's career from his early work with Fellini and Rossellini, through his production of the unsettling and explosively controversial *Salo,* to his brutal murder, allegedly at the hands of a street hustler, in 1975. (Lacking is a discussion of this notorious murder; the crime sparked speculation that Pasolini was the victim of a political assassination, and Italy's yellow press made much of its more sordid aspects, emphasizing the director's homosexuality.) Interviews with others, including Bernardo Bertolucci, round out the set.

But the unique and engrossing feature film remains the best reason to plunge into the *Mamma Rosa* Criterion edition. Lovers of film will find in it a formidable entertainment. And scholars could conceivably keep themselves busy for years.

EVALUATING CHILDREN'S MOVIES

The hallmark of any good "kid flick" review is that it discusses both the movie's appropriateness for children *and* for adults. Remember: Little kids don't often go to the movies by themselves, they go with their parents. The best kiddie fare has something to keep both children and adults amused, without turning either party off. It's also always a good idea to include a discussion of how old children should be in order to enjoy the film. Remember that in aiding the buying decision here, parents will be weighing specifically not just whether the movie is appropriate for them but whether it's appropriate for their kids, too.

Pixar has done the best job of the aforementioned balancing act with its entire canon of films. A review of one of these is included below as an example of how they're best written.

Finding Nemo (2003), ★ ★ ★ ★*1/2, by Sean O'Connell*

The Pixar logo – which is the company's name with a desk lamp in place of the "I" – has become the cinematic equivalent of a "Prime" stamp on a side of beef. Once we see it, we know we're in for breathtaking animation, clever scripts, and wholesome family entertainment. The cynic in me waits for the geniuses responsible for the *Toy Story* features, *A Bug's Life*, and *Monsters, Inc.* to slip up and release a flop. Looks like I'll be waiting a few more years.

The latest Pixar pearl, *Finding Nemo*, ventures under the sea, where single dad Marlin (voice of Albert Brooks) overprotects his only son, Nemo (voice of Alexander Gould). One day, Nemo wades into uncharted waters on a dare, only to be snatched up by a scuba diver and placed in the tank of an Australian dentist. For the remainder of the film, Marlin and a forgetful fish named Dory (voice of Ellen DeGeneres) scour the ocean floor in an effort to bring Nemo home, a task that's easier said than done.

You won't need a map to unearth the treasures buried in *Nemo*. Pixar continues its streak of casting eclectic atypical stars and marrying them to the right visuals to create memorable characters. Brooks is pitch-perfect when conveying Marlin's neurotic insecurities and DeGeneres hooks the humor in Dory's sporadic mental flights. The fact that her fish suffers short-term memory loss reeks of "tired comedic device," but DeGeneres bucks the odds and gets enormous and consistent laughs here.

The vast ocean setting only broadens the array of creatures available for animation, and the Pixar team responds in kind with wildly vivid designs. Their most spectacular achievement has to be the way they capture a fish's swaying motions. *Nemo* convinces us we're underwater. You may have to remind yourself that it's safe to breathe. That is, if you can catch your breath between fits of laughter generated by writer/director Andrew Stanton's sharp script.

With concurrent plotlines being played in both the ocean and the fish tank, *Nemo* is able to introduce and develop more characters than you'd expect. My current favorite is Jacques, a French shrimp with a cleaning fetish, but that could change after my next viewing. Miraculously, they're not just characters on screen; they stay with us long after the theater has gone dark.

Despite its "G" rating, it's worth mentioning that *Nemo* occasionally backstrokes through the deep end of the adult content pool. A tragic death of *Bambi* proportions starts the film, and Marlin and Dory face an ocean of dangers – from toothy sharks to sting-happy jellyfish. Kids may be spooked by the urgency of certain chase scenes, but it's only temporary, and the fear factors are immediately followed up with safe, giggle-inducing head clunks.

The number of obstacles placed between father and son will eventually exhaust even the most attentive child, and the inevitable reunion could've arrived a tad bit earlier. But these quibbles are miniscule in the face of the big picture. *Nemo* swims with the finest fish. This catch is certainly a keeper.

EVALUATING ODDBALL MOVIES

Finally we enter into what are categorically the most difficult movies to review. Consider Richard Linklater's *Slacker* (1991), which spends 60 seconds to a few minutes with each of its characters before jumping on to another one.

You can't develop a character in 60 seconds, there's no plot to speak of, and the direction is highly dependent on the individual scene Linklater is staging.

The three films in the *Koyaanisqatsi* (1983) series have no dialogue; each consists solely of themed images set to music.

In his infamous *Lost Highway* (1997), David Lynch offers a sketchy narrative about an accused murderer who strangely morphs into another person halfway through the film.

How do you review something like this?

Reviews of oddball films are your chance to let your freak flag fly. My theory is that if a director is going to break the rules, you can break the rules, too. Call it like you see it. Run fast and loose with language. Have fun.

When it comes down to it, avant garde cinema like this is often an "either you get it or you don't" affair. This is not meant to imply that if you *don't* get it you're somehow stupid. I've panned a number of movies like this for the simple reason that they fail as both art and entertainment. When a director is too busy putting "his stamp" on a movie to make an impression on the audience, that's a failure.

At the same time, boundary-breaking cinema like *Slacker* can be a great success. Watching hundreds of movies a year desensitizes you to the three-act plot structure, the traditional character arc, the deep traditions of establishing shot-action shot-reaction shot. Once in awhile it can be very refreshing to see a film that takes a new approach to moviemaking. Consider *Memento* (2001), a film that is traditional in every way but one: It's told in reverse. This little touch turned what would have been an ordinary (even boring) thriller into a masterpiece.

Still, one man's masterpiece is another man's contrivance, and reviewing oddball films like these can be both the most gratifying and contentious reviews you'll ever write. Below you'll find two very different reviews of Lynch's *Mulholland Drive*, a film that ultimately earned Lynch an Oscar nomination alongside plenty of razzing. Who's right? It's all in the mind of the audience and the critic. You be the judge. (For more reading and context, Jeremiah Kipp and I continued our debate about this film in a feature story which you can find archived on filmcritic.com.)

Mulholland Drive (2001), ★ ★ ★, *by Christopher Null*
>   *Twin Peaks* stands as one of my favorite television series ever
>   made. But if you slapped the first three episodes together and
>   called it a movie, I doubt I'd feel the same way. *Mulholland*

Drive was originally intended as David Lynch's return to TV. Rumored to be a creepy and atmospheric drama, I had anticipated another *Peaks* — and prayed for something better than Lynch's disastrous "sitcom" *On The Air.*

Trouble began when ABC abruptly pulled the plug on *Mulholland*, but Lynch, ever the trooper, decided to take the footage he'd shot so far and turn it into a movie. Of course, a few things would have to be added — namely a lot of nudity and oozing sexuality and, well, an *ending* — so it was back to the set for extra shooting. The result is archetypical Lynch — creepy, uncomfortable, erotic, and devoid of all logic whatsoever.

The story, as much as there is one to describe, is told much like any TV pilot would do. Characters are fed to us slowly — remember, this was supposed to carry us over 13 hours or so — and plot details are drawn with a large brush. We witness a Hollywood car crash and meet its amnesiac victim (Laura Harring), we see a farm girl/aspiring starlet (Naomi Watts) take her in and befriend her, and we sit in on a series of strange meetings surrounding the making of an artsy, difficult director's (Justin Theroux) Big Movie. And somewhere among the apartment buildings, the dingy diner, the studio lot, and Mulholland Drive itself, these stories will intersect.

Whether those stories will be comprehensible (and whether that's an important quality for a film to have) are something else entirely, and as with any Lynch movie, it's pretty much up to the viewer to decide all that on his own. Personally, I think that story *does* matter, and I'd also say that *Mulholland Drive* simply doesn't make sense when looked at with a critical eye. You can make up your own mind, but between the mystical matter-transference box and its triangular key, a pair of giggling seniors, a yeti that lives in a parking lot, and a good dozen character identity changes a la the boneheaded *Lost Highway*, even the most patient moviegoer will be utterly lost starting right at the fade in.

I realize that faulting Lynch for not making sense is a bit like being mad at the dog for digging in the garbage. It's in his nature to be random. But *Twin Peaks* and movies like *Blue Velvet* are masterworks because they managed to be cryptic think-pieces and still satisfy you in the end, backwards-talking dwarfs or no. To be certain, *Mulholland Drive* is gutsy and has moments of greatness: Watts' virtuoso audition with a far-too-tanned leading man shows how truly magnificent the movie could have been. Other vignettes are just as memorable — like when a perfectly ordinary event like coming home from work suddenly turns into a nightmare — but they end up being islands in an ocean of overly pregnant pauses and wild tangents.

But again, I have to harp on this: Far, far too much of the film (clocking in at almost 2 1/2 hours long) is nonsense. Most notably, near the hurried finale, Harring drags Watts to a way-after-hours performance wherein musicians *don't* play their instruments. Watts ends up shaking violently until a magic box appears in her lap. Um, okaaaaayyyyy.... It all sounds like some silly dream Lynch once had and scribbled down during the middle of the night. Who knows, maybe that was the point.

Technically, the film is assured and reasonably memorable. The actors' performances (virtually all unknowns) are good but hardly career-making — with the dual exceptions of Watts and Lafayette Montgomery's miniscule yet thunderous role as a cowboy somehow pulling all the strings. The camerawork is typical of Lynch but his use of out-of-focus shots — presumably meant to make us question our perspective — ends up being distracting more than anything else. The music, by longtime Lynch collaborator Angelo Badalamenti and Lynch himself, is appropriately creepy when it needs to be and fun when levity is needed.

To his credit, Lynch at least *tried* to wrap everything up in the last 20 minutes. It all involves that damn magic box, but still, he does pay lip service to the notion of plot structure. It's no "Who killed Laura Palmer?", but it's something to chew on. It's just too bad that trying to make heads or tails of the dozen last-minute plot twists is a bit like trying to analyze jazz — the more you think about it, the less sense it makes. Let the movie go, and you'll find it far more enjoyable.

Mulholland Drive (2001), ★ ★ ★ ★ ★, *by Jeremiah Kipp*
The dream resembles a TV-movie, and reality itself is

fragmented and torn. David Lynch's *Mulholland Drive* is more than just a curiosity piece expanded from a scrapped TV-pilot, though it uses the forms and conventions of television to explore the increasingly addled fantasies of a would-be starlet. Those who found *Lost Highway* an audacious stunt, transforming its protagonist into someone else at the midway point, will be flummoxed by Lynch's askew storytelling methods here. Not only do the characters morph into deeper representations of their secret selves, the entire schematic approach to the mini-series dissipates into an altered state.

To the tune of composer Angelo Badalamenti's wine-dark funereal melodies, Lynch forages his way into the nocturnal avenues and expressways of Los Angeles. On Mulholland Drive, a beautiful, raven-haired amnesiac (Laura Harring) staggers from the twisted wreckage of a black limosine and makes her way through the night-shadowed Hollywood Hills toward the beckoning city lights. The sound of her high heels is preternaturally loud as she evades impending pursuers, hiding away in the tangled bushes surrounding a residential apartment complex.

The clear light of day brings no comfort. Two men (Patrick Fischler and Michael Cooke) in a coffee shop recount a nightmare about some strange, shadowy figure that peers through walls and lurks behind the diner, a controlling force that brings death. To prove there's no such thing as phantoms, the men investigate the neighboring alleyway and make a startling discovery.

Arriving in L.A. for the first time is a bright-eyed innocent named Betty (Naomi Watts), filled with naïve dreams of becoming a movie star. Temporarily staying at her aunt's opulent home at 1612 Havenhurst (a Lynch preoccupation: showing us Where We Are), her first brush with Hollywood may shatter those illusions. Before this fledgling has a chance to spread her wings, she finds a newfound friend and roommate in the helpless amnesiac. Drawn into the mystery of "Rita's" identity, the two women attempt to uncover the truth. Along the way, a savage attraction blooms between them that could be the start of something exquisite and hazardous.

To delve further into this labyrinth would be a disservice to any audience open to forming their own subjective connections and analysis. Suffice to say, these subplots merge together, involving gangsters and studio moguls, magicians and chanteuses, detectives and assassins, red curtains and pinheaded villains, spare hotel rooms with hissing radiators. There are spontaneous bursts of violence (like when a film director, played by intense, bespectacled Jason Theroux, smashes the windows and headlights of a posh limo with his trusty golf club) and sexual forays that might be described as subterranean. Lynch's preoccupations with noir's form and graphic design prove an ideal match for the impassive, sparse cityscapes of the west coast. "Welcome To Los Angeles" is one of the first signs glimpsed in transit; it has rarely felt so foreboding.

Presuming that *Mulholland Drive* takes us deeper into fantasy is more than shortsighted; it's a misnomer. Inner feelings of sentiment and dread directly affect the external images, remaining truthful to Lynch's heartfelt observation of the world. Setting aside logic, it's better to consider the Lynchian mold as an emotional, musical tapestry, one that filters into collective anxieties. There's nothing obscure about the question of self, an obstacle Betty and Rita both must confront. Romance and betrayal morph them into new roles. Lingering underneath the starlet might be a calculating rube, under the seemingly timid amnesiac stirs an ever-ripening sensuality.

Sketched in muted colors and pervasive darkness by superb cinematographer Peter Deming (who also lensed *Lost Highway*), the standards of television rely on conventional medium-shots and close-ups to fit the small screen. Lynch makes advantageous use of those unwritten rules, though he contorts them through his unusual camera placements and penchant for lingering on obscure beats (who else would linger on a cup of espresso during a confrontation scene, thereby making the *cup of espresso* into a menacing artifact?) As the characters merge into something Other (or, alternately, become fully realized versions of themselves), Deming's photography becomes more ragged and hyperreal, accompanied by Mary Sweeney's serrated knife-edge editing technique of shock cuts.

Holding this bundle of nerve ends together are remarkable ensemble performances from startling newcomers and established veterans: legendary Amy Miller as a freakishly maternal hotel caretaker; Dan Hedaya as a volcanic movie financier; Lafayette Montgomery as a soft-spoken cowboy with murder in his eyes ("You'll see me one more time if you're good. You'll see me two more times if you're bad."). The real finds are Naomi Watts and Laura Harring, whose balancing act recalls Shelley Duvall and Sissy Spacek in Robert Altman's *Three Women*. They're the lifeblood of *Mulholland Drive*, offering richly calibrated incarnations of womanhood. Watts and Haring are poised for triumphant careers, two more reasons why Lynch and his collaborators have created a masterpiece. As they say in show business, this is where the magic happens.

COMPARATIVE ANALYSIS

As I've mentioned before, it's always a good idea to talk about a movie's predecessors, inspirations, and direct connections (especially with sequels and remakes), but how do you bring in more obscure connections to your discussion of a movie? It's easy!

- When introducing cast and crew, include a parenthetical statement or short note about other recent films with which the star or director has been involved. The more obscure the actor or director is, the more important it is to make these connections for the reader, if for no other reason than to help familiarize them with the stars of the show. Example: "One of the more frightening portrayals of life in the '70s to hit screens recently, *Boogie Nights* is full of kitsch and sprawls over a full decade of excess. Writer/director Paul Thomas Anderson, who hit-and-missed with *Hard Eight*, takes a dozen characters through 2 1/2 hours of meandering storylines, supporting players, drug/sex binges, and more costume changes than you can fathom."

- Another good option for referencing other films is when you're exploring films with a common theme: "One common recurring narrative in many of King's better-known novel-to-screen adaptations – such as *Stand by Me*, *The Green Mile*, and *The Shawshank Redemption* – incorporates an older gentleman recalling his youth or a life-changing incident of his life. *Hearts in Atlantis* follows this to a tee."

- For in-depth reviews (especially of classic films), you may want to devote a full paragraph or more to talking about the film's influences, its place in cinema of its era, or the work of its director before and since. A review of a mid-career movie like Martin Scorsese's *After Hours* might discuss his growth from violence-driven films, his foray into comedy, his angst from directing and attempting to distribute *The Last Temptation of Christ*, and his later return to more violent fare.

The possibilities are truly endless. In the following review of *The Company*, Jeremiah Kipp writes about director Robert Altman's career and other films, his contemporaries, and other popular cinema of the day, contrasting it with this film. Had he been so inclined, he might have broadened the comparative analysis into other movies about dancing (*All That Jazz, Flashdance*), and discussed more of Altman's previous films. The sky's the limit!

The Company (2003), ★ ★ ★ ★*1/2, by Jeremiah Kipp*

Thank you, Robert Altman. Coming fast on the heels of one of the worst moviegoing years of recent memory, *The Company* appears like a wondrous beacon of light. (It even trumps Altman protégé Alan Rudolph's clear-eyed ode to middle class challenges, *The Secret Lives of Dentists*.) Altman casts his gaze upon the Joffrey Ballet of Chicago: their days and nights, their strict regime and straight-ahead pursuit of artistic expression, and the grueling physical toll of stretching their bodies to the limit. Opening with a modern dance number with performers in skin-tight costumes racing across the stage with multi-colored banners, *The Company* is like a direct appeal to the heart and mind, to which I can only exclaim, "Wonderful!" and "Beautiful!" It's a reminder of what cinema can do, and the poetry of the dancer's movements is corresponded to with Altman's visual panache, his use of vivid colors, his vividly imaginative framing.

It shames flashy movies like *The Matrix* sequels, which adopt surface style and frenetic movement but lack sheer, sumptuous vision. Altman's movie isn't just a pretty sheen ("I hate pretty!" snaps Malcolm McDowell as the head of the ballet company), it's a full audio-visual experience. For all the limbs blown apart in *The Matrix Revolutions* it's got nothing on the *Company* dancers bandaging their bruised heels and toes, or the horrifying moment when a tendon snaps during a rehearsal. It's something we can respond to, relate to. It's emotion pictures, corresponding to the vibrant, emotive images of the dance.

Though the narrative seems tenuous, *The Company* is a well-observed and enticing portrait of artists at work and at play. It's punctuated by elaborate dance sequences (Altman shows a dancer performing on and around a swing, cutting to images of her feet gliding inches above the floor—a moment among many of transcendence and grace); moved along by rehearsals and the occasional push from McDowell's benevolent tyrant shaking off preconceptions, guiding toward the organic and spontaneous within the tight parameters of dance.

The show that's detailed from start to finish in *The Company* is an elaborate feat called "Blue Snake," which pushes the dance sequences into (intentional) stylistic excess. Grotesque? Perhaps. But it's an ironic counterpoint to all the sensual pieces that came before, and to his credit Altman takes the frankly overcooked production seriously. He doesn't mock the creators; in fact he embraces them and applauds them. (The closing credits are seen over images of the company dancers taking their bows.) Though I wouldn't argue *The Company* is a metaphor for Altman's own process, his identification with his fellow craftsmen is palpable, direct, and warts 'n' all honest.

Co-producer Neve Campbell has one of the more substantial roles as Ry, a peripheral dancer who is allowed to cross over into center stage during a few key points in *The Company*. It's a performance free of vanity, with Campbell literally giving herself over to the ensemble. Ry frequently blends in with her colleagues (mostly actual ballet dancers from the Joffrey company), and is identifiable more as the woman dating another artist (James Franco, not playing a dancer but a master chef). The concept of dancing, or performance, extends into Franco's dexterous cooking — or during the game of pool where Campbell winsomely looks across the barroom at her future boyfriend sipping a beer, silently admiring her. Words are fleeting, movement and moments seem more palpable and identifiable. The morning after their first night together, spent making breakfast, is mostly played silent.

The Company is one of the more erotic movies of the year, not because of the occasional backstage nudity as dancers change but because of the palpable heat generated by the actors and their physicality. It feels intimate even within the public forum of a staged performance. Altman frequently shoots in long takes, with wide angles showing the full length of the human form. Occasional close-ups show details of hands or feet, or the shuffling of the craftsmen backstage; tracking shots from the audience capture the vibrancy of their enthusiasm. When Campbell is given her first big shot dancing during a wind and rainstorm, leaves scattering across the stage, even Mother Nature swoons.

The Company has all that and more, finding space for an elegy to AIDS, deflation of cultural machismo, a nod to the experienced old in contrast to the impetuous young, safe sex (in an amusing throwaway moment that Altman doesn't throw away), and of harsh and dear life lessons. Altman sometimes claims that he ends his movie with a death (*McCabe & Mrs. Miller; Brewster McCloud*) because otherwise the film, like a life, would simply go on forever. *The Company* finds an artful way of handling a death of another kind, and through a few sensitive words and a gesture of romantic bravado suggests the beginning of something new. In a movie that's sexually charged and humane in its intention, what better place to end than the origin of love?

PERSONAL TASTES

Don't care for Johnny Knoxville's tattoos? Does Rosie O'Donnell's voice make you want to tear your hair out? Personal distastes that have nothing to do with the actual movie can be tricky in a review. Done right, they can provide a fun lead or interesting aside. But most of the time, they simply detract from the review and make you look petty.

I've taken more than one movie to task for Bette Midler's grating presence in it. I can tolerate Midler in small doses, but when she headlines a film and screeches her way through the entire movie, it's just too much for me to bear. On one hand, mentioning this is simply a discussion of both bad acting and bad casting: It's fair game to attack what is essentially Midler's real-life personality because the filmmakers knew it would show up in the final film. I don't mean to pick on Midler. A number of high-maintenance stars are like this. You don't cast Marlon Brando (rest in peace) in your movie if you don't want him to go nuts, take control of the set, and ignore your direction. Brando is Brando – if he acts up on set, it's your fault.

As well, it's fair game – encouraged, even – to admit your personal tastes and distastes in print. If you have a secret crush on Julianne Moore that might make you love an otherwise iffy film, say so. Ditto on the flipside if you're just not a fan of Will Smith.

In the end, though, you should try to be as objective (and as brief) as possible when considering how these personal likes and dislikes affect your writing. No one wants to read your review of *The Day After Tomorrow* if a quarter of it is mooning over how dreamy you think Jake Gyllenhaal is. Crushes and vendettas are fine. Just keep them confined to a sentence or two, at most.

As well, you've probably got movies you like which are critically and commercially loathed – and vice versa. Say you're doing a retrospective of *Gigli*, which you inexplicably adore. Best to fess up and admit the bizarre situation from the start. When you're writing something wildly contrarian that's already been around the block a few times, it's fair game to freely acknowledge other critics' opinions; you'll want to in order to make light of your own odd peccadilloes and put the review on a lighthearted keel.

If you're not a fan of *The Godfather* or another classic and you write up a savage review, expect lots of hate mail no matter what. But you can minimize it by explaining yourself from the start and acknowledging you're in the minority. Don't get high and mighty, be humble. Back up your points with examples, cover your bases, and leave it in the end as a matter of personal taste. Take the high road and you'll still get the hate mail, but at least it'll be a touch more intelligent.

HOW MUCH TO WRITE

Earlier I noted that 600 words represents the "sweet spot" for a movie review. But depending on the constraints of the publication, you may be forced to write a much shorter review of 300, 150, or even 50 words. If you're writing for online or for a magazine which wants a feature-length review, you could be asked to fill 1,000 words or more.

For short reviews, you'll need to cut to the chase. Lead in with one sentence and conclude with one sentence.

For long reviews, your lead and conclusion sections will be roughly the same length as a 600-word review

For both, you'll need to split up the remainder of your write-up between plot summary and analysis appropriately.

In general, try to keep the split at 200 words of analysis for every 100 words of plot summary. So for a five-sentence review, you'll want one sentence outlining the plot and two sentences quickly outlining the highs and lows afterward, and so on. Once you get into much longer reviews, your plot synopsis will probably start to peter out around 500 words or so. If you're writing a movie review of more than 1,500 words, you'll want to move beyond mere plot and analysis and start to look more deeply at the historical context of the film, societal concerns it raises, deep thematic discussions, and secondary works of the cast and crew. As very, very few reviews are written to this length (and even fewer are read), I'll leave exploring them further as an exercise for the reader.

COMMON WRITING MISTAKES

The devil is in the details. Little mistakes make your work look sloppy and rob it of credibility. Proofread everything before you go to press. Likewise, avoid these little problems, which can slowly eat away at your review: Here are some of my pet peeves as a longtime editor of entertainment journalism.

- **Don't switch into past tense.** This is my biggest complaint with inexperienced writers' reviews. Movie reviews should be written in *present tense*. For example, "Tom Cruise shines in a surprising role that is a radical departure from his usual character." You wouldn't say, "Tom Cruise shined in a surprising role that was a radical departure from his usual character." It sounds awkward and it makes the review feel like a research paper, not a conversation between friends.

  A bigger problem occurs when a critic switches between present and past tense willy-nilly. Even if you're writing for an outlet that mandates past tense, switching between tenses makes you look like an amateur and violates the first rule of grammar. Pay close attention to this and eventually it will become second nature.

  There is one major exception to this rule: You do use past tense if you're detailing something about the making of the movie that happened prior to release. For example, you would write "To give the film a more authentic look, the tennis scenes of *Wimbledon* were actually filmed at the

All England Lawn Tennis & Croquet Club during the 2003 Wimbledon Championships."

Also note that if you do find you need to use a structure like "I found myself falling asleep" or "My date kept asking me who was who," those sentences should be written in past perfect tense.

But when you're writing straightforward analysis, keep it in the present.

- **It's written: '70s, '80s, '90s.** If you're going to contract decades, do it right. *70's* is a possessive that implies something belongs to "70." Just about the only time you would use a contraction like this is in a sentence like, "2001's top-grossing film was *Harry Potter and the Sorcerer's Stone*." The film belongs to the year 2001. The contraction *'70s* refers to dropping the "19" from the front of it. Thus, 1970s and 1980s are grammatically correct, as well. This crops up in movie reviews more than you'd expect, so pay close attention.

- **Standardize italics and punctuation.** Whatever you do, be consistent. At filmcritic.com, we use the serial comma ("Bob, Sid, and Nancy" instead of "Bob, Sid and Nancy") and we italicize movie titles, TV shows, magazines, and newspaper names. Some outlets use all caps for movie titles and put other items in quotation marks – a throwback to the days when reviews appeared in plain text, without formatting (as is still the case on Usenet, discussed in Chapter 9). Most of the world has moved on to more sophisticated usage, though.

- **Spelling counts, especially when it comes to people.** Accuracy is critical to establishing your credibility, especially when it comes to identifying actors and spelling their names right. This means getting the funky accents and umlauts correct, like it or not. It's Stellan Skarsgård, Téa Leoni, and Rachael Leigh Cook. At Northwestern University's journalism school, students get an automatic F if they misspell the name of a person in an assignment. If you play loose with spelling, you'll quickly find yourself lumped in with gossip rags and "fanboy" sites. While you're at it, make sure you get your facts (dates, places, and so on) straight. Proofread and double-check everything!

KNOWING WHEN AND HOW TO BREAK THE RULES

Goofing off can be the most fun you'll have as a critic. The key is to not overdo it – and don't do it too often. Too much lunacy can try the patience of even the most loyal reader.

In film criticism, breaking the rules means foregoing a plot synopsis, a lead, or any kind of real analysis – or all of them. Why would you do such a thing? Usually because a movie is so abhorrently bad that you simply can't review it in a serious manner.

There's no rhyme or reason on how to do this, but when the urge strikes you, let loose. I'd recommend maybe two times a year, at most. I haven't gone bananas on a movie review since Tom Green's *Freddy Got Fingered* in 2001. The review is written as lyrics to his then-popular "The Bum-Bum Song," and is meant to imply that the movie is utter excrement.

Freddy Got Fingered (2001), ★, *by Christopher Null*
   (sung to the tune of Tom Green's "The Bum-Bum Song")

   My bum is in the chair
   My bum is in the chair
   Look at me
   I'm watching Tom Green's hair!

   Tom plays Rip Torn's son
   Tom plays Rip Torn's son
   Once respectable? Rip, where's your career? (hee hee hee!)

   Look at Tom, he's raw
   Look at Tom, he's raw
   Get a job?
   No, he just wants to draw!

   Watch Tom go berserk
   Watch Tom go berserk
   Stuff his face
   Or give a horse a jerk!

   An organ made of meat
   Or a woman he can beat
   They don't make much sense, but try not to worry too much
   about that!

A HA HA HA HA HA HA!!!

They're walking out in droves
They're running for their cars
Don't look back
Away from here they go!

Hi my name is Tom
Hi my name is Tom
I can't tie my shoes but I can write a movie script!

Poo! Poo! (repeat)

While I got a lot of appreciative, "that was funny" fan mail, I received a handful of letters from people who said that being juvenile in a movie review was just as bad as being juvenile in the movie itself. How could I be taken seriously if I wasn't willing to take the review seriously?

My response is that a handful of films don't merit any intellectual thought at all, and are incapable of serious review. Again, everything in moderation: I wouldn't try reviewing any other film that I've ever seen this way, but *Freddy Got Fingered* was so appallingly bad and so absurd that it merited a uniquely insulting method of reviewing. It's a question of taste, but in this case, I felt the movie deserved it.

Goofing off doesn't have to mean throwing the standard review structure out the window entirely. It can also mean writing in a style that's appropriate for the film you're covering. A review of *Wall Street* might be written as if it's an article in the *Wall Street Journal*. A review of *Like Water for Chocolate* might be written as a recipe. Pete Croatto took it the opposite direction and wrote a review of *The Joy Luck Club* as a dialogue between two men on a basketball court, turning the "goofing off" idea on its head.

This review of *8 Mile* is written as if it was penned by a streetwise fan of its star, Eminem. It's not a terribly serious film or a wholly astute review, but it gives the reader a chuckle.

8 Mile (2002), ★ ★ ★*1/2, by Sean O'Connell*
What up, dawg? Rolled wit my boys to the *8 Mile* screening to see my homey Eminem's new movie. Man, that shiznit was off da *hook*. At first, I was worried that Eminem might sell out,

'cuz I seen him everywhere talkin' about this movie, man. He showed the love on MTV's *Movie House,* and was on the cover of my father's *Entertainment Weekly* wearin' boxing gloves. But no worries, this ain't no *Glitter II.* Em kept his cool, and his new movie was straight dope.

Word.

The movie starts with a freestyle rap battle, which is kind of like a boxing match held during a taping of Russell Simmons' *Def Comedy Jam.* Eminem's the challenger, but he backs down without rapping, and loses. It looks like he's got stage fright, but I know better. Eminem's not scared of nothing.

People call Eminem a lot of different things in this movie, like Rabbit or Bunny Rabbit, which is confusing. Then I remember he likes to take on new personalities all the time, like Slim Shady or Stan, the obsessed fan who tied up his pregnant wife, threw her in the trunk of a car and then drove off a bridge. That was awesome. So I guess Rabbit is just another identity for Em. Whatevs.

The middle of the movie covers Em's life on 8 Mile, a nasty-ass stretch of run-down buildings in Detroit that separates the poor areas from the rich areas. Detroit's cool because Kid Rock and Eminem are from there. When I save up enough money, I'm gonna go. Em hangs out with a cool crew who are funny and smart. They all tell Eminem, uh Rabbit, that he's the best rapper in the world, and think that once he lets people know about his skills, he'll be the hottest star in the world.

Until then, Em has to keep workin' at a factory, which sux. That's where he meets Alex, who's played by that girl who says "I'll never tell" in the trailer for that movie. Except here she wears trashy outfits and talks real dirty. She's awesome, and she loves to have sex. Eminem does her in the back of the factory. Yo, I need to get me a woman like that. Bring her home to meet my mom.

Speaking of moms, Eminem's old lady lives in a trailer park and dates a redneck who used to go to Eminem's, uh Rabbit's, school. She's played by the hot old lady from *Bless the Child,* which was so bad. In this movie, she swears in front of her youngest daughter and smokes and drinks constantly, which was cool. She's waiting for her boyfriend's settlement check to come in so she can pay the rent. She's always tellin' Em what to do, and sayin' his life ain't worth crap. "Biotch, look in the mirror sometime," is what I'm sayin' to her. She also talks with a Southern accent the entire time, which is stupid. She's supposed to be from Detroit, which is in, like, New England or something.

Anyway, the movie ends with another battle, and Eminem finally gets to rap and show us why his friends think he's so dope. One guy called Slim "Leave it to Beaver" and said he raps like Vanilla Ice. But Em gets to embarrass this posse of player-haters on stage, and everybody in the theater started clapping and yelling. It was the best.

On our way out, some old men with pens and notebooks in their hands were talkin' outside the theater about *8 Mile*. They said Eminem had a lot of screen presence, and talked about the director's ability to capture the poverty of metro Detroit. One old dude kept talking about Eminem's come-from-behind mentality, and another raved about the energy powering the inspired rap battles. They all kept repeating the name Tony Manero over and over, but I didn't know who that was, so I left.

Whatever, dawg. I don't care. I just need to get me to a pay phone so I can call up *TRL* and request "Lose Yourself" from the movie soundtrack. I'm gonna dedicate it to my girl Kelly in Paramus, because she's so hot and she loves to listen to Eminem when we're hangin' out at the mall, yo. True dat.

Goofing off can also mean throwing little touches on your reviews to make them memorably silly, too. Many critics have had success writing reviews as memos to the studio that made the movie. "Memo to Harvey Weinstein:" (the president of Miramax) is an especially popular introduction. The line between a creative lead and goofing off is a very broad one. Use your best judgment, and try not to overdo it.

CHAPTER 7:
GRADING AND STAR RATINGS

When people read your reviews, the thing they'll see first will be the star rating. Many people will stop right there: They simply want to know if you liked it or not. And even if they do read your review, if your writing doesn't back up your star rating or grade, you'll catch heat for it, too. Grading films appropriately is one of the most important parts of your job as a critic. It's also one of the most difficult parts of the job.

TO STAR OR NOT TO STAR

The question of whether to assign grades of any kind is an epic one, and the answer is tricky.

The argument against star ratings and grades is an obvious corollary to what I stated above: If you assign a star rating, many people will look at the rating alone and stop reading. So why bother writing a full-blown review if no one's going to read it? No one becomes a film critic so they can just throw out star ratings, do they? I know I didn't.

The other common argument against ratings is that a movie review can't be condensed into a rating, or that a work of art is too complex for such a simple summary. It's like Robin Williams' speech in *Dead Poets Society*: You wouldn't assign a grade to a poem to represent its "greatness," and if movies really are a work of art, you shouldn't treat them that way either.

Fair argument, but the other side is a more compelling one.

The primary argument for star ratings is the flipside of the argument against them: If you *do* assign ratings, some people won't read your review. But if you *don't* assign ratings, even more people won't read your review! Why? Because, like it or not, people need signposts to help them through written material. Star ratings are part of what is known in journalism as an "entry point," a jumping-off point to encourage people to read more of your material. Without this entry point, your review will be daunting and off-putting to the casual reader. How will you compel him to read this large block of text? Well, a star rating is a tantalizing summary of what's to come. Nothing's more exciting than seeing a one-star rating, cueing you in that a juicy trashfest is on the way. Without that single element, the reader won't know what's in store. A star rating simply helps you set the stage for the review to come.

Another argument is that the competition will nearly always use star ratings, so you should, too. I wrote before about the need to keep readers coming back to your reviews, given the saturation of the film criticism market. If everyone else uses star ratings and you don't, you're dramatically discouraging time-pressed readers from coming back to your material.

Ultimately, I recommend every critic adopt some rating scheme (even if it's as simple as "thumbs up/thumbs down"). If you decide it's not working for you later in your career, you can always drop it or play it down, but grading systems offer so many benefits that you'd be foolish to forego one.

GRADING SYSTEMS

Grading systems come in a variety of shapes and sizes. Here's what to consider when choosing one. Remember to pick one that you're comfortable sticking with for the long term: It's extremely difficult to change to another system once you've established yourself on one of them.

- **Yea/Nay Systems**. This is the classic "thumbs up/thumbs down" critique, and it cuts right to the chase: Should the reader see this movie? Yes or no. The problem is of course that thumbs up/thumbs down doesn't have any leeway in it to allow for really bad or really good movies (although you will often hear Ebert and Roeper give a "big" or "enthusiastic" thumbs up). How urgently should a reader rush out to see this film you're recommending? All yeas and all nays end up the same, and it becomes difficult for a casual reader to understand exactly how much you like a "thumbs up" film.

  The other problem is the middle ground: films you cautiously recommend or those you believe certain audiences may enjoy. How do you treat middling movies? Ebert tends to give them a "thumbs up" rating and explains himself during his review. This unfortunately leads to severe grade inflation (see below), and homogenizes the review. Some critics throw in a "thumbs middle" category to mitigate this. Often you'll see it manifest in a "red light/yellow light/green light" system of three-rating tiers.

- **Star Ratings**. My system of choice, and a system favored by most critics. It's popular for good reason: We're used to star ratings of movies, restaurants, hotels, just about everything. When you see a four-star rating, you immediately understand it's a good thing, even if you don't know the exact scale of the system.

  Determining the scale of a star-rating system is the trickiest part. Do you offer four stars at most or five stars at most? Do you stop at one-star minimum or zero-stars minimum. Some critics have a zero to five star scale, plus a "bomb" rating for true cellar dwellers. In general, I find this needlessly complicated. Zero to five with a bomb turns the scale into a system with seven levels of good and bad (not including half stars). This is unintuitive and difficult to keep consistent. In star ratings, simplicity is best, which is why I greatly prefer a 0 to 4 star system or a 1 to 5 star system (the latter of which filmcritic.com uses). Note that both systems give you the same number of discrete levels on which to grade. 1 star to 4 stars only gives you 7 grading levels (including half stars) on which to grade, so I tend to avoid it.

Half stars can be contentious, but I like them. Having only 5 grading levels makes it very difficult to draw a line when a film is clearly in between categories. A 3 star rating is typically not a recommended film, but 3½ stars is. At the same time, bumping the rating up to 4 stars is too generous. Sometimes you'll be so torn that only a half star will do, and on a 1 to 5 star scale, this gives you 9 levels on which to assign a grade.

- **Letter Grades.** A few populist outlets (notably *Entertainment Weekly*) assign letter grades instead of star ratings, due to their easy understandability among readers who became accustomed to them in school. This is unfortunately the biggest failing with letter grades: Readers have also become accustomed to grade inflation, where a B means average and anything below a C+ is a failure. Honest letter grades should center around a C rating, with genuinely good films earning a B and great films earning an A. But grade inflation invariably affects everyone who uses them in movie reviews: Flip through any issue of Entertainment Weekly and you'll see almost every movie receives a B or a B+ rating, with a smattering of A- ratings. This homogenizes reviews and ultimately makes the entire system irrelevant. I find EW's ratings laughably predictable these days, as every film ultimately gets the same grade. I recommend avoiding this system.

- **1 to 10 Points**. On paper, a 1-to-10-point rating system is about the same as a 1-to-5-star system with half stars. Unfortunately a 10 point system is less intuitive. What does a 6 really mean? Is that good or bad? Instinctively it sounds bad – but it translates into a 3½ star rating on a five-star scale, which is recommended. The 10 point scale just doesn't work well for films, in my opinion.

- **1 to 100 Points.** This is another school-inspired grading system that's fraught with problems. Why? Because 70 points is typically a passing grade in school. Anything below that is a failure. So does the 100-point movie scale center on an average of 80 points or an average of 50? Do you really want to have to explain this repeatedly to readers upset when you recommend a film but give it a 69-point rating, which looks like a failure in traditional school terminology? Also, do you really need 100 grading levels upon which to rate a film? What's the difference between a movie that gets 44 points and one that gets 45 points? Does it matter? Anything over 10 discrete rating points is overkill. (The same argument follows for 1.0 to 10.0 rating systems, where tenths of a point are assigned, as in a diving competition. It's just silly.)

- **Oddball Ratings Systems.** Here are a few other strange systems I've encountered, with opinions on each. A few outlets assign a dollar value to each movie – if it's a high number (say, $10), they recommend seeing it theatrically. Low prices (say, $3.50) suggest it's a good video rental or something you should see on cable. It's cute, but it doesn't work consistently since putting any price on a film implies you should, at some point, pay money to see it. There's also a problem with financial inflation, as movie ticket prices go up. In 10 years, all of your high ratings will look like medium ones.

  The *San Francisco Chronicle* uses a five-star scale disguised by what's known as "the little man." If he's standing on his chair applauding, that's a five-star grade. If he's asleep in the chair, it's two stars. If the chair is empty, he left: one star. It's clever, but it's hard to explain this to new readers and may be a barrier to understanding.

  One of the worst systems I've ever seen is a scale that went from -4 points to +4 points, with half-points in between. Not only did this have the problematic effect of making zero points the average, no one is accustomed to negative numbers in reviews. What's the point? As with the hundred-point scale, once you're below, say, 50 points, isn't it moot? This scale is so absurd that the critic in question eventually shied away from it and adopted two separate ratings systems in his reviews.

HOW TO ASSIGN A GRADE

Once you've settled on a system, how do you assign a grade within that system? As with the tone of your movie reviews, the key to grading movies is also *consistency*: Grading all films on the same basis. This is far harder than it sounds, but experience and careful thought will generally lead you to an appropriate grade. Think about similar films and how you rated them. Which was better and why?

One good way to think about assigning grades is to enter any movie with a three-star expectation, then start adding or subtracting from there. If the story is taut and the characters are well-acted, I start adding stars. If clichés erupt and I get bored, I subtract stars. By the end, I've figured out roughly where the movie will land on the star scale, give or take a half-star. Later, once I'm done writing the review, I assign a final star rating.

Some critics start with a perfect score and start subtracting from there. One bad character or bad act in the script equals, say, a half-star deduction. Or for every negative item noted in the write-up, half a star comes off the review. For unredeemable movies, you might start at the one star minimum rating and add half-stars for any good points in the film (say, good special effects, perfect music, or an interesting supporting character).

Assigning star ratings and grades is unfortunately more art than science, and it's one that takes practice and some history to judge against. It's a good idea to assign ratings to 100 or so films you've seen previously (or you can start with the movies in Appendix A) before you start trying to write full-fledged reviews. A good base of ratings will give you a better feel for what's excellent, what's horrible, and what's merely average. If you start cold, you'll spend years writing reviews with inconsistent ratings before you settle on a good median. This is one area in particular where advance planning pays off.

Here are some additional tips for ensuring you give the correct grade every time.

- **Compare the grade to other films in the genre.** Failure to do this is a common mistake made by many critics. Grade ratings should be assigned so that horror is ranked against horror, comedy vs. comedy, and so on. A five-star comedy is a much different experience than a five-star drama. Comparing the two against each other only leads to headaches and botched star ratings. If your favorite sci-fi movie is *Star Wars*, you should consider that movie as the five-star benchmark and compare other sci-fi movies against it.

- **Embrace the bell curve.** Enemy of high schoolers, friend to the film critic. Your review ratings, over time, should follow a low bell curve pattern.

Assuming a five-star scale, the bulk of your reviews should be in the 2.5 to 3.5 star range, with progressively fewer reviews at the edges. How many of these you shunt to the edges is up to you (and I'll discuss "breaking the 3-star habit" later). Typically you should aim for a relatively flat curve as opposed to one with an enormous spike in the middle and very few high and low ratings. This keeps variety in your reviews and ratings, and it will help avoid the 3-star quagmire. What you want to avoid is an inverted bell curve or a dramatically skewed curve with most of your ratings at one end or the other: Over time you should develop a generally equal number of good and bad ratings to keep each other in check. (Note that many critics try to avoid seeing bad movies, so reviews tend to skew higher. This is acceptable, as long as it isn't too extreme. Painful though it may be, you need to review some bad movies in order to put your positive reviews in context. No pleasure without pain, no love without hate.)

• **Ensure your write-up matches the rating.** Nothing's more maddening for an editor than reading a scathing review and finding it's been summarily tacked with a middling or even a positive grade – and vice versa. If you plan to give a movie a positive rating, you should spend more time writing about the good things in a movie than the bad. Likewise, don't gush over minor details in a movie which you plan to ultimately pan. This can be hard, especially in the case of reviews of movies you modestly recommend – but careful planning before you sit down to write will aid you greatly here.

GRADE INFLATION

Why do so many critics tend to grade on the high side?

According to the good people at entertainment website Rotten Tomatoes (www.rottentomatoes.com), Ken Henke of the Asheville, NC *Mountain Xpress* recommends a full 75% of the movies he reviews. Netflix house critic James Rocchi provides nearly 82% of his reviewed films with a positive rating. And Carol Cling of the *Las Vegas Review-Journal* recommends 85% of the films she reviews! (By comparison, my personal "recommended" rating percentage stands at 52%, just about perfect.)

Why are these guys so soft on movies?

Sure, Cling and Co. may gravitate away from films they know are going to be bad, leaving them for second-string critics, but that can only explain part of this dilemma. The main reason has more to do with simple human nature.

Put yourself in the shoes of a new (and hypothetical) critic: You're being invited to see a movie in advance, for free, possibly with a guest and in a reserved row of a packed cinema. The publicist is gracious and earnestly supportive of the film she's representing. She even gives you a free t-shirt with the movie's logo on it.

After viewing the film, you have to write a review. What has 25 years of good upbringing taught you to do? Well, if you're like most people, you haven't been taught to rip the film to shreds by insulting everyone involved with it! On the contrary: Society has taught us that if we don't like a meal, we graciously eat it anyway or quietly excuse ourselves. We don't spit in the chef's face and punch him in the stomach. But that's exactly what writing a bad review can feel like: A direct insult to those involved with the film, even if you're political in your approach to the review.

This effect is compounded by the fact that many movie stars and directors take negative criticism to heart. I've seen dozens of instances of angry filmmakers who write letters and even make threatening phone calls to critics who pan their work. Critics are insulted as worthless leeches who thrive on other people's creativity. (This is also a common refrain in hate mail. I'll discuss this phenomenon at length in Chapter 13.) "If you're such a know-it-all," they ask, "why don't you make your own movie!?"

Advertising is another big issue: If you write for a magazine and review a film negatively, odds are slim that the company distributing that movie will buy an ad in your magazine. Many writers are religious (no pun intended) about the separation between church and state (editorial and ad sales) in their business, but more than you would believe aren't so scrupulous about it. Ad sales are unfortunately a huge driver in why many bad films receive strangely positive reviews.

Over time, fear of backlash (verbal and financial) plus good-hearted human nature can cause your average rating to creep up. Before you know it, you might be giving four-star ratings to everything you see, simply because the print showed up. This is why technical magazines rarely give anything worse than a three-star rating out of five to the products they review: Editors are afraid of backlash and of losing advertising dollars (and thus, their jobs). This is also why college grades have slowly inflated to the point where a 3.09 GPA is now the national average, vs. a 2.94 GPA only 10 years ago, according to a study posted by Stuart Rojstaczer at gradeinflation.com.

Another issue often crops up with critics who don't review a broad enough range of movies. If you find you're constantly giving reviews of four stars and up to everything, ask yourself a few questions. Are you seeking out only movies in genres you especially like? This is a particular problem with writers who only cover a certain field – horror films, Japanese animation, or sci-fi/fantasy movies. Many die-hard fans of these movies like *everything* in the genre, and they end up with a crush of highly-rated films and only a handful of negative reviews. You may need to seek out more films in other genres or "bad" examples in order to temper your enthusiasm appropriately.

Finally, grade inflation is most severe among the cottage industry of critics who give nothing but good reviews. Seriously: No matter how bad a movie is, these guys are on hand to praise it.

Who are these people? You see them quoted constantly in ads for the very worst movies, writing for outlets you've never heard of and obscure TV and radio stations (none of which I'll name here). For them, film criticism is a business: They provide good quotes for the studios to use in their advertisements; in exchange, the studios provide lots of trips to movie junkets (I'll cover these in Chapter 15). These people are called *quote whores*, and that's how they get their kicks. About 20 quote whores work in the field today. *Do not add to their ranks.* (The most egregious of these was David Manning, who was revealed in 2001 to not even be a real person at all; he was made up by Sony's marketing department.)

There's only one way to combat these effects, and that's with your mind. Be neutral. Don't be co-opted by schwag like free t-shirts and posters (you'll get sick of that stuff soon enough). Suppress your gut instinct to "be nice." Reset your expectations so that average movies get average ratings. It's tough, but you can do it.

I can't really advise you on what happens if you get pressure from an advertiser or editor to make a review nicer. If you work for a venue that supports advertising, this will happen eventually, so prepare yourself for it someday. My only counsel is to hold your ground (unless your editor has a valid point about an unfairly negative review). Accept that your work may indeed create friction between the publication and the advertiser. Believe me, advertisers have been dealing with this for over a century. It's part of the game they play in an attempt to turn publicity to their favor. (If you'd made a movie, you'd want people to like it, too!)

But studios also understand, for the most part, that people will review any film negatively. You can't win 'em all, and only truly evil publicists and media planners will take vengeance on you for simply speaking an honest opinion.

And that, of course, is the ultimate takeaway: Be honest – the fundamental rule of good film criticism. Simply use your best judgment. Don't be nice just because you're afraid of the consequences. Get too soft, and you'll lose the respect of your audience, and then where will you be?

THE THREE STAR HABIT

Here we see a related phenomenon to the grade inflation issue.

Many critics tend to give a lot of middling reviews, and for good reason. Whether you're grading on a curve or not, as you see more and more movies, they begin to occupy this vast middle ground of "just OK" movies that are distinguished by very little that's good or bad. Maybe there's a good performance, a few funny scenes, or some big explosions that catch your eye. Invariably, your review touches on a lot of goods and a lot of bads... and you give the film three or three-and-a-half stars.

The problem is that you end up with a lot of mediocrity, and by extension, a lot of truly boring movie reviews that all read the same. This is especially troubling for your readers, who have to read between the lines to figure out whether you like something or not.

Homogenization of reviews is a tricky problem because if you're doing your job right, you should have a decent cluster of reviews around the three-star level. The key is keeping that cluster as small as possible without betraying your honesty and blowing the bell curve completely.

How do you break the three star habit? Train yourself to be more critical and more accepting of different genres. Remember the rules of rating – you may be holding a film to an impossibly high standard that isn't necessarily appropriate. Or you may simply not have seen enough truly horrible movies. Follow the advice in one of the following two sections, depending on where you find the bulk of your reviews falling. (If they're all falling in the middle, follow the advice in both sections.)

ARE YOU RATING TOO HARSHLY?

Finally, there's a third phenomenon you'll probably encounter, especially during the historically dead movie months of February and September. (These are two of the worst months for the box office, so studios dump relatively unworthy movies here.)

We've all had that feeling that despite having dozens of movies available on TV at once and dozens more in theaters, there's just "nothing good" on. How many hours have you walked the shelves at Blockbuster, looking for a perfect movie?

Well, the perfect movie doesn't exist. Even the greatest of films have flaws, and while it's your job to find and note those flaws, it's also your job to dismiss them when they have no bearing on your enjoyment of a film.

Start by thinking of your favorite films and what's wrong with them. Mark Hamill's inexperience as an actor shows in *Star Wars*, as do the rough special effects. Yet the film ranks on many moviegoers' top ten lists despite some obvious flaws. Why? Because the film as a whole transcends the little issues. If you overanalyze any movie, you're likely to keep whittling away at the film's rating until it arrives at a mediocre rating.

Don't be overly nitpicky. Remember that a movie is a collaborative process among hundreds of people with finite budgets and limitations that you may not be aware of. In *Clerks* (1994), a key scene (the misadventures in the funeral home) was cut because it would have been prohibitive to shoot on the movie's paltry $28,000 budget. Costumes can't always be made of historically perfect thread. Sometimes it's just not feasible to dress thousands of extras in suits of armor; shortcuts have to be taken.

Consider issues like this and dismiss them if, in the end, they didn't ultimately impact your overall opinion of a movie. In Chapter 4, I mentioned a key plot hole in the film *Sneakers*, but in the end it doesn't ruin your enjoyment of the film. I took it into account, and let it go. Here's another "nitpicky" example from the movie *Tadpole* (2002). In this low-budget film, a distraught Sigourney Weaver nervously washes dishes by hand in the sink. One critic pointed this out as sloppy filmmaking: A dishwasher was visible right next to her.

Comments like that are absurd. For one, you can explain this away by rationalizing that the dishwasher was full or broken. But realistically, it's a simple decision made by the director: The plot point was written that way in the script, and the crew couldn't find the perfect set that didn't have a dishwasher in the kitchen. Comments at this level are rationalizations: The critic simply didn't like the movie and he was looking for an excuse to ding it with a lower rating. This is simply bad criticism.

Over time and with practice you'll learn where to draw the line between a genuine flaw and a permissible mistake.

WHEN TO WRITE YOUR REVIEW

How long after you see a film should you wait to write your review? Some critics write as soon as they get home from the theater. Some wait for weeks before doing their write-ups.

Deadlines may force your hand on this. If a film screens on Thursday evening before opening on Friday, you may have to write your review that night in order to get it online or in print in a timely manner. But if you saw the film weeks before opening and you're really busy, you may not have time to get to the write-up immediately.

In an ideal scenario, I try to write reviews about 24 hours after seeing the film. This gives me a full day to "marinate" on the movie while being soon enough so that I don't forget important details. (Taking notes will help extend the shelf life of your thoughts; I'll cover note-taking etiquette in Chapter 12.)

If you write immediately after seeing a film, you'll find that your comments are more a product of gut instinct and less analysis. You'll still have a frustrating drive or a long wait for popcorn in mind, or the kid who was kicking your chair will still be fresh in your thoughts. What you did see on the screen will be vivid – but you'll focus on the highlights and you'll miss out on some of the nuances that come with critical thought about a film. First impressions are always best, but first impressions tempered by a bit of serious thought are better.

If you wait too long to write your review, the major problem is that you'll start to forget about the movie. Films you see in the interim will get jumbled together, and your review will probably start to veer toward that neutral middle ground as it becomes homogenized with other films and experiences in your life. Similarly, the longer you "think it over," the more nitpicky problems you're going to turn up. Tiny plot holes may be uncovered, for example. And while it's the job of a critic to seek these out, you don't want to come across as a freak obsessed with movie minutiae. The big picture is more important, so get your thoughts out while they're fresh and full of passion.

You're also at risk of stumbling upon other reviews in the meantime, a strict no-no when it comes to film criticism. I try to avoid any advance information about a film – and usually I don't even see the trailers for movies – before going into a screening. But reading another review before you've written yours is anathema. (I covered this in more detail in Chapter 4.)

TUNING OUT THE AUDIENCE

I mentioned the chair-kicking phenomenon in the previous section in passing, but it merits a more serious mention: Movie audiences can really ruin a movie for critics.

At advance screenings, radio stations give out hundreds of passes to listeners (typically far more than the theater can hold), and after the press is seated, these folks are herded in to the theater, as well. Preview audiences can be surly and loud – who can blame them, since they've been waiting to get in for hours. Once inside, every available seat is slowly filled, and the level of chatter and cell-phone ringing can be maddening. Preview audiences are just as rowdy as real ones: There's plenty of talking, seat kicking, and trips to the bathroom. It's actually worse, since publicists try to fill every seat in a theater during preview screenings.

All together, this can really get aggravating for a critic who is supposed to concentrate on the screen.

I occasionally mention my gripes with rowdy audiences in my reviews, but by and large any serious critic has to try his hardest to put the audience out of his mind. Remember that it's not the movie's fault that a wailing child is sitting behind you. It's not the movie's fault that you're seated next to an old man with an iffy bladder who keeps getting up or a woman who brought in her smelly garlic noodles from home.

On the other hand, if you experience an audience that is talking back to the screen, laughing when you should be crying, and otherwise reacting in some notable way to a movie (whether good or bad), this is fair game in your review. I'm especially keen to note audience reactions to comedies: If I'm not laughing but everyone else is, I tend to make note of this in the review, as my sense of humor may be much different from that of the rest of the world.

In any event, however, don't let the audience overly impact your ultimate grade for a film.

SECOND THOUGHTS

Like it or not, film critics are human. And as humans, we make mistakes. When it comes to the highly subjective task of reviewing a movie, a lot of things come into play beyond what you see on the screen and hear from the speakers. Was the critic in a bad mood? Was some kid kicking the chair? Was the reviewer on medication? Or did he simply have an unhealthy fascination with one of the main characters?

Whatever the reason, I occasionally go back and tweak my reviews as they mellow in my mind or my appreciation for them matures. This is actually an unpopular habit. Pauline Kael, the late, relentlessly celebrated film critic, was well known to never watch a film more than once or revise her opinion on a film. Her reviews were her gut instincts, and once they were put down on paper, they were sacrosanct, never to be revisited.

I believe this is an unhealthy way to approach one's craft and to live one's life, unwilling to accept that our first impressions may be wrong. Imagine if you never changed your mind about any person you met, any food you tasted, or any music you heard. You'd have no friends and the same tastes and interests you had when you were eight years old. That's hardly an enlightened way to live. We're humans, not androids.

The beauty of the internet is that you can revise things whenever you want. I've rewritten a handful of reviews over the years as my tastes have matured and my understanding of film has deepened. Likewise, I've written mea culpas for reviews I later regretted.

There's really no shame in reconsidering a film, nor is there any shame in simply letting sleeping dogs lie. Whether you decide to revisit your reviews from time to time or not is completely up to you.

Also note that simple corrections like typos and cast and crew errors merit immediate attention. Everyone makes mistakes – whether it's subbing in "who's" for "whose" or mistaking an oddly named female director as a man. At filmcritic.com, we get a trickle of letters alerting us to these mistakes (some of which have been left undiscovered on the site for five years or longer), and we always correct them as soon as possible. Not only is 100% accuracy the only tenable goal for any journalistic endeavor, but correcting mistakes like these quickly engenders reader affinity as people feel their comments are being heeded.

I also make the occasional change to a plot synopsis when readers tell us that too much has been given away. Sometimes critics get over-eager in their synopsizing and they accidentally spoil too much of the plot — but that's hard to notice if you're editing a review written by another writer about a movie you haven't seen yet. Some simple trimming usually resolves this problem quickly.

CHAPTER 8:
GETTING STARTED WITH A CAREER - ADVICE FOR BEGINNERS AND FREELANCE WRITERS

You've patiently made it this far. You understand the history of movies and the mechanics of moviemaking. And you know how to write a review and grade a film.

Now it's time to put that talent to work and prepare for your first steps as a professional film critic.

FIRST STEPS

Before you start sending resumes out, here's how to prepare for the task of reviewing movies professionally. As with much of this book, I'll assume that you're an absolute beginner (and probably in school) with no professional writing experience. More seasoned writers should skip ahead to the next section, Exploring Freelance Opportunities, and beyond.

How do I recommend absolute beginners get started as professional film critics? Simple:

- **Go to college.** But don't major in film unless you really want to be a filmmaker instead of a critic. Your parents always told you to get a practical degree, and they were right. Chances are, even if you do become a film critic, it will never become a full-time job. So focus your collegiate efforts on a more down-to-Earth vocation. Take a few film classes if you feel the need, but don't expect school to prepare you for film criticism.

- **See lots of movies.** This probably goes without saying, but take it to heart. See movies from different genres. Don't ignore the classics. Compare remakes with their originals. Experiment with art house and foreign films, and check out big blockbusters, too. Don't even start writing practice reviews until you've seen at least 100 of the movies in the Appendix.

- **Practice writing.** Practice writing movie reviews, but practice writing other kinds of stories (from fiction to regular news reporting), too. If you're in school, this is the *perfect* opportunity to get some experience painlessly. Chances are your school paper will let you review movies to your heart's content. Find the Arts & Entertainment editor and ask about the application process. If you've written some sample reviews, this is the perfect opportunity to trot out the very best of them. Get all the practice you can while you're young. In five years you'll inevitably look back at that material and cringe, so it's best to get the bad writing out of the way early.

• **Read!** While it's a bad idea to read reviews of a movie you plan on reviewing yourself, you should gorge yourself on other people's reviews, especially while you're getting started. Don't just read movie reviews, though. You'll get bored quickly, I promise – there simply aren't that many interesting writers working in the field. Rather, seek out journalism that you like in all subjects (especially magazine journalism, where the best writers can usually be found) and soak it up. Reading material other than film reviews will improve your own writing as much as reading film reviews will, and it isn't as repetitive as that 15th review of *Spider-Man 2*. And read this book again.

EXPLORING FREELANCE OPPORTUNITIES

Your first experiences as a critic will probably come as a freelance writer for another medium, whether that's a local newspaper or an internet site. Even if you're intent on starting your own website (as I'll discuss in the next chapter), it's a good idea to get some professional experience with an established outlet. This will not only help you hone your writing style, you'll also make valuable industry contacts (namely with local publicists who can get you into advance screenings), and you might earn a little money, too.

How does freelance writing work? Newspapers, magazines, and websites are all staffed by *editors*, who manage the content they publish. In the case of a large newspaper or magazine, there may be hundreds of editors. A separate staff of dozens of salespeople and marketing wizards handle business, like selling advertising and subscriptions. In the case of most websites, there is probably just one editor who also handles the business side of the company, too.

Many publications have *staff writers* as well, people who are dedicated to creating original content. Editors may also work as writers and vice versa.

But in virtually every enterprise there comes a need for additional content that the staff can't produce. This can be generated in one of several ways. In the case of newspapers or internet sites, they can run *syndicated material*, also known as *wire stories*, provided by a content syndicate like the Associated Press or UPI. These outlets provide professional copy at a low cost. Many smaller newspapers rely on the AP and UPI for the bulk of their content.

The other option is using *freelancers*, which is where you come in. Freelance writers are independent contractors who work on a contract basis instead of on staff. A freelancer generally takes an *assignment* from one of the aforementioned editors, or he may *pitch* his own story to the publication. Once approved, he writes the story as assigned and turns it in to the editor on or before the agreed-upon deadline. A round of editing usually then transpires, as the editor applies his magazine's style to the story and sends queries and revisions back to the freelancer. Eventually, a final version of the story is reached, which is printed in the publication or posted on the website.

Sometimes, a freelancer will write a story without an assignment. This is called *writing on spec*, and it differs in that the writer will submit a completed story to an editor in the hopes that he'll buy it outright. Spec work is tough because it involves a lot of writing without any assurance of payment. As such, only beginning writers typically work on spec, but in the beginning of your career you may have little opportunity otherwise.

At some point in the process you'll have to sign a *contract* that outlines the rights you grant to the publisher of your content. Most outlets today require *all rights* to be signed over, also known as *work for hire* writing. In a work for hire situation, the publisher owns the work completely; you no longer have any rights to it after it is bought: If you resell the work later, you may be liable for copyright infringement.

Some publishers (namely those with more money) will buy one of a variety of rights to the work instead of all rights. The vagaries of publishing contracts are outside the scope of this book, but typical rights clauses might call for you to sell 90-day exclusive worldwide publication rights, all North American rights, print only (vs. web) rights, or a combination of these. Rights clauses are rarely negotiable (at filmcritic.com we buy all rights, take it or leave it), so make sure you understand what you're getting into, or consult an attorney if you need help.

Finally, you'll want to get paid for your writing. You may be asked to prepare an *invoice* for the publisher; make sure you include all requested information when you submit it or your payment will be delayed. Publications generally pay between 30 and 90 days after you submit your piece. This will be specified in your contract: *Payment on acceptance* means your invoice will be processed after your story is accepted by the editor. *Payment on publication* means you won't be paid until after the story appears in print or on the web.

Finally, if you're working on assignment and your story does not run, you may receive a *kill fee* for your trouble, typically about 25 percent of the contracted fee. When you are paid a kill fee, the rights to the story return to you, so you can shop it around to another publication if you are so inclined.

And at last, the process begins again. The life of the freelancer means hustling constantly for work, so always keep pitching stories to keep the system rolling.

FINDING THE RIGHT EDITOR

One of the most critical challenges of any freelancer's career is finding the right assigning editor. So how do you find the right editor for your pitch? Read on.

At newspapers and alternative weeklies, your first stop should be the *masthead*, the section which indicates who edits which part of the paper. The editor you want will be the "entertainment editor" or the "arts editor," depending on what your paper calls its movie section. The smaller the paper, the easier this will be to find.

In some cases you won't be able to find this editor from the masthead, which is often the case with very small regional papers that don't have section editors. In this case, you might simply query the managing editor; either he may be directly responsible for the section, or he can refer you to the appropriate contact.

The process is similar at magazines, though magazine editors are even less likely to have section authority noted in their titles. You may try to contact an editorial assistant or lower-level editor to inquire who the appropriate contact is for movie coverage.

Finally, there's the web, which is essentially a free for all. Many websites note their primary editorial contacts (as filmcritic.com does) if you click the "About Us" or "Contact" links. A little searching around will make this evident without too much trouble. If all else fails, you could e-mail webmaster@website.com or postmaster@website.com and inquire who the correct contact is that way, though don't always expect a response.

As a last resort for any publication, whether online or offline, you can always try web searches to find the right contact. Searching for "Nowheresville City News entertainment editor" will probably give you some clues about who the right contact is. You could also take the direct route and simply phone the main switchboard of the publication and ask who the entertainment editor is and how best to contact him.

THE QUERY LETTER

Once you've found the right editor, you need to pitch them with a *query letter*. Some sites have an extensive list of criteria for aspiring freelance writers, and some have no guidance at all. At filmcritic.com, we don't accept general freelance work unless a writer is accepted to join the staff as a whole. The submission process requires applicants to send a resume, several writing samples, and a number of lists of favorite films and directors. This is plainly outlined on our site where even casual visitors can find it.

Other sites don't outline a specific application process for new writers, so you'll want to send a general *query letter* to the editor you've identified. Here's a good, general-purpose query letter that should at least get you a response from the editor, if not an assignment.

Dear Sir or Madam,

My name is Bob Critic, and I'm interested in contributing to your website as a film critic and entertainment writer. I've been writing reviews for six months and would love to start working with Filmegaplex.com, which has a style and approach to film writing that deeply resonates with me.

Would it be possible to obtain a copy of your writer's guidelines and/or more information on any freelance needs you might have? I am available for film reviews and general assignments and can provide a very quick turnaround on anything you might need. I'm a full member of the local media corps here in Nowheresville, NC, and have regular access to movie screenings. I am also happy to contribute DVD reviews if you need them.

If there's any way I can contribute to the site, please let me know.

Thanks for your time,

Bob Critic
bob@bobcritic.com
619-555-9393

Note that this should be used as a rough outline, not verbatim. Customize the letter appropriately (or they'll quickly see you simply copied it out of this book!), and have as much fun to suit your style and that of the site you're pitching. Avoid hammy clichés like, "Have I got a story for you!" Editors have seen this kind of writing so much that it immediately turns them off, and they'll quit reading your letter.

Don't include additional clips and writing samples at this time unless the site specifically requests them in advance. Many editors won't accept attachments from strangers due to the risk of viruses. If the editor wants writing samples, he'll ask for them and will specify a delivery method.

Above all: Be professional. Check your spelling. Know your target audience. If the site only prints celebrity interviews, don't pitch yourself as a movie reviewer. Use common sense. Also: If you have a website with clips of your sample works, by all means include a link to it in the letter. A page of clips is a sign of a professional who has obviously spent some energy on a freelance career. It looks exceptional as part of your portfolio. (For those inclined, you can see my personal clip page at www.chrisnull.com/clips.html.)

Finally, if you have a specific story to pitch (for example, if you just interviewed a star with a movie coming out in the next two weeks), mention it in your letter. Don't go overboard by pitching numerous stories on your first contact, but sometimes a specific piece like this can serendipitously fill a nagging hole in the editor's calendar. If your timing is perfect, you just might get the assignment on the spot!

FOLLOWING UP

What happens next can be any number of things. Many editors will ignore your query letter: These are typically people who have no need for additional writers or are simply swamped with too much work. Don't worry too much about the no-response types. Focus on those who do get back to you.

If you are contacted (and it's not an outright rejection), the editor will typically ask for samples and/or story ideas. Once you've made it this far, simply follow the train of messages that ensues and give the editor what he needs. Responding quickly and with the requested materials will always increase your chances of getting that coveted assignment. Once you've reached this point, you're in the home stretch. Keep at it and you'll eventually get the assignment.

How many editors should you pitch at a time? In the old days, it used to be preferred that you pitch only one editor at a time. Times have changed, and those informal rules have relaxed. Today you're safe pitching as many editors simultaneously as you'd like, as long as you can keep track of them. (One caveat: Only pitch one person at a time at a given publication. There's nothing worse than carpet-bombing every editor on staff because you were too lazy to do your homework to find the right editor to pitch.)

On a related topic, keep a database of all the publications you approach. Use Microsoft Outlook, Act!, or some other computerized contact manager to keep detailed notes on names, phone numbers, and e-mail addresses, along with commentary on when you pitched them and the results of those pitches. You can also use the software's calendar tool to alert you when to pester an editor again for follow up.

How often should you follow up? No more than once a month, unless an editor is actively contacting you or you have an established rapport. Editors loathe overly enthusiastic freelancers who can't take a hint. If you aren't getting responses after several months, you might want to move on to greener pastures. Of course, if an exclusive interview with Steven Spielberg lands in your lap, feel free to break the rules!

Meanwhile, don't stop writing. Pitch other ideas – once your foot is in the door, you need to keep it there. Editors will quickly forget about you. Once they find someone whose style they like and who they know can hit deadlines, they like to work with that person over and over. This is why breaking in is tough. Keep hammering away at it!

WHERE TO PITCH: BEST BETS FOR BEGINNERS

I discussed newspapers and magazines earlier, but frankly, you're wasting your time trying to break into either of these industries until you have several years of experience.

Newcomers to criticism should start with the world's great media liberator: The internet.

Why look to the web for your initial clips? First of all, there are far more outlets online than will ever exist in the print world. Online sites are easier to contact, are generally more open to freelancers, rarely care where you live, and have a much faster turnaround. You could pitch a website in the morning and have your story published that afternoon. And if an onliner isn't interested in your material, he'll often e-mail you back promptly. Newcomers pitching a major magazine will be lucky to get a response in the mail three months later.

The major drawback with online is pay: That is, there's not much of it. Filmcritic.com pays very little to its writers, and we're the exception: Most websites don't pay anything at all. Still, it's an excellent place to get started, and if you're interested in reviewing a movie every other week instead of diving into film criticism as a full-time job, an online site like filmcritic.com is the perfect place to work out your appetite for reviewing movies.

If you're tired of online or have established a couple of standby web outlets where you're a contributor, you might then try your local weekly newspaper. Every city of reasonable size has one or more of these. Typically they are distributed for free from bins located strategically throughout the city. Coverage runs toward local politics and arts & entertainment – so any local angle you can bring to your pitches, the better. (For example: An interview with a local filmmaker, or a review of a locally made movie.)

With newspapers, it often *does* matter where you live, so don't bother pitching a paper that's out of town. Also, don't limit your pitches to just theatrical reviews. Chances are your paper doesn't need any more film critics, but it may be interested in adding to the roster of home video writers, especially if you're willing to review obscure films that are newly issued on DVD.

Finally, there's local radio and television. This shouldn't be a first stop, but a number of writers have parlayed an understanding of film and a good camera face into a spot on TV doing movie reviews. You may be required to show up at 5:30 on Sunday morning to do a five-minute live spot, and the gig may not pay anything other than exposure for your writing, but TV and radio spots are a fun way to play *Ebert & Roeper* and get a taste of the limelight, even if you aren't being paid for it. Check out Sean O'Connell's story "How One Critic Did It" on the following pages for more background on how you might break into the world of television. It might be easier than you think!

MOVING UP THE LADDER

At some point in your career, you're going to want to evolve beyond the static world of freelancing. How do you move up the ladder, and where do you go once you're climbing the rungs?

Many writers will be searching for that elusive *staff position*, a la Roger Ebert. The bad news is that these jobs are impossible to come by, and in many cases they don't exist. Very, very few newspapers are in a position to pay a full-time salary to someone to write movie reviews. When these scant few jobs do become available, they're almost always given to existing staff members who've been there for years. If it's your goal to become a staff critic for a newspaper, your best bet is to seek an entry-level job there and work your way up the ladder.

Most writers will be more successful seeking a regular writing job or possibly a weekly column with a website or newspaper. These are still freelance jobs but carry more responsibility, more respect, more consistency, and (generally) more pay. How do you go from occasional writer to regular contributor? By pitching your editor. After you've been writing for a website for a year, for example, you might reiterate your skills and ask if you could formalize your work with the site, contributing a guaranteed review every week or offering a regular opinion piece for the site. Editors are constantly on the lookout for new and interesting ideas like this, and if you take the initiative to offer your services, you might find yourself rewarded. Remember that most of your competition is lazy: Distinguish yourself not only by your writing but by your ambition level, too.

Finally, if you aren't getting anywhere with your existing sites, explore other venues. Save your best clips, and use them to wiggle your way into bigger and better-paying publications. It takes hard work and persistence, but it can be done.

HOW ONE CRITIC DID IT

Sean O'Connell, a senior critic at filmcritic.com, was kind enough to relate his experiences as a budding film journalist for this book. Here are his unfiltered comments.

Like most lazy slobs, I took communications classes at my liberal arts college, The Catholic University of America in Washington, D.C. I was a history major, originally pre-law before I realized I had no business becoming a lawyer. I grew up a movie junkie, but never gave it a thought that I could make a living off of my love for films.

What I didn't realize was I was cultivating a base of knowledge that I could consistently refer back to in current reviews. I kept watching movies on a regular basis, and had steady girlfriends throughout grade school and high school, and always took them to the movies. Again, adding to the base without ever really acknowledging it.

I started taking film study classes my sophomore year at college. That's when it clicked. We, as a class, discussed the different career paths one could pursue in the communications field. Every job related to television, film, theater… all of the things I adored in my free time. Why not try to combine these interests with my professional aspirations? Now, while still in college, was the right time to try.

My communications teachers emphasized the importance of clips. Getting your work published was key. The campus paper had a film critic, so that was no good. At the time, the internet seemed like the great unknown, the frontier that needed to be tamed. Plus, websites needed content and they didn't care who wrote for them. Perfect for a fledgling writer such as myself.

I found out about an opening at EclipseMagazine.com by combing the classifieds of Washington's alternative weekly newspaper, *The City Paper*. The site wasn't paying, but it was recognized by the city's one and only publicist house, Allied Advertising. These were the "keepers of the screenings" who decided whether you'd be able to see a movie in advance or not. Getting on their list was next to impossible. Staying on it was equally difficult, especially for an online writer.

My reviews from this era completely sucked. They're childish, with no structure or relevant thought stream. But they're fun to read, for the most part, because I was so enthusiastic about seeing the films and voicing my opinion.

The only way you can improve as a writer is to keep on writing. Maintaining a commitment to publish reviews on Eclipse got me into a weekly routine of seeing a movie, coming home and writing about it. Don't put it off. Write your review. I've been in that cycle for 10 years now.

Eclipse also gave me a folder of published clips. When a job opened up at *USA Today*, I sent these clips to a friend of a family friend. As is true with most things in life, it's not what you know, it's who you know. I interviewed with the folks at USA Today Online. They asked me what section I preferred to write and edit for, and I told them Life. As luck would have it, that was the only section that had an opening – most people want to be in Sports or News, it seems. They can have it.

Each new job opened yet another door. I only worked at *USA Today* for 8 months before I got married. Michele and I were looking to move to North Carolina, and I found an ad on Yahoo Classifieds hiring writers for Citysearch.com. I don't think they would have hired me if I didn't have USA Today Online on my resume. But I got the job and took over the network's Charlotte portal, covering its Movies, Sports, and City & Visitors pages.

Here's something you need to know about being a movie critic. Very few of us get to be "just a movie critic." If you work at a small outlet, be it a newspaper or website, you're going to have to write additional content in a different field. Often its sports, but it could be business, faith, health, or something that you have a remote interest in and the outlet needs covered. Roger Ebert started out as a sports writer in Illinois. Be prepared to do so, only because it means you're getting your reviews published, and that's all that matters.

I covered Sports and C&V for Citysearch, but I drove home the point that Movies were my thing. Working for Citysearch got me on the regional publicist lists for Charlotte – they're based out of Atlanta for the entire Southeast. It also (and I can not stress this enough) kept me in the habit of seeing movies and writing each and every week. I met and worked with Charlotte's two other working movie critics, who in turn kept me in the loop on art house screenings, floating screener tapes, and more. From what I understand, relationships between critics can be harsh, but the two guys writing in Charlotte (Lawrence Toppman of the *Charlotte Observer* and Matt Brunson of *Creative Loafing*) couldn't have been nicer.

After a year of toiling on the local Charlotte site, I was promoted to a leadership position as Associate National Movies Editor for Citysearch's whole operation.

Working full time as a movie critic and editor allowed me the opportunity to read plenty of other people's work. Constant internet surfing of the top criticism sites put me in touch with filmcritic.com. Time for another lesson: While you're surfing the classifieds of all those weekly and monthly newspapers, try tabbing over to the "About Us" sections of websites you frequent. Quite often, the people you enjoy reading are looking for submissions. As stated earlier, websites everywhere are in dire need of content.

At the time, filmcritic.com had a "Want to write for us?" tease at the bottom of a page. I e-mailed Christopher Null on a whim, made up some nonsense about why I thought I was qualified to contribute to his site, and waited. Not long, as it turned out. Chris contacted me shortly after and invited me to start contributing. It helped that I had access to screenings and a willingness to review just about anything that came down the pipe.

Luck shined down when a new publication, *The South Charlotte Weekly*, launched locally. I hit them with a resume and clips basically the day they opened. Again, it paid off to have fresh samples, and a passion for movies and arts. It took some convincing, but they hired me on to write movie reviews and local sports. As the paper grew, my entertainment section grew. Two years after I joined the paper, it hired a full-time sports editor. Now I only write arts and movie content for the weekly paper.

By a fluke, I got onto TV. Basically, I entered a Trading Jobs contest with the NBC news anchor. I did the morning news show, and he wrote a review of *The Matrix*. It was a gimmick slot, but it stuck. They liked me, and worked out a partnership through the newspaper where I'd appear once a week (on Saturday mornings) to do a review. That gig lasted almost two years before an opposing affiliate, CBS, contacted our newspaper about setting up a partnership. Now I'm on Friday mornings, which makes more sense, and I work for people who appreciate fresh movie content. These gigs are out there, if you remain patient and stay persistent.

Basically, I just keep trying to move forward. I always make sure I have an outlet (any outlet) for my reviews. I stay in my weekly routine. I fight to stay on press lists, and I maintain contact with regional southern reps, even after I moved away.

CHAPTER 9:
STARTING YOUR OWN SITE

You've done the freelance thing. You're tired of fitting your writing into someone else's style. You want the glory – and all the pay – for yourself.

It's time to launch your own website, and for many of you, I expect that's why you've picked up this book in the first place.

Filmcritic.com was one of the first movie review websites on the internet – if not the very first. As such, I have 10 years of lessons to offer those who want to follow in our footsteps, from picking a name for your site to turning a profit on it down the line. Although the details of web technologies and advanced layout are outside the scope of this book, I'll touch on each of those issues to at least familiarize you with the unique challenges of running a movie review website.

Here's what to do to launch your site, step by step.

CHOOSING A NAME

Naming your website is as difficult as naming your child, and picking the right URL and name can make or break your endeavor. (A URL or a domain name is just another term for the letters you type in to visit a website – such as www. filmcritic.com. I use the term synonymously with "name" in this book.)

Finding a website name that isn't already in use is extremely difficult, as 10 years of rabid buying has sucked up the pool of short and appropriate names. In other words, there aren't many great and obvious domains like filmcritic. com left any more, which is why you see so many websites with names like Goatdog's Movie Reviews (yes, that's an actual website, as are all the sites mentioned in this chapter).

Coming up with a name often ends in an exercise in visiting domain registration sites like Register.com, NetNameOne.com, or NameBoy.com to search for something that's reasonably appropriate and still available. But before you get to that point, here are some tips to help you find a name for your site – if not the perfect name, then at least a good one.

- **Your name should be the same as your URL**. Filmcritic.com's original name in 1995 was "The Movie Emporium." This was unfortunate because not only was it a dull name, but it also forced the reader to remember two separate details (the name and a much different URL). We dropped the Movie Emporium and stuck with filmcritic.com shortly thereafter.

- **Make sure no one's using it already.** This may go without saying, but it merits repeating: Search all you can to make sure no one is already publishing reviews under your chosen name. If you name your site to be the same as your URL, this usually isn't a problem, but steer away from trademarked names like "Disney" and avoid taking an existing name (like filmcritic.com) and tweaking it with a hyphen or spelling trick (say, "filmkritic.com" or "film-critic.com"). Not only will this get you sued by the owner of the original site, most people will mistakenly go to the site you're trying to rip off anyway.

- **Don't plan to use a freebie hosting site.** Sites like Geocities, Blogspot, and Angelfire offer free hosting services, but they come at a hefty non-financial cost. Not only do they insert a lot of ads into your site and limit your bandwidth, they often require you to use their name as part of your URL. Getting people to remember "The Cavalcade of Schlock" is hard. Getting them to remember www.geocities.com/tyrannorabbit is impossible. (Yes, that's an actual website and its URL, too.)

- **Be memorable and easy to type.** Film.com, movies.com, filmcritic.com – these are excellent names because they're so easy to type and remember. Linnearreflections.com is not so good because it's tough to type without making a mistake. Sick-boy.com is so-so, but hyphens can cause a real problem as most people will forget to type them. Filethirteen.com is problematic because most people will try to type it as file13.com.

- **Don't make up a word.** What does salocin.com mean? Say the name of your site out loud. If you have to spell your URL letter by letter, you've got a lousy name. It's OK to run two words together a la filmcritic.com or moviejuice.com, but don't delve too deeply into crazy combinations that have nothing to do with film.

- **Play into your genre.** Do you cover horror exclusively? Sites like horrorview.com, buried.com, and horrorseek.com all make it obvious what you're getting when you visit.

- **For God's sake, don't use your personal name.** Who is Crazy Ralph of crazyralph.com? I don't know, and I don't care. Names have a place on the web: in personal weblogs, and that's about it. Use your name anywhere else and it will come across as a vanity project.

- **Imagine saying it on the phone.** Picture calling a publicist and saying "Hi, this is Ralph from crazyralph.com. I'd like to attend the Friday screening of *Star Wars*." They'll hang up on you. Come up with something respectable.

- **Use .com at all costs.** There are many good domain names that use the .net, .org, or some other obscure suffix. Unfortunately, no one can ever remember that part of the equation. Anyone launching film.cc will lose all their traffic to film.com thanks to the habits of web users.

If you can't find a good name that isn't taken already, you can always attempt to buy one, especially if the name isn't in active use and the owner is simply sitting on it. GreatDomains.com is a site that specializes in reselling domain names, but don't drop by unless you've got $10,000 or more to spend on one. Better to approach the owner of the site directly (you can find out who owns any website by visiting whois.net). Many people who own unused domain names will often sell them for $500 or less, especially if they aren't obvious terms with mass appeal.

TECHNOLOGY AND WEB HOSTING

You've got your name and now you're ready to start putting together a site. You need to make two important decisions here: What will you use to build the site and where will you host it?

The answers to both questions are interlocked and depend on your familiarity with the tech world as well as your interest level in maintaining web servers and other hardcore back-end technologies.

The simplest form of site technology is a *completely hosted solution*. Companies like Blogger (www.blogger.com) and Geocities (www.geocities. com) let you build a website with completely web-driven tools and provide hosting on their own servers. Both are also free: You don't pay a thing for the service unless (in the case of Geocities) you need more than 15MB of storage and surpass 3GB of bandwidth per month (that translates to about 15,000 page views per month if your site has image content). For comparison, filmcritic.com consumes 300MB and sends 250GB of data every month – so obviously this is a solution only for those of you just starting out.

With these solutions, there's not even any software to download: You want to design a web page, you just visit the Geocities website, log in, and work on the site via a web browser window.

On the flipside, free websites also require ads to be placed on your site – ads for which the hosting company earns revenue, not you – and you often have minimal control over the way your site will look. Still, because the price is right, it won't hurt to get your feet wet with a 100% hosted solution. Just make sure you keep backups of all your reviews and layouts, as you'll probably want to migrate to a more permanent solution down the line.

Screening logs are an up-and-coming and very popular form of the hosted solution. Essentially, these are weblogs served by Blogger and the like, with short and informal movie reviews attached as they are covered. Filmcritic. com contributor Mark Athitakis runs an occasional screening log at runningobard.blogspot.com (note the awkward spelling), featuring a random collection of capsule reviews mixed in with spicy film commentary. Not quite full-blown reviews sites, screening logs are becoming more accepted by the mainstream press and by publicists as genuine journalism, but they have a long way to go before they gather serious audiences — if they ever get there.

The next tier of web design is a *simple hosted web service.* You design all the pages on your end and upload them to a remote web server via the internet. The hosting company takes care of the back-end technology while you worry only about the front end. You pay by the month: Fees run from less than $10 to $100 and up, largely depending on the amount of bandwidth you require. Get into really heavy usage, where you're sending more than 50GB of data per month, and you can rent a *dedicated server,* which means your website lives on its own piece of hardware. In a standard $10-a-month hosting service, you share a web server with a number of other websites.

In either case, the back end works the same for you: The company maintains the web server and ensures everything runs well, but it doesn't supply any web design tools or help. You will have to obtain these yourself; applications like Microsoft FrontPage and Macromedia Dreamweaver are two of the industry standards. You might also look at Movable Type (www. movabletype.org), which offers an inexpensive platform for development of your site.

Finally, there's an *in-house server* solution, like the one filmcritic. com uses. This is undoubtedly overkill for most of you, and if your site is genuinely this big, you'll have long since outgrown this book. At this point, you'll need in-house technical staff to set up a file server, a fast network connection, and redundancy features in your own offices. You may even invest in a database to make advanced searching on your website possible. Find a local consultant to get you up to speed and go over your options.

DESIGN

With any type of technology aside from a simple hosted web service, you'll need to also invest in a design program like FrontPage or Dreamweaver, which will cost $100 to $400. Free web design software programs are also available if you scour the web for them.

Mastering web design takes time and a lot of trial and error, but I've collected my lessons learned from 10 years in the business. Here's what I know about the unique needs of a movie review website.

The Home Page

Your home page is the most critical page on your site. About half of your visitors will glance at the home page and never even bother to click on any of the reviews you've slaved over. So make the home page count and encourage them to click. Here's how:

- **Make sure new releases are on top**. Don't make the reader scroll around or have to hunt to find the new info. Most people are interested in what's playing that week, not your thoughts on *Citizen Kane*. If you offer video/ DVD reviews, make sure these are easy to find, too. Also, having a bunch of old reviews on your home page makes your site look dated.

- **Include your star ratings on the home page**. It discourages people from clicking-through to read the full review, but it encourages them to keep coming back. In the end, your easily-digested ratings are more compelling and will help you build an audience, and eventually they'll start clicking on the reviews.

- **Offer a search function**. This technology can be added in by a handful of services and plug-in technologies, and it's definitely worth it, *especially* if you plan on maintaining an archive of old or classic reviews. Approximately 60% of filmcritic.com's merchandising revenues come from sales of old DVDs, books, and soundtracks related to movies that haven't ever appeared on our home page.

- **Make sure you can reach every page without searching from the home page**. Check out the home page of filmcritic.com: We have links to master lists of all of our 5,000 stories from the home page. These links aren't really designed for people, they're designed for search engines. But since search engine spiders can't actively search your site, they need pages of static links to scour. This way, you can be sure that every search engine can find every page of your site. It also makes it easy for people who want access to everything you've ever written to find it.

- **Keep relevant "top 10" lists**. At filmcritic.com we maintain links to reviews of both the top 10 theatrical movies for the previous week, plus the top 10 selling DVDs. We generate a substantial number of hits from these lists. You might also add top video rentals, top soundtrack sales, and more. It's a great way to leverage your existing content without doing much extra work. Another good idea: Keep a calendar of upcoming content (such as upcoming reviews on the site). This encourages readers to come back at a later date.

- **Include appropriate META tags on all pages**. But don't overdo it. If you don't know what a META tag is, keep researching the web.

- **Offer contact and business links**. If you're selling advertising, syndication, or other services, make sure you offer a way for interested parties to contact you. You also need a privacy policy, which should be linked from every page of your site.

The Reviews Pages

The rules are a lot less strict when it comes to individual reviews. Again, here is some wisdom from my years of experimentation.

- **Focus on the text**. Make sure the review starts near the top of the page. You don't want readers scrolling around to find the actual review.

- **Make the rating nice and big**. Really, it can't be too big. Some sites put it at the bottom of the review. We put the rating at the top.

- **Include an image from the film if you can**. Images eat bandwidth but they really make your review look more professional. You can find images (aka *stills*) in a number of places. I usually start by searching for them at IMDB.com (the Internet Movie Database) and/or looking on the movie's website directly. Some studios have special websites and send out CD-ROMs with images where you can obtain artwork. (More on these later.)

You could also try a general search engine if none of those methods pan out. Note that legally it's OK to use a still image on your website without special permission: Studios make stills available expressly for that purpose, so don't feel like you're violating the law if you republish a still you found elsewhere. A final note: IMDB, in an effort to save bandwidth, does not let you directly save images from its website. To grab an image from IMDB, take a screenshot of the page (using the *print screen* button), paste it into your favorite image editor, then crop the shot appropriately.

- **Include cast and crew info**. Even if you mention all relevant cast and crew in the review, it's a good idea for both readers and search engine spiders to include that information in a separate part of the review. You can get cast and crew info at IMDB or from the movie's website, but IMDB is often faster.

- **Split up large documents**. If your review sprawls past 1,000 words, consider breaking it up into two or more pages. With a two-page review, you make it easier for a reader to digest your review and you double the number of ad impressions while easing the feeling of fatigue on the reader.

- **Link back to home and other parts of the site**. Always make sure your reader can get to the most popular areas with one click – especially the home page. You might also link to special pages which keep tabs on the latest releases, new DVD releases, interviews, and other digest-style content.

BUILDING TRAFFIC

What if someone launched a movie review web site and nobody came? Even if you're writing the most thoughtful, entertaining criticism on the net, no one will read it if they can't find it. Promoting your site is key to getting visitors, yet it goes without saying that a multimillion dollar ad campaign is out of the question.

Here are some grassroots ideas for getting people to come to your site.

Search engines. Foremost, you have to be listed in the big search engines. It's easy to get listed; it's difficult to get ranked. And more and more, search engines are penalizing those who try to game the system. My best advice is to simply submit your site for listing to each of the below locations and hope for the best. If you've organized your site the way I've outlined above, you won't need to worry about "search optimization" or other tactics. (It probably goes without saying, but avoid services that promise to get you a top ranking on the search engines. They don't work, they cost a lot, and they often hurt more than they help.)

Each page noted here contains the submission information for new sites. In most cases, you simply fill out the form once your site is launched, and that's it! Also note that the world of search engines changes all the time, just as the web itself does, so this list should not be considered exhaustive. As well, the URLs for the submission pages are also subject to change.

- Open Directory – www.dmoz.com/add.html – Listing your site here will land you in most search engine's results, including Google, Yahoo, and AOL.
- Google - www.google.com/addurl.html – For good measure, it's a wise idea to submit your site to Google directly as well. Google also runs a popular pay-for-hits advertising service called AdWords (adwords.google.com), which is good to toy with if you're looking for low-cost advertising.
- Yahoo – submit.search.yahoo.com/free/request – Yahoo incorporates results from other search engines, too, but you can submit directly here.
- Zeal – www.zeal.com, click "add a site" – This is a human-edited list of sites mainly used by the Looksmart search engine.
- Snap – www.snap.com – Results feed into Snap from other sites, but once you're listed here, you'll want to send them your logo to enhance your site's profile listing.

If you've covered these bases, you really needn't worry about submitting your site elsewhere. Over time, you'll find that your website shows up in countless random places as it's linked and re-linked across the web. Don't panic. This is normal. In fact, this is good. The more incoming links your website has, the more traffic you'll eventually generate.

Movie review databases. Beyond general search engines, you want to get your site listed on as many specialized movie databases as possible, as these are already well-known destinations for movie lovers. Note that with some of these sites, you need to be a major web presence before even approaching them for a link. I've made note of these concerns and more under each listing.

- IMDB – www.imdb.com – The Internet Movie Database is without a doubt the most important site for you to get to link to your reviews. Not only is it a major destination, it's the world's largest movie database, so virtually any movie you review will have a listing at IMDB, and you'll be able to submit a link back to your site. Free traffic! To get an IMDB link, search for a film, then click "external reviews" on the left side of the page. At the bottom of that page click "Update" and walk through the steps to enter the URL to your review and the name of your site. That's it! Links normally appear within a week. Note that the IMDB is unfortunately erratic, and the site loses about one of every 20 external reviews submitted. You can always resubmit later if you find your link is gone, but this is impossible to track, so try not to sweat it too much.

- Movie Review Query Engine – www.mrqe.com – The MRQE spiders sites automatically and maintains lists of links to reviews, authors, and overall star ratings. The MRQE uses a home-made spidering system; once you have a good handful of reviews, contact the site operators at cinema@mrqe.com to find out how best to organize a master list of reviews to make it easy for the site to index your content. (This is another great reason to keep such a page on your site!)

- Rotten Tomatoes – www.rottentomatoes.com – Rotten Tomatoes is a major aggregator of movie reviews, often linking to more than 100 websites for a big Hollywood release. Rotten Tomatoes then calculates a "Tomatometer" rating based on the percentage of critics who recommend the movie. Very useful, and relatively open to new critics and sites. To be considered, read their criteria here: www.rottentomatoes.com/pages/critics. If you're eligible, submit your information on the web form at the bottom of the page.

Those are the major outlets that accept links from independent critics. Other sources like Yahoo Movies, Movies.com, and Metacritic are also great sources of incoming links if you can obtain placement on them, but none of these sites appears to be accepting new websites for its review listings. (I can't even get filmcritic.com on Metacritic!) If you're serious about getting listed on sites like this, the key is *quality* and *quantity*. Once you've published more than 1,000 quality reviews (and you run a well-designed site), the big guys will start to take notice.

Usenet. Usenet is a text-only discussion group system that predates the web by many years. It's now run and managed by Google. Usenet can be a good place for absolute beginners to find an audience, as the Usenet group rec.

arts.movies.reviews (aka RAMR) allows *anyone* to post reviews online (it's part of the Rotten Tomatoes system now). The reviews are automatically and permanently archived at IMDB (check under "newsgroup reviews") and on Google Groups (groups.google.com). The catch, of course, is that reviews can consist of text only and they aren't hosted on your own pages. In other words, you're providing free content to someone else when you write for RAMR – though of course you may link back to your own site within the review.

You'll see on IMDB that not many people use RAMR any more, because text-based internet groups have long since fallen into disuse. (AOL recently abandoned Usenet altogether.) The type of reader Usenet attracts is rarely the kind of person who will become a regular reader of your site, and traffic doesn't seem to rise much with a RAMR posting. As well, any posting on Usenet invariably nets you tons of spam, so if you decide to go for it, don't post with your primary e-mail address.

If you're interested in experimenting with RAMR, send an e-mail to rec-arts-movies-reviews@moderators.isc.org to get full instructions on formatting (which are strict) and submission guidelines on how to send in your reviews.

Link exchanges. Getting traffic often comes down to getting good placement on search engines. Getting placement on search engines is by and large a game of getting links to your site. Getting links can be done a number of ways, but the easiest is to offer a link exchange with your peers. Filmcritic. com has an open link policy with any entertainment site that reciprocates with a link back. It's a simple way to build traffic through the sheer number of links into your site, but it's very slow – most search engines discount "reciprocal links" to the point where they're barely relevant.

The other way to get incoming links requires much more work and is equally slow at building traffic, but it avoids the reciprocal link discounting problem. If you've written a feature on a popular (or obscure) celebrity, an interview, or even a review in which a certain performance or crew position is discussed in depth, let those people's fans know. A simple Google search will turn up dozens of sites written by fans of Mark Harmon. Mark Harmon! If you've got a paragraph in a review about good old Mark's performance in a recent film (or even an old one), chances are several of these sites will link to your writeup if you ask them to. Sure, this amounts to begging, and it takes a lot of effort for minimal reward, but if you've got the time to do it and don't mind e-mailing innocent people with your groveling, it's relatively foolproof.

This is especially successful if you have a celebrity interview, as fan sites will always link to them.

Mailing lists. Filmcritic.com has long offered a mailing list for those readers uninterested in visiting or unable to get to the website. This is good for them, since they can read reviews in the format they prefer, and it's good for us, since we embed the same advertising into each page sent via e-mail. The easiest way to set up a mailing list is to use a service like Yahoo Groups (groups.yahoo.com), which completely handles the subscription process for you. Managing a mailing list yourself is sheer folly. Don't do it.

Message boards. Don't ask me why, but people love to jabber endlessly on message boards. You can obtain free software to add forums/discussion groups/message boards to your website with relative ease. We don't have them on filmcritic.com because managing them can be a headache, but many website owners have experienced great success with this technology.

Contests. Contests and giveaways are a great way to build your readership. People will do just about anything for a free DVD or a t-shirt. Filmcritic.com once received more than 1,000 entries for a contest giving away a handful of little mirrors with *The Manchurian Candidate* logo imprinted on them.

Filmcritic.com's contests are typically simple giveaways: You send us your address and we draw winners at random once the contest has run its course. But you can easily create more hoops for readers to jump through in order to earn merchandise: Filling out a demographic survey, clicking a certain number of reviews to find a "secret word" they have to submit with their entry, or subscribing to your mailing list. The more barriers you set up, the fewer entries you'll receive (and the less likely you'll be to generate return readers), so don't go overboard with the obstacles.

Merchandise for giveaways can be obtained in a number of ways. Once you become established, publicity companies will seek you out to run promotions. These are the easiest giveaways to run, since all you need to do is set up the contest, then send the publicity company the names and addresses of the winners. The company handles the shipping for you.

If you're just starting out, this won't be an option, so you'll have to be more inventive in your giveaway materials. DVDs you've reviewed and aren't interested in keeping make great giveaways, especially if they're recent releases. You could also make t-shirts for your site at a local print shop (or online at sites like cafepress.com) and give those away: A logo t-shirt has a secondary function of working as free advertising for your site!

Be creative. Everybody loves free stuff. The more you can give away, the more readers you'll earn from it.

FINDING AN AUDIENCE

Filmcritic.com's goal is to be the most comprehensive movie review website online, with reviews of every release, large or small, that plays in any movie theater anywhere. As a result, we're often visited by people who discover we are the *only* source of a review of a number of films. Meanwhile, we also review the big Hollywood releases and have exhaustive coverage of the latest DVDs.

This, in a sense, is our *niche*: Breadth of coverage and total comprehensiveness for the deep cinema buff.

That niche doesn't make a lot of sense for a lot of websites. Why? It's extremely time-consuming (we post over 500 reviews a year) and each added review generates only a small increase in the number of visitors.

So how do you get people to pay attention to what you have to say, elevating your work above the noise of the web? Focus, focus, focus:

- **What are your interests?** If you decide to take a niche route, ask what you're especially knowledgeable about. Is it lesbian horror films? 1980s teen comedies? Slacker films? These are all niches that would sustain a small, part-time website with a rabid audience. They won't earn you more than a few thousand dollars a year, but they'll let you indulge your love of movies and get some free DVDs.

- **What niches aren't exploited?** Classic and foreign movies have a dearth of coverage online. Oscar winner *Going My Way* has only nine reviews linked from IMDB. *All the King's Men* only has 11. Foreign films are even more ignored. Most of Antonioni's early films have no reviews online at all. The problem with filling niches is often getting copies of the films to watch. You'll spend a lot of time at art house cinemas and avant garde video stores tracking down these movies. Bring lots of patience, but having a monopoly on reviews of these films will ensure you are rewarded. Other unfilled niches exist; just hunt for them.

- **What unique perspective can you offer?** In the late 1990s, the "teen film critic" made headlines and countless TV appearances because he was, well,

169

a teenage film critic. Readers might be bored with the middle-aged white guy perspective and can look for a minority point of view. You might offer reviews from a specific gender, ethnicity, age, or sexual orientation. The website Three Black Chicks (www.3blackchicks.com) is a very successful example of this phenomenon. Even if you are a bland, middle-aged white guy, you can still build a perspective. Consider Joe Bob Briggs, whose irreverent southern character has charmed thousands. Chuck Schwartz's Cranky Critic website (www.crankycritic.com) – while considerably less cranky than it used to be – made its name on crotchety perspectives on film. You might also consider reviewing a film from a visual effects or soundtrack point of view. These are all interesting niche perspectives that can reach interested audiences.

- **Build the archive.** Nothing good in theaters this week? Build that archive! Volume equals traffic. There's no way to cheat it.

- **What kind of review does your audience want to read?** Are you trying to reach a "fast food" crowd or a "sushi bar" crowd? Or are you just writing for yourself? There's an expectation that if you review an art house movie, you should write it with the audience in mind. Mooning over how cute the lead actress is won't win you respect, but deconstructing the film appropriately probably will. Understand that writing for a niche audience requires adopting a niche-appropriate writing style. You can always break the rules and simply write what your heart desires, but understand that you'll be limiting your audience unless you work toward a style that's appropriate for that specific subset of reader.

BASIC WEB MARKETING

Beyond getting incoming links, mailing lists, and contests, what can you do to get your site known? It's tough to do much without spending a lot of money, but here are a few guerilla-style suggestions that might generate some traffic for your site.

- **Plug your site all the time.** Include a link to the site in your e-mail signature. Tell everyone you know. Make the site your home page. If you use a public computer, set that computer to use your site as its home page. Wear a t-shirt with your site's logo when you go to the movies. Spread the word loudly and constantly.

- **Post on message boards.** Visit forums like those at Rotten Tomatoes or the IMDB and plug your site whenever you post a message. Be relentless. If you have a review of a hot movie or an interview with a big celebrity, plug it. No one else is going to promote your site. You need to do it yourself.

- **Embrace public relations.** Make yourself available for interviews from other media sources. You'd be surprised how often newspapers and magazines (including major ones like *The New York Times* and *USA Today*) are looking for quotes from film critics, especially when movies intersect with hot topics like terrorism, human cloning, and global warming. I was interviewed by the *Times* regarding my review of *The Recruit* and the unlikely way it treated computers and technology. Typically, press comes to you, but you can also check out services like Profnet (www.profnet. com) and Response Source (www.responsesource.com), where journalists post questions and solicit answers from experts. You have to pay to receive questions at most of these services, but if you're a growing site it might be worth it.

- **Review independent films.** Offer to review indies on your site, and request (or require) a link back to your site when you write up a review. You'll receive a flood of VHS tapes and DVDs, and since indie filmmakers are always promoting their work, their efforts will indirectly promote your website as well.

- **Advertise.** It doesn't have to cost a fortune. Text ads, small button sponsorships, and e-mail advertisements can often be had for a very affordable rate. (Check out AdBrite (www.adbrite.com) and Google AdWords (adwords.google.com) to experiment with cheap and targeted advertising.) Web advertising is a very nebulous topic and results are erratic, so tread lightly in this area.

EARNING MONEY

What, you want people to pay you to write movie reviews? Of course you do! Here's how websites make money, and here's how you can do it to.

- **Advertising.** The banner ad isn't dead, but it doesn't pay much any more. Once you have a substantial user base (at least 1,000 page views a day and preferably more), you can expect to make a little money by selling advertising on your website. The good news is you don't have to sell ads directly to advertisers. You can simply join an ad network and let them do the selling. Typically they keep about half of the money earned, and you get the rest. There are literally hundreds of advertising networks out there. Filmcritic.com has used Burst! Media (www.burstmedia.com) in the past and present quite successfully. Most of our ads today are placed with Gorilla Nation (www.gorillanation.com), which specializes in larger entertainment sites. Burst accepts most new applicants and can provide ads in virtually any format, including banners, towers, large cubes, and pop-up advertisements (which pay the best). We also use Adbrite (www.adbrite.com) for text ads, which are less intrusive and available to just about anyone. Check out your favorite websites and see what ad services they use (you can usually tell by hovering over the ads and looking at the URL). Advertising networks can be slow to pay and the revenues aren't that great, but they are generally consistent and don't require much maintenance. Just drop some code onto your web pages and you're done.

- **Merchandising and affiliate sales.** You review DVDs, why not sell them too? Companies like Amazon.com and hundreds of others from Disney to eBay make it easy for you to hawk their wares in return for a cut of the profits (usually about five percent). You can sign up for countless affiliate deals at Linkshare.com, or check out Amazon Associates to participate in its selling program. Amazon, alone, presents a myriad of opportunities for sales: In addition to DVDs and VHS videos, filmcritic.com also sells soundtracks and books upon which movies were based. We even sell video games from time to time when we review films like *Resident Evil*. Netflix is also a great movie review site affiliate, as is AllPosters.com (or one of the countless other poster sales companies), for those seeking memorabilia. Amazon is definitely the site's highest-grossing affiliate deal; in any given month, the site often makes more money from Amazon sales than it does from advertising. Special note: Make sure your merchandising links are kept up to date. Links change without warning, and you won't earn a commission if your links don't work!

- **Syndication.** This is a tough business to crack, but it can be a lucrative one once you get into it. Filmcritic.com syndicates its reviews and interviews to other websites and offline publications, a popular content strategy when that site/newspaper doesn't have the resources to hire its own critic.

172

Finding syndicate partners is tricky and difficult. Expect serious financial negotiations once you do find leads: Pricing can be set per review or for "all access" rights to your archives. You might also offer discounts for small outlets. Syndication can make you a good amount of money — and if you're big enough, you can approach a syndication service like Universal Press Syndicate, but note that not even filmcritic.com is important enough to merit inclusion in that service.

- **Charging for subscriptions.** This is a very controversial and unproven strategy, but it does guarantee some revenues if you have a loyal readership, since you charge them to access your site. Michael Elliot (www. christiancritic.com) charges $9 a year for access to his website, which reviews movies from (obviously) a religious point of view. In 2003, he took his site from free to paid-access, converting about 10 percent of his readers to the subscription model. Elliott reports modest success: He no longer has to deal with advertising issues, receives a steady flow of new subscribers, no longer receives hate mail, and has received no negative fallout from publicists. Often considered a strategy of last resort, charging for access can in reality be a very smart way to stabilize your revenues and better serve a fiercely loyal audience. Recognizing whether that audience is willing to pay, and how much, is the tricky part.

LEGAL ISSUES

Remember: Once you start collecting money for your reviews, you are a business. Act like one:

- **File a DBA.** You'll probably receive checks made out to your website, and your bank won't accept them unless you have a DBA ("doing business as") document. You can get a DBA for about $30 at your local city hall. You simply go there, search the local records to make sure no one is already using your business name, and file some paperwork. You may also need to file to pay local taxes — which are typically nil if you have no employees. Take your DBA paperwork to your bank; they'll add the record to your checking account, and you can deposit checks which are made out to your website.

- **Incorporation.** You can avoid liability for certain crimes by incorporating your operation or becoming a Limited Liability Company (LLC). This doesn't really make a lot of sense for a small operation, so only consider this once you've outgrown your checking account.

- **Get business cards and make letterhead.** You'll be meeting a lot of people, and the professional thing to do is get a business card with your logo on it. You can obtain cards affordably online at sites like vistaprint.com.

- **Get a fax number.** You may not need it — most press releases come via e-mail now — but a few publicists still send faxes, and it adds to your professionalism if you have one. You can always get a cheap efax number (www.efax.com) if you don't want the expense and hassle of a second line and fax hardware.

- **Copyrights.** By law, anything you write is copyrighted by you. Contrary to popular belief, you do not have to file a copyright document with the U.S. Copyright Office, though this will strengthen your case if you encounter a violation of your copyright (aka plagiarism, see the next section). Copyrighting a document costs $30, so it makes little financial sense to waste money on a formal copyright when you don't really need one. You should, however, include a full copyright notice on every page of your website. The standard notation should read: Copyright © 2005 yourwebsite. com (or you may use your name if you haven't filed your DBA yet).

PLAGIARISM

Plagiarism — the intentional duplication of another writer's work without attribution — is the most serious crime a writer can commit (at least, in the course of duty). There are two issues at hand regarding this heinous act.

The first is *plagiarism by you* of another's work. It can be tempting to lift a sentence or two from another review. Who'll find out? Who gets hurt?

Well, on the internet, someone *will* find out, since search engines make it painfully simple to track down plagiarism, and I've seen countless people get caught over the years. Readers also help out. Fans of another writer will tell them if you've stolen their work.

The penalties are stiff. You'll never work for a reputable publisher again, and you could face a severe financial judgment in court. Put simply, don't do it. Ever. If a critic that works for you does it, fire that critic and carefully check over all of his collected works for plagiarism, permanently deleting anything that's even remotely fishy. An apology is also in order for your readers and definitely for the victim of the crime.

Since I *know* you'd never plagiarize another person's work, the thornier issue becomes *plagiarism of you* by another writer.

Write for long enough on the internet, and people will inevitably start stealing your work. How you discover it may be a bit random, but dealing with it is invariably difficult.

Once I find a plagiarized review from filmcritic.com, I begin by sending an e-mail to the owner of the website and/or the writer of the review – anyone I can find that's involved with the website. It's basically a form letter that looks like this:

> Dear Sir or Madam,
>
> You may not be aware of this, but someone has posted our material on your website without our permission. Our review of *Kill Bill* appears here on your website: www.yourlousysite. com/killbill.htm
>
> This material is in violation of our copyright.
>
> We understand that mistakes can be made, but we do request that you remove the review immediately.
>
> Alternately you may enter into a syndication agreement with us. We have many affordable plans available and can make our content readily available to you legally for your website or other purposes.
>
> Please contact me at your earliest convenience to discuss a remedy for this situation. Thank you.
>
> Sincerely,
>
> Christopher Null
> Editor in Chief
> filmcritic.com

The goal is to be as non-confrontational as possible while still being forceful. The letter mentions the law but doesn't explicitly threaten legal action, which gets people feeling combative quickly.

About half the time I won't receive a response. A quarter of the time the person immediately apologizes – often it was posted to the site without the owner's knowledge or the page was used as a test that was later forgotten

– and the page is immediately removed.

The other quarter of the time results in people who eventually set up a syndication deal with us or some other legal form of licensing our content. These are usually people who think that they're "helping us out" by copying an entire page of our content and posting it on their site, with credit and a link back to filmcritic.com. After explaining this is not the case, discussions about how we can work out a legal (read: paid) syndication deal follow.

If the plagiarism is just one article that a fan of a film or an actor has posted (with credit and a link back to our site), I'll usually let it go. The hassle just isn't worth it, and the link back (as mentioned earlier in the chapter) is worth something. If I spent all day chasing down plagiarists, I wouldn't have time to watch movies.

How you deal with the silent majority, those who don't respond to your letter, is up to you. You can consider legal action, but this is expensive and the reward will be minimal. You generally have to prove damages, and unless your site is raking in cash *and* the copyright violation has cost you income, that's hard to do. Consult a lawyer if you are so inclined, but in most cases, even serious plagiarism won't be worth the cost and headache of a full-blown lawsuit. You may have better luck filing complaints with the Better Business Bureau or by sending a letter to the site owner's ISP explaining the situation, but these steps don't often provide results.

I feel your pain. It's depressing – especially if your review is twisted to work against you (as occurred when a filmcritic.com review was stolen by a Holocaust revisionist group) – but as a small operator, your options are unfortunately limited.

CHAPTER 10:
GETTING ACCESS

OK, this chapter is probably why you bought this book: You want to see movies and get DVDs for free, right?

No sweat, just read along.

Getting into advance screenings can save you thousands of dollars a year, so it's worth it to expend substantial effort in getting on the press lists of your local PR agencies. But first you have to understand how the PR system works. (Note that this chapter largely assumes you're starting your own website or otherwise going it alone. If you're writing for another outlet, they'll typically handle PR for you if you live locally. If you're writing for an out-of-town outlet, these lessons will also apply to you.)

PUBLIC RELATIONS 101

Traditionally, PR — alternately *press relations* or *public relations* — has a love-and-hate relationship with journalism. Entertainment PR is especially tense: Film critics can't work without publicists (at least not very well), but without film critics to write about their movies, publicists wouldn't exist at all!

Movie studios do recognize that film critics provide a valuable service for them: We offer free advertising of their films. In exchange we get to see the movies early and sometimes get access to the cast and crew. The studio doesn't care much about how positive your review is: Even a bad review is publicity, and for virtually every film released, the studios are willing to take the chance that some critics — even if it's a minority of them — will give a film enough good press to positively impact the box office of that film. It's rare that a film won't screen for the press; if it doesn't, you can be sure the film is so terrible it shouldn't have been released to begin with.

Of course, sometimes bad reviews do raise hackles, and some legendary battles have been fought over bad reviews given out by critics. (More on this later.)

But the studios don't fight these battles, they have mouthpieces to do it for them. *PR agencies* represent 90 percent of who you'll be dealing with as a member of the press. Rarely, if ever, will you talk to anyone from an actual studio once you've found out who the proper PR agency contact is.

There's a good reason that studios outsource the bulk of their PR work: There are thousands of members of the press throughout the country, and hundreds of thousands of press screenings to organize every year. It would be an impossible task for a studio in Los Angeles to manage a screening in Topeka, and even if it could find a theater to rent and ensure a print arrived at the theater in time, it would have to have an employee fly to Topeka to usher guests in and out of the movie. Multiply this by the hundred-plus cities in which these screenings take place — often on the same night — and you'll understand why studios outsource this job to local PR agencies.

Dozens of PR agencies can be found in every city, and agencies specialize in certain types of publicity — technology, restaurants, personalities, and of course, entertainment. Over the last few years, PR agencies have consolidated to the point where you'll probably need to deal with only two or three agencies in your area to cover every studio and independent release. In San Francisco, two large agencies now handle the work of every major studio. One additional, smaller agency handles independent releases, and two or three one-man companies handle even smaller independent films and self-distributed works. Once you get on this handful of mailing lists, you're typically covered for every movie that gets released in your town. Some publicists — even within the same company — manage their own mailing lists, though, so be prepared to contact various publicists within each company.

Depending on how large your town is, the agency may not be located in the city limits. PR for Sacramento is handled out of San Francisco — and SF publicists have been known to arrange screenings for places as far away as Hawaii, Salt Lake City, and Las Vegas. Screenings may not be local either, so expect to have to drive to your nearest major urban center to attend a press screening.

As a new critic, your first goal will be to get on the mailing lists of your local publicity companies. If you're reviewing DVDs, you'll want to contact these studios as well to get on their lists for screeners. (Detailed home video contacts can be found later in the chapter.)

The trick, of course, is that you can't just call up a publicist and demand to be placed on a mailing list. Sending out all those screening passes and — especially — DVDs is expensive. You have to prove you're worthy before they put you on the list. So get your ducks in a row before you start calling the contacts listed in the next section. At the very least, I recommend you have the following things to show for yourself, or publicists won't return your calls:

- **Six months of current releases (theatrical or DVD, as appropriate) covered with substantial, well-written reviews.** If you're reviewing new releases, make sure you have reviews of new releases. Classics, DVDs, and video game reviews won't count. If you're reviewing DVDs, review as many newly released discs as you can before you start pestering PR agents for freebies. Aim for at least 30 reviews under your belt as a bare minimum. Again, it goes without saying that these reviews should be written to the absolute best of your ability, proofread, double-checked, and perfectly formatted.

- **A well-designed site that's rich in content.** Do whatever you can to keep your site from looking threadbare. Add capsule reviews to supplement major reviews. Include news blurbs, top ten lists, or other "easy" content to make your site look beefy, even if it isn't yet. Most publicists will check it out carefully before they make a decision about adding you to the mailing list.

- **Some statistics about your site's popularity.** And no, you can't just make them up. The absolute easiest thing to do is get rated by Alexa.com, but that takes time and is notoriously inaccurate. Sign up with an advertising service, though, and you'll be able to get traffic reports through it which you can use in contacting publicists. Other traffic reports can be generated by your server's logs or through third-party applications like the one offered by eXTReMe Tracking (www.extreme-dm.com). Don't bother talking to publicists unless you're getting — again, at a bare minimum — several thousand visitors per day.

- **Some demographic information.** If you can get demographic data (through a poll or survey, usually), that's even better than traffic numbers alone. Many publicists will specifically ask for information about the age, gender, income, and other habits of your readers. If you don't have this information, just say so — but also say you're working on it.

I'm serious about these minimum requirements. Don't call before you have completed the list or it will seriously impact your chances of getting recognized later on. Publicists will remember you as an amateur instead of a professional, and it will be infinitely more difficult to overcome that stigma.

GETTING ON THE LIST

You've completed the minimum requirements, now you're ready to start making some phone calls and sending some e-mails.

The first step is easy: Call the studio to find out who handles publicity for your area. In the following sections you'll find the phone numbers for the main switchboard of each of the major studios. (I haven't included direct lines to the PR departments because 1) they would kill me and 2) they change all the time.) This is a very simple affair:

Dial the number, hit whatever key sequence you need to reach the operator. Ask the operator for "the publicity department." When you're transferred to the publicity department, just ask whoever picks up the phone the following: "Hello, I'm trying to find out who handles theatrical publicity for Whatever City." Nine times out of 10, they'll give you a name and a phone number (or they may give you the company name for you to look up the number). If they want to know who you are, just tell them, "I'm a film critic with Whatever Movie Reviews." Most studio publicists won't ask a lot of questions; they'll let the local PR reps deal with you.

Now you have a local contact for that studio. You should probably gather all the local contacts from the various studios before you start calling local reps, to save yourself time and trouble from having to call the same local rep more than once. Your next step is to start calling local reps and introducing yourself and your site.

For each local publicity company, call the number you were given and ask for the appropriate contact. If you don't have a contact name, just ask the operator, "Can you transfer me to the publicist that handles Studio X?" Once you get a human voice or a mailbox, simply say something to this effect: "Hi, my name is Bob Critic, and I was talking to the folks over at Studio X. They said I should definitely talk to you about getting on your list for local screenings. I run a site called Whatever Movie Reviews, and we'd love to start covering your releases."

This introduction has the effect of making you seem like a veteran, like you already have a relationship with the studio, and like you generally know what you're doing. You'll probably have to answer a few questions about your site — they'll want to know traffic stats and the general demographics of your site at the very least.

Remember, the publicist doesn't really want to add you to the list. It's not just that it's a lot of work, it costs money in stamps and man-hours, too.

Most studios are interested in getting as many critics as possible to review their films, but with the rise of the internet, mailing list rosters have grown substantially. I used to attend press screenings with two or three other people in the audience. Now, even "press-only" screenings are packed with dozens or hundreds of people: Some are alleged "VIPs," but many are genuine members of the press, often from obscure outlets, only a handful of which will actually review the film at all. So publicists try to keep the size of the mailing list down.

You may also be asked to send a fax or e-mail with the aforementioned information to the PR company to formalize your request. The publicist will tell you what to include in that message, but a general sample e-mail or fax follows:

Dear Publicist,

Thank you for talking to me on the phone earlier today. As requested, here's the information about our website for your consideration.

Whatever Movie Reviews was launched in 2004 and has steadily grown its readership since. Today we reach 50,000 devoted followers and receive 200,000 page views a month. Alexa ranks us as a top 100,000 website. We specialize in action films, but we also try to review every major and independent movie release. You can find us at www.whatevermoviereviews.com.

Our readers are predominantly males in their 20s. Our demographic survey shows that they are college educated with an average income of $60,000, and they go to the movies an average of twice a month. I can provide additional demographic information at your request.

I hope you'll consider our request to be added to your mailing list, as it will allow our reviews to be posted in a more timely fashion instead of days or weeks after a film is released. If I can be of any more service, please don't hesitate to write or call. My contact information follows.

I'll check in with you in a couple of weeks. Until then, thanks for considering Whatever Movie Reviews.

Sincerely,

Bob Critic
Whatever Movie Reviews
bob@whatevermovies.com
619-555-9393
619-555-9394 fax
123 Main St.
Whatever, CA 94100

Again, don't follow this script exactly — customize it to work for you. Getting on a press mailing list isn't rocket science. It simply takes persistence and the highest degree of professionalism. I've said it before, but I'll say it again: Make sure your website is sophisticated and thorough. Check your spelling. Don't use a lot of flashing graphics. You don't want the PR agency to close their web browser in disgust.

Some publicists put everyone on the list. Some will add virtually no one. Chances are you won't get on every mailing list your first time out, but you'll get on some. Keep trying every few months, and send *tear sheets* (discussed later in this chapter) to the publicists of the films you're reviewing, just so they know you're still alive. It will impress a publicist greatly that you are willing to spend your own money to review a film, even if you weren't invited to a screening. Eventually you'll get on the list, though it may take some time. (Also note that once you're on the list, screening passes are non-transferable. Start giving them to your friends and you'll find yourself booted immediately.)

Finally, be aware that contacts, phone numbers, websites, and agencies change *all the time*. One studio may fire its publicity company and move the whole operation somewhere else. There's no guarantee that you will survive that transition — even if you've been on the mailing list for years. Publicists quit jobs and change agencies just as much as regular workers. People get sick. People retire. Agencies worry about costs and they audit their lists, trimming people off at random.

Staying on the mailing list is as much of a task as getting on it to start with. If you suddenly find that you're not receiving invitations from one studio, give your contact a call and find out what's going on. There may be a mistake, or you may need to reapply. I've had countless experiences where I had been on a mailing list for years, only to suddenly stop receiving screeners. Six months of pestering later, I would be back on the list. It happens all the time, so don't get upset. Be firm and persistent, and nine times out of 10 you'll get back on the list.

STUDIO PR CONTACTS

The following 10 listings represent about 90 percent of the films that you'll probably want to review theatrically. The main switchboard numbers are listed for each company. Remember: Call, ask for the publicity department, then ask who the publicist is for your region. *That's* the person you'll want to deal with in getting on the mailing list, *not* the person who answers the phone at the studio.

20th Century Fox – 310-369-1000 or visit www.fox.com

DreamWorks SKG – 818-733-9600 or visit www.dreamworks.com

MGM – 310-449-3000 or visit www.mgm.com

Miramax – 212-941-3800 or visit www.miramax.com (Though Miramax is part of Disney, theatrical publicity is often handled by a different company. DVDs are distributed by the same company.)

New Line – 310-854-5811 or visit www.newline.com

Paramount – 323-956-5000 or visit www.paramount.com

Sony Pictures Entertainment/Columbia TriStar – 310-244-4000 or visit www.sonypictures.com

Universal Studios – 818-777-1000 or visit www.universal.com

Walt Disney Pictures (aka Buena Vista) – 818-560-5151 or visit www.disney.com

Warner Brothers – 818-954-6000 or visit www.warnerbros.com

INDEPENDENT DISTRIBUTORS

The following 10 distributors are smaller outlets that are typically more anxious to have critics review their films. Getting on these studios' mailing lists is often easier than the majors. If you're nervous or aren't having any luck with the large distributors, you may want to give these companies a shot. E-mail addresses are included where appropriate (again, simply ask who handles publicity for your region), but the phone will often get better (and faster) results. Most also have video divisions, as well.

First Look Media – 323-337-1000 or visit www.flp.com – Independent studio and distributor on the rise.

First Run Features – 212-243-0600 or visit www.firstrunfeatures.com – Well-regarded independent distributor.

Focus Features – 818-777-7373 or visit www.focusfeatures.com – This is a specialty unit of Universal (which released *Lost in Translation*); if you get in with Universal, you probably don't need to contact Focus directly.

Indican Pictures – 323-650-0832 or visit www.indicanpictures.com – A very small distributor, but worth a call.

Lions Gate Entertainment – 310-314-2000 or visit www.lionsgatefilms.com – The biggest indie distributor; responsible for *The Cooler, Girl with a Pearl Earring*, and other titles.

Magnolia Pictures – 212-924-6701 or info@magpictures.com or visit www.magpictures.com – Released *Capturing the Friedmans* and a number of foreign films.

New Yorker Films – 212-645-4600 or info@newyorkerfilms.com or visit www.newyorkerfilms.com – Releases smaller films theatrically and on video.

Newmarket Films – 212-303-1700 or info@newmarketfilms.com or visit www.newmarketfilms.com – Released *Monster* and *Donnie Darko*.

Seventh Art Releasing – 323-845-1455, or seventhart@7thart.com or visit www.7thart.com and click Contact Us.

THINKFilm — 646-293-9400 or dfenkel@thinkfilmcompany.com (David Fenkel) or visit www.thinkfilmcompany.com – Focuses on documentaries; released *Spellbound* and *Going Upriver.*

Wellspring – dgoldberg@wellspring.com or visit www.wellspring.com – Handles a number of highly regarding foreign and independent films.

Also note that in most cities, independent movie theaters run their own press screenings, especially if they book obscure, revival, or art house films that aren't nationally promoted. Almost every city also has an independent publicist who handles screenings for movies that fall in between the national releases and the single-cinema movies. If you can locate this publicist, you'll likely find yourself drowning in screening passes … for movies you've never heard of. Simply call your local art theater to ask if they have a publicist. The theater may also point you to an independent publicist who handles various indie films for a variety of cinemas.

SPECIALTY VIDEO/DVD DISTRIBUTORS

The following list represents the dozens of companies that handle their own home video/DVD distributors. Distributing video is easy compared to distributing in theaters, so there are many more of them. They also come and go quickly, release films erratically, and generally have smaller budgets. Most specialize in one genre of film, so don't expect a flood of *screeners* (advance copies of DVDs sent out for review). These aren't exactly large companies, either, so if you don't intend to review that company's movies, don't request screeners.

I'll discuss some of the intricacies of reviewing DVDs in Chapter 14, but don't expect reviewing many of these titles to generate much traffic for your site. Right or not, people are more interested in seeing your review of the latest *Star Wars* film than the latest Dolph Lundgren action vehicle. On the other hand, if yours is the only site that has a review of an obscure French mystery or a cult classic DVD, you might see more traffic for that review than for a major release. Choose which companies you contact appropriately, based on the descriptions below.

Finally, the procedure for getting on the video/DVD mailing list is a bit different than getting on the theatrical list. The major theatrical studios (as noted in the above two sections) use external PR agencies to handle their lists, but the companies listed below typically do not. (Note also that because DVD reviews aren't dependent on local contacts, virtually every major studio uses a *national* publicity company to handle mailings – so home video PR contacts are almost always different than theatrical PR contacts.)

Most studios don't automatically send DVDs, either. They send press releases announcing their DVDs, then you have to request a copy of each one you want to review. Again, use restraint and don't request every single title. You won't possibly be able to review them all.

Paradoxically, it's more difficult to get on a DVD screener list than it is a theatrical list, because of the expense involved in producing and mailing a DVD to you. But DVD reviews are comparably less important for the studio than a theatrical review, so really they don't care what you say: The critical consensus has been reached long ago. At the DVD level, they're far more interested in simply getting coverage than in getting positive reviews.

The companies below largely handle screeners by themselves, so when you make first contact, you'll simply want to ask who you need to talk to in order to get on the screener mailing list, bypassing the "who handles local publicity" step altogether. E-mail is usually fine for your first introduction to each company. And here they are:

A&E – 212-210-1331 or see website at www.aetv.com – Provides mostly made-for-TV documentaries and copies of its television shows.

A.D. Vision/ADV Films – 713-341-7105 or see website at www.advfilms. com – Distributes Japanese anime films.

Anchor Bay – fax 248-816-3335 or visit www.anchorbayentertainment. com – Primarily a horror film distributor with some fitness and children's titles mixed in.

Ardustry – 818-784-3337 ext. 300 or visit www.ardustry.com – Distributes a variety of titles, heavy on documentaries.

Ariztical – 800-356-4386 or customerservice@ariztical.com or visit www.artiztical.com — Gay and lesbian video distributor.

Avalanche Home Entertainment – 310-314-2000

Buena Vista Home Entertainment – 818-295-5200 – Part of the world of Disney. I'm including it here because Buena Vista handles *all* home video products for Disney, Miramax, and affiliated companies. Don't call Disney's theatrical division to reach them. The company handles an awful lot of specialty children's titles, too, including baby videos. I've had an excellent relationship with the folks at BVHE for years.

Central Park Media – info@teamcpm.com or see websites at www. centralparkmedia.com and www.anime18.com – Specializes in adult Japanese manga and anime titles.

Criterion Collection – see web forms at www.criterionco.com — If you get on one mailing list, this is the one to be on. Criterion's distribution of rare, important, and classic films is second to none.

Eclectic DVD/Music Video Distributors – 800-888-0486 or visit www. eclecticdvd.com – Specializes in, well, music videos, but also releases some cult and independent films.

Empire Pictures – 212-629-3097 or info@empirepicturesusa.com or visit www.empirepicturesusa.com

Excel Entertainment – 801-355.1771 or info@xelent.com or visit www. xelent.com – Specializes in Mormon-oriented films.

Facets Multimedia – e-mail chrisk@facets.org or visit www.facets.org – Primarily a video retailer, Facets also distributes a small number of classic and obscure films itself.

Funimation – pr@funimation.com or visit www.funimation.com – Anime distributor.

Hart Sharp Video – 917-847-2918 or visit www.hartsharpvideo.com – Hart Sharp releases films like *Boys Don't Cry* theatrically through other distributors; it also puts out a substantial number of home video releases on its own.

HBO Home Video – visit www.hbo.com – I've never been able to get on the HBO mailing list because the company claims it is "full." Frankly, I wouldn't bother.

Home Vision Entertainment – 773-878-2600 or pr@homevision.com or visit www.homevision.com – Pumps out a steady flow of foreign, documentary, and cult films on DVD.

Image Entertainment – 818-407-9100 or publicity@image-entertainment.com or visit www.image-entertainment.com – Releases a wide variety of films in various genres.

Kino International – visit www.kino.com – Absolutely hates film critics and won't return your calls or e-mails at all. Don't bother.

Koch Lorber – videomarketing@kochent.com or visit www. kochlorberfilms.com – Handles a variety of classics, often foreign.

Lightyear Entertainment – 212-353-5084 or mail@lightyear.com or visit www.lightyear.com – Portfolio is heavy on music titles.

Maverick – 954-422-8811 or info@maverickentertainment.cc or visit www.maverickentertainment.cc – Distributes urban and Latino films.

Media Blasters – sales@media-blasters.com or visit www.media-blasters.com – Handles anime, cult, and adult titles.

Monarch Home Video – 615-287-4632 or visit www.monarchvideo.com

Monterey Media – 800-424-2593 or visit www.montereymedia.com

New Concorde – 310-820-6733 or info@newconcorde.com or visit www.newconcorde.com – Roger Corman's company, specializing in action and horror.

Olive Films – contact@olivefilms.com or visit www.olivefilms.com – Mostly a DVD retailer; distributes a few of its own titles, like Facets.

Palm Pictures – 212-320-3644 or visit www.palmpictures.com – Releases a steady stream of independent films.

Pathfinder Pictures – pr@pathfinderpictures.com or visit www. pathfinderpictures.com

Picture This! – 888-604-8301 or info@picturethisent.com or visit www. picturethisent.com – Primarily gay and lesbian films.

Plexifilm – 718-622-5757 or media@plexifilm.com or visit www. plexifilm.com – Releases documentaries.

R2 Entertainment – 503-276-4094 or bberry@respond2.com or visit www.respond2entertainment.com – Reissues classic television programs.

Shout! Factory – press@shoutfactory.com or visit www.shoutfactory. com – Primarily releases music and enthusiast titles.

Showtime – visit www.sho.com – Distributes the network's original programming on DVD.

Spanner Films – press@spannerfilms.net or visit www.spannerfilms. net – UK company that specializes in human rights and environmental documentaries.

Strand Releasing – 310-836-7500 or strand@strandreleasing.com or visit www.strandrel.com – Home video company also does some theatrical distribution.

Subversive Cinema – 206-524-4851 or visit www.surbversivecinema. com – This new outlet distributes heavy-duty horror and experimental films.

Tartan Video – visit www.tartanvideo.com

TLA Entertainment – 215-733-0608 or press@tlareleasing.com or visit www.tlareleasing.com – Specializes in gay and lesbian films.

Vanguard Cinema – info@vanguardcinema.com or visit www. vanguardcinema.com – Puts out a steady stream of independent and Spanish-language features.

Ventura Distribution – visit www.venturadistribution.com – Operates a number of subsidiary specialty studios, including UrbanWorks and Studio Latino.

Woodhaven Entertainment – 818-882-3073 or visit www. intermediavideo.com/woodhaven.html – Offers a strange collection of children's, specialty, and martial arts videos.

Xenon Pictures – visit www.xenonpictures.com

If you come across a company that isn't on this list, use your best judgment in tracking them down. A simple web search will usually give you an e-mail address or phone number for the corporate headquarters. (Try adding "pictures," "movies," and/or "film" to your search criteria if you're getting too many unrelated results.) Online services like Switchboard.com can also help you locate phone numbers if web searches are coming up dry. And as a last resort, you could simply try calling Los Angeles information at 310-555-1212 and ask for any listings under that company's name.

Even more so than other industries, entertainment companies are merging and going out of business all the time. They also move a lot, which means these phone numbers may suddenly become disconnected. When in doubt, call information, or simply check on the web for updates.

You will be helped immensely if you maintain a database of entertainment contacts which you can frequently refer to. Individual contacts come and go, people get promoted and fired, and accounts change hands all the time. That means that when it comes time to request a screener or send a tear sheet, you don't want to have to start all over from scratch with a call to the studio. I have used both Microsoft Outlook and Best Software ACT! to maintain my contacts database (which now runs to several hundred people). Start a database from the very beginning so you won't experience the sizable pain of trying to reconstruct it later.

HOW SCREENINGS WORK

Once you've got the screening invitation, now you have to actually attend the screening. Here's how screenings operate.

Screenings typically take place earlier in the same week that a movie opens. (In other words, most movies are screened for the press on Monday, Tuesday, and Wednesday for films that open that Friday.) Sometimes screenings take place weeks or even months in advance. Just keeping track of screenings can be difficult. I use the same contact management program to keep track of when and where each screening is. In order to attend a screening, you must RSVP for it. The number to call will be listed on the pass you receive in the mail, along with other information about the screening (when to arrive, how many guests you can bring, and so on).

The bulk of screenings occur in the evening, and these are nearly always *promotional screenings*, the same screenings that you might hear being given away as prizes on local radio stations. Promotional screenings offset the cost of the screening for the distributor and help to build word of mouth for the movie. But promotional screenings can be annoying for a number of reasons.

Some publicists reserve rows of seats for the press, and some do not. If you're a member of the press, you're entitled to sit in the *press row*, and the publicist will direct you to the seats or a roped-off area will indicate where the press can sit. When in doubt, ask a publicist: Some roped-off seats will be reserved for "VIPs" (read: your local newspaper critic and/or friends of the publicist), and you'll promptly get kicked out of them.

When you arrive at the theater, you'll assuredly see a long line of people waiting to get in. These are people that won their passes on the radio or, as is frequently the case, people that are on a mailing list to receive passes to every movie that has a sneak preview in your town. *Preview junkies* are a very strange breed, as they appear to have endless patience (waiting for hours in the cold or the rain nearly every day) and an equally endless appetite for movies, no matter how bad they might be. Attend enough screenings, and you'll see the same people in the audience over and over again, often saving multiple rows of seats at a time for their friends and family and hauling in bags full of food from home. Avoid them.

At the typical promotional screening, you need to arrive 30 minutes before show time. Why? Because that's when the regular audience is usually admitted to the theater. Before that time, you'll be able to leisurely find a seat and get popcorn if you're so inclined. Once the regular audience is admitted, the theater becomes madness. If there was no press row saved (as is often the case), you'll be lucky to find a seat in the very first row. As well, people start jumping into

189

the press row, and eventually the publicist will give away those seats to the stragglers. All told, you're far better off arriving 30 minutes ahead of time. If you know you're going to be late, speak to the publicist and explain your problem. He or she *may* reserve a special seat for you and your guest. (Passes typically admit two people, unless noted.)

Also note that you do not have to wait in the general admission line. Simply enter the theater normally and try to find the publicist (if you don't recognize her, she's the person with the clipboard). She will typically check your name against the RSVP list, then usher you in. If you can't find the publicist, ask the usher. If he tries to get you to get in the line, explain that you're with the press and you need to find the publicist for the screening.

Eventually you'll find a seat and the movie will start (usually after some comments from the radio station sponsor and a t-shirt giveaway or two), and you can watch the film like you would at a normal screening. Congratulations: You're watching your first free movie!

The minority of screenings are *press-only screenings*. Typically these happen during the day at a local theater or a *screening room*, which is a very small theater located somewhere in your town. Most press-only screenings occur during working hours, so if you have a day job these will probably be out of bounds for you, unless you use sick and vacation time judiciously. You do not need to arrive early for press-only screenings, nor are there reserved seats. If you have the ability to attend them, the relaxed pace and lighter time commitment of a press-only screening is highly recommended. Plus, there's just something to be said for being one of a handful of people in a theater screening a movie: If nothing else, it's far quieter in the audience.

Occasionally, a film will screen on Thursday night before opening on Friday. This is a cue that the film is not going to be very good; distributors arrange for Thursday screenings because they know newspaper critics won't have time to write a (bad) review before the newspaper is printed for the following morning. But they still want coverage, just at a later date, after a (hopefully) strong opening weekend.

With the rise of the internet, the Thursday screening has become less effective, since internet critics can publish their reviews whenever they want. As a result, studios have been moving toward not having screenings at all for their worst movies. Again, this is a sign that the movie in question is terrible and doesn't even have the faith of the studio behind it. It's hard not to pre-judge films based on the time of their press screenings, but do your best if you end up reviewing them. In the end, the movie will speak for itself.

PUBLICIST ETIQUETTE

As much as writers like to complain about them, publicists are key people for getting our jobs done. More importantly, they're people, too: Treat them respectfully and they'll return the favor.

The job of a publicist is largely an organizational one, so to stay on their good sides, you should do everything in your power to aid that organization.

Meet deadlines. Screening passes note specific deadlines for RSVPing, along with the specific time when you should arrive at the theater. Don't mess up either one or you'll risk falling off the press list.

Send tear sheets and/or links. This is a real must. Publicists are tasked with gathering up reviews of the movies they're representing and sending copies of the reviews back to the studio. The studios analyze the reviews (for whatever reason) and use them in the marketing campaigns, and so on. The publicists have too much to do to track down the reviews individually: It's up to you to send them a copy of your review once it is published. In the print world, these copies are called *tear sheets* (reflecting the fact that you tear pages out of a newspaper or magazine). For online reviews, you can simply e-mail a link to the publicist. I often fax a printout of the web page instead, but links work just fine.

Yes, you even have to send a tear sheet for bad reviews. However, I don't always send a tear sheet for some negative reviews of home video releases, especially direct-to-video releases or films that we're reviewing weeks after they were released. No one ever seems to mind if the film has already been out for a long time.

It's especially important for your website to send tear sheets to any independent filmmakers whose movie you review. Why? Because if you ask nicely, they'll probably link to your review from their website. That's a free link for you and great publicity for your site, since the filmmaker will likely be expending considerable energy promoting his film through the internet. Big studios won't link to you, of course, but the little guys will usually be happy to – especially if you ask them to do so.

Be polite. Say please and thank you – all the time.

EMBARGOES

Embargoes are restrictions against publishing reviews of a movie before a certain date. Semi-officially, *every studio has an embargo policy*: Reviews should not be posted before midnight the day a movie opens. Failure to comply with this policy by posting reviews earlier than that will likely get you banned from screenings (see the next section). Paradoxically, you should note that very few publicists will explicitly state an embargo policy, unless you ask them for one. And if you do, you'll be told that no reviews can be posted until Friday.

Why do studios embargo reviews like this? Sadly, it's due to the power of weekly magazines like *Time, Newsweek,* and *Entertainment Weekly,* which are only published on Fridays. Each of these magazines boasts large audiences of millions of readers, and as such they have substantial power in the publicity world. Over the years, they have strong-armed the studios into a policy that puts them on equal footing with daily newspapers and the internet, which can publish at any time. Hence, the studios try to ensure that every review of a movie lands on the same day out of "fairness" to the weeklies.

Why is this policy a problem for you? Mainly because by waiting to post your review, you are missing out on traffic that you'd otherwise be getting. Posting early has significant advantages. The first reviews of a movie posted often get the lion's share of the traffic. After a movie has been out for a week, traffic to that review drops considerably. Even after opening weekend, traffic will begin to fall off. (This isn't to say that archive reviews aren't important – I still regularly get letters for films I reviewed in 1995 – but since most of your traffic will come from current releases, you will always want to be as timely as possible with your postings.)

Meanwhile, if you are sitting on a completed review, you'll feel the frustration that other sites are gleefully breaking the embargo policy and posting their reviews early. Gossip sites openly violate this rule by publishing reviews of test screenings months before a film opens – and yet they have Hollywood eating out of their lap! But if you post a review a week early, you'll feel the wrath of that very same studio and their local PR reps.

Is this a double standard? You bet it is. Is there anything you can do about it? Not really. Take your anger and refocus it into your writing.

Unofficially, there is substantial leeway in the embargo policy. Publicists simply can't track every website every day, so generally, the smaller your website is, the more leeway you can get, simply because you will sneak under the radar of the publicist and the studio. But as your site grows, more and more eyes will fall upon it, and eventually the embargo will hit you square in the face (and often through a heated exchange with a publicist).

How you deal with embargoes is a tricky issue that's up to you. Many sites set a time of day and day of the week when that week's reviews are automatically posted. In most cases, Thursday evening is fine. Usually, you can post on Wednesday and not face any sanctions. Filmcritic.com has had a Wednesday-posting policy for several years now (after many years of publishing reviews whenever we felt like it). We haven't received any heat from the studios or publicists for our new posting schedule (though our old one is another story, see below).

In any case, you shouldn't send tear sheets out until late the Thursday night before or the Friday morning a film actually opens. No need to call attention to yourself, no matter when you're posting reviews.

Finally, very rarely you'll be faced with an embargo that says you can't review a film until, say, a week after it opens. Even more rarely, studios will try to enact a "no reviews allowed" policy for a film. I've never honored these embargoes. If it means skipping a screening and seeing it when the film opens in general release, that's far preferable to letting the studio control everything you do.

GETTING BLACKLISTED

Yep, studios will blacklist you (that is, they'll stop sending you screening passes) if you don't play ball their way. The good news is that if you ever merit a spot on the blacklist, that means you've earned enough clout for the studio to care what you think. Even better: Blacklists are invariably temporary. Follow the advice earlier in this chapter for getting back on the press list.

I've seen blacklists applied for two reasons:

1) *Breaking embargoes.* I discussed this above. If you get caught posting reviews too early, you'll usually face a temporary blacklist of a month or two. To get off it, keep reviewing that studios films (yes, you'll have to pay for them in general release) and prove to the studio that you're honoring embargoes by posting at sanctioned times and sending tear sheets afterwards. The easier way to remedy this is to simply honor the embargo from the start.

2) *Writing too many negative reviews.* This is a tricky one. Studios rarely care whether you liked a movie or not, but eventually you're bound to offend someone with one of your more-scathing reviews. Studios will *never* tell you this is why you've been blacklisted – and chances are they won't tell you you've been blacklisted at all. You'll simply stop receiving passes in the mail. Ask the publicist and they'll tell you, "We're reevaluating our press list" or some other excuse. To get reinstated, continue to follow the advice I've outlined in the book: Keep sending tear sheets to the publicist, and ask every month or so if you can be reinstated to the mailing list. Eventually the publicist will relent.

BLURBS

"More terrifying than *The Ring*!"

So reads a large slug of text on an ad for *The Grudge* that's sitting in front of me, along with a nice plug for the author of that movie review.

For some, *blurbs* are a nice perk to the job of a film critic and a fun (if vain) way to get recognition by the general public. They're also free advertising for your publication, of course, and they lend legitimacy to your work. After all, if the studio quotes you, they must respect you, right?

Not quite. Many critics loathe blurbs, and for good reason. First is that they are often taken out of context. The *Grudge* reviewer may have really said "*The Grudge* is more terrifying than *The Ring*, but that's not saying much – I thought *The Ring* was awful!" Or he may have meant the sentiment genuinely. You'll never know, but a good portion of the time, critics find their words twisted into a positive message where one was not previously implied.

Ballsy studios sometimes simply invent quotes wholesale and attribute them to critics who they hope won't notice or whom are so minor that they won't be able to make a fuss. I've even had publicists call me and ask if I can rewrite a review with more positive language. Handling this can be awkward, to say the least.

How do studios get blurbs? They pull them from your tear sheets. Although some publicists will occasionally call critics for a quote they can use on a poster, that's by far the exception to the rule. By and large, the process of getting blurbed is something you'll never come in contact with.

If blurbs are your thing, be sure you don't fall into the trap of being outrageously positive all the time. (I covered quote whores in Chapter 7 and needn't dredge up that sorry subject again here.) It's bad enough to see your name in print on a movie poster next to the fawning thoughts of quote whores, but it's another thing altogether to become one of them. Of course, if you go down that path I'll have failed you altogether.

ACCREDITATION

When you arrive at a screening, how do you prove you are who you say you are? Most of the time just having the pass with your name on it is enough, but in rare cases, you may need to prove you're a member of the press in order to get into a screening – and some studios may require you to become accredited before adding you to their mailing list. This is by far the exception to the rule, as most of you will never have to deal with accreditation of any kind. But when someone does ask you about it, here's what you'll need to know.

Local press cards. You've probably seen pictures of reporters wearing hats with a card reading "PRESS" stuck in the hat band. Press cards like these have become outdated in most locales, as have "press badges," actual sheriff-like metal pins that could be affixed to your clothing. Some cities still offer press cards – check with your local police department and/or city hall, but by and large, a business card will suffice when it comes to getting into screenings and other physical events. If you're brand new to the field, you might also print out some copies of published works, which can be helpful in proving you are who you say you are. (Always bring a photo ID like a driver's license, too.)

Writers organization IDs. If you're pressed for more credentials than simply vouching for yourself with a home-made business card, you might consider joining a professional writers organization like the National Writers Union (www.nwu.org) or the Society of Professional Journalists (www.spj. org). (Numerous other organizations exist; check the web to find others.) Membership fees are usually less than $100 a year and get you other perks like members-only job postings, access to health plans, and other benefits.

Film critics groups. If you're big enough, you might consider applying to your local film critics group or applying to international groups like the Online Film Critics Society (www.ofcs.org). Membership is often tough to achieve, but if you do get in, you'll receive perks like advance copies of movies on DVD at the end of the year, plus the street cred from voting in your group's Best of the Year awards.

MPAA accreditation. Some studio publicists (but never third-party publicists) in the Los Angeles area ask for critics to become accredited by the MPAA in order to be granted access to screenings and press materials. MPAA accreditation has a strange and sordid past: In the 1990s, there was no such thing, and publicists would use the demand of MPAA accreditation to get pesky junior writers off their backs. When the writer called the MPAA, the group would say there was no such thing, and the writer would report back to the publicist, who would claim there was. The cycle would continue until the writer gave up. Cut to today: MPAA accreditation now does exist for real, though how it came to be is unclear. The bottom line is when L.A. publicists demand MPAA accreditation, you can actually go out and get it by sending a letter of introduction here:

Public Relations
Motion Picture Association of America, Inc.
15503 Ventura Boulevard
Encino, CA 91436

The letter should follow the same basic structure and contain similar information as the introductory letter outlined earlier in this chapter.

OBTAINING PRESS KITS AND PHOTOS

In the old days, you'd receive a printed press kit and a packet of photos (prints and a CD-ROM) to use in putting together your review. That doesn't happen much any more: Major studios maintain online websites where they deposit electronic press kits (also known as EPKs) and high-res images for the media to use.

Some of these sites require registration; don't bother registering until your site is up and running, as most will check to make sure you're a legitimate outlet before granting you access. Here's a directory to the major and mini-major online press sites. (Note that registering at these sites will *not* get you on the mailing list for screenings or video screeners; these sites are solely repositories for text and photos about the movies.)

20th Century Fox – press.foxmovies.com, www.foxpressroom.com (for home video), and www.foxsearchlight.com/press (for Fox Searchlight films)

DreamWorks SKG – www.dreamworkspresskits.com

Lions Gate – www.lionsgatepublicity.com

MGM – www.mgmhe-art.com (for home video only)

Miramax and Dimension – www.miramaxpublicity.com

New Line – www.moviepublicity.com

Newmarket – www.nmextranet.com

Paramount – www.phepromo.com (for home video only)

Sony Pictures/Columbia TriStar – www.sonyclassics.com/press.php (for Sony Classics films) and www.cthead.com (for home video only)

Universal Studios – www.ximage.net and www.ushvpublicity.com (for home video only)

Walt Disney Pictures (aka Buena Vista) – www.bvpublicity.com and www.bvhepublicity.com (for home video only)

Warner Brothers – movies.warnerbros.com/pub and www.whvdirect.com (for home video only)

FILM FESTIVALS

Is there a film festival going on in your neck of the woods? This is your chance to get in for free and see a dozen films or more!

Getting press access to a film festival works just like getting access to regular press screenings. As soon as you find out that a film festival will be playing, check the website and find out who the press contact is. Send them an introductory e-mail or call them on the phone. Typically they ask for an introductory letter about your outlet, and that's it.

It's important to do this is early as possible: Film festivals always face the problem of limited seating, and they try to limit the number of press badges they hand out. Avoid the hemming and hawing of a reluctant festival organizer by being at the top of the list.

CHAPTER 11:
EDITING OTHER CRITICS

Perhaps you're sick of having to review *every single movie* that comes out. Perhaps your stack of DVDs has reached the ceiling, with more coming in than you can dispatch with reviews. Or perhaps you've been promoted from writer to editor.

For every critic there comes a time — and it usually doesn't take long — when you have to start editing other writers.

This chapter will explain how to find other critics to help you increase the amount of content on your site without tearing your hair out, plus how to edit their work once they start writing for you.

THE RECRUITING PROCESS

To be honest, I've never had to recruit anyone — they always come looking for me! In the old days, I simply considered applicants on an ad hoc basis, reading their clips and informally deciding if they were good enough writers and if they fit into the style of filmcritic.com.

Today, we've formalized the application process due to the heavy influx of applicants. As a result, we created a simple web page that outlines how to apply. When you're ready to start recruiting, you might model your own applicant page after ours (you can find it by looking under the About Us section on the site). Here's what we request from applicants on that page, which are then voted on by the seven senior members of filmcritic.com:

- Your current resume.
- At least one sample review of about 600 words (published or unpublished — unpublished preferred), preferably of a current release. Please read a few reviews on the site and submit material in the same format, with star rating, etc. Spelling, grammar, and punctuation all count — a lot. Style counts the most — we are looking for critics who match the sarcastic, tongue-in-cheek, off-the-cuff style of filmcritic.com.
- A cover letter outlining your background in film and criticism (i.e. why should we pick you?)
- One-sentence reviews and ratings on our five-star scale for the following films (classics and recent releases alike): *A Clockwork Orange, Brazil, Annie Hall, Mulholland Drive, The Crying Game, Little Nicky, The Lord*

of the Rings: The Fellowship of the Ring, Fahrenheit 9/11, Dancer in the Dark, Heavenly Creatures, and *Y Tu Mamá También*. (You are advised *not* to check our reviews on these films before writing your own — we aren't looking for yes men! We're looking for a sense of your general tastes, your ability to succinctly explain why you do or do not like certain movies, the breadth of your film knowledge, and whether you can follow instructions.) Also send your top 10 list for the most recent calendar year (theatrical releases only) and tell us in general terms about some of your favorite films, directors, and/or actors.

- Finally, please tell us where you live and if you are recognized as a member of your local media (i.e. are you already invited to screenings?).

Asking for all of this stuff accomplishes a number of things. First, it ensures that only serious writers will bother to apply. If a critic hasn't seen the bulk of the movies on the one-sentence review list, he won't apply, and that list represents a decent collection of movies — good and bad, old and new — which lets us know immediately where his expertise and tastes lie.

Most of all, we look closely at the review samples, asking ourselves a number of questions. Does this writer really understand movies? Does he know how to write well? How much editing is he going to need? Does his tone fit in with the rest of the site?

This last point can be a deal breaker. We regularly receive perfectly acceptable writing samples from critics whose style is dead wrong for the lighthearted, vaguely sarcastic, conversational tone of filmcritic.com.

Finally, we get to see if the critic will be able to contribute reviews before they are released, or if he'll be relegated to reviewing only DVDs and the occasional film that we didn't get around to reviewing before it came out. Where the critic lives is also important here, as we give preference to those who live in major metro areas and, thus, have access to more films than those in smaller towns.

CONTRACTS

As discussed in Chapter 8, as a freelance writer, you are asked to sign a contract outlining the rights you're selling to the publication. As an editor or site owner, you will want your writers to sign a contract granting *you* those rights.

Contracts may be intimidating at first, but they're vital for ensuring everyone's on the same page when it comes to publishing stories. If you're syndicating content, you will need explicit resale rights. If you're archiving it permanently, you'll need to specify those rights as well.

The easiest way to do this is to require contributors to grant *all rights* to their stories, or contribute on a *work for hire* basis. This gives the writer no copyrights after he files the review: You own the work and can do with it what you want.

Another tact is to require all rights be sold to you, but you may grant back some rights to the author. This way, you can allow writers the possibility of reprinting their content in other publications or on their personal websites — if this is something you're interested in allowing. You can also specify what kind of publications might be allowed to reprint the content, how long they must wait before reselling it, or set limits on the number of words that can be resold. The key, of course, is that you obtain all rights up front and then re-grant those rights back to the author.

Filmcritic.com uses work for hire due to its numerous syndication agreements, and it has always worked well for us. The entire filmcritic.com contract follows for your perusal. Comments are included after the relevant sections where they might be useful to you. Your contract needn't be this long or in-depth, but make sure you cover all the same points along the way.

Whatever you do, don't fall into the trap of thinking that a handshake or an e-mail is enough to hire a writer. Time passes, memories and hard drives fail, and misunderstandings are rampant. You need to outline specifically what you will be doing with the writer's reviews.

FILMCRITIC.COM

Master Agreement on Contributions

Date: _____

Dear _____:

Welcome to the ranks of filmcritic.com contributors. Please take a moment to read this letter carefully. It sets forth the terms governing your submissions of contributions to filmcritic.com. If you agree to the terms provided below, please sign the duplicate copy of this letter and return it to the undersigned.

1. Scope of Master Agreement; Definition of Contributions:

This agreement shall cover all reviews, articles, and all other contributions submitted by you to filmcritic.com which are accepted or rejected by filmcritic.com on or after the commencement date of this agreement and all ancillary materials. All of the foregoing contributions and ancillary materials are sometimes hereinafter referred to individually as a "contribution" and collectively as the "contributions."

2. Assignments of Contributions:

An editor of filmcritic.com may assign a contribution to you orally, electronically, or in writing. You will use your own facilities and equipment in creating each contribution. The assigning editor must approve the topic, deadline, and fee structure for each contribution. You are expected and required to create each contribution to meet the assigning editor's specifications (objective, length, etc.). Contributions will be considered for publication on an individual basis. Your submission of an assigned contribution shall be deemed acceptance of the terms approved or designated by the assigning editor with respect to that contribution (e.g., terms such as delivery date, which are not specified in this agreement) and shall confirm that the terms and conditions of this agreement apply to such contribution. The terms and conditions of this agreement shall also apply to any unassigned contribution that you may submit and filmcritic.com accepts.

In the above paragraph, we specify that all reviews must be assigned by the editor and that unsolicited submissions will not be accepted.

3. Delivery of Contributions:

Contributions must be delivered complete and in a form suitable for publication. Filmcritic.com reserves the right of final approval of both the form and content of each contribution. Filmcritic.com may adapt and edit and authorize this adaptation and editing of each contribution as it deems desirable. Filmcritic. com may or may not publish a contribution at its sole discretion. If a contribution is not accepted, you are free to seek publication of that contribution elsewhere, though that contribution must not appear to be affiliated with filmcritic.com.

This clause states that we can do whatever we like to the content and can mandate its delivery in the form of our choosing.

4. Payment:

Filmcritic.com pays quarterly via PayPal. We do not pay via any other form of payment. Please note that filmcritic.com will not reimburse you for any expenses whatsoever. All costs associated with producing a contribution, including travel (local or otherwise), ticket costs, concessions, or any other expenses are the sole responsibility of the contributor. Filmcritic. com, at its discretion, may make free film passes available to contributors as a courtesy. These are not to be considered as reimbursement of expenses. Filmcritic.com does not offer any "kill fee." Even if a contribution has been delivered on schedule and you are in compliance with the terms and conditions of this agreement, if the piece is not accepted by the editors of filmcritic.com, for any reason whatsoever, no payment will be made.

Fairly straightforward; here we explain that we don't pay you aside from purchasing the reviews. We don't specify payment here; that's covered in the writer's guidelines and is flexible.

5. Assignment of Rights:

You hereby grant and assign exclusively to filmcritic.com all your copyright and all other rights throughout the world, in all forms and media, whether now or hereafter known, for the entire duration of such rights and any renewals and extensions thereof, in each contribution which filmcritic.com accepts, insofar as any copyright or any part thereof in each such contribution is not considered to vest in or to be owned by filmcritic.com by operation of law. Filmcritic.com may grant you the rights to reprint your contribution at its sole discretion, and on a case by case basis. Any such requests must be made, in writing, to filmcritic.com management.

The critical clause: This states that all work is work for hire.

6. Representations and Warranties and Covenants:
You represent and warrant and agree that:

A. Each contribution will be original and previously unpublished;

B. You will not publish, distribute or otherwise exploit any contribution, in full or in part, in final, preliminary or modified form, or authorize the foregoing, in any media prior to, concurrent with or, except as specifically provided in paragraph 5 above, subsequent to its acceptance by filmcritic.com;

C. You will be the sole author of each contribution except as otherwise agreed by filmcritic.com, your execution and delivery of this agreement will not violate any contractual or other obligation and you have the right to enter into this agreement and to grant and assign all of the rights granted and assigned in this agreement;

D. No contributions will be false and defamatory or falsely disparage any product, service or company or violate or infringe any right of privacy, copyright, or any other rights of any third party or any applicable law;

E. You will not directly or indirectly accept any gratuities or gifts of products or services from any supplier in connection with the preparation of any contribution. You will not accept any royalties, fees or other payments from any third party for any rights or services that may suggest an endorsement of that party's products or services;

F. You will disclose to your assigning editor any relationship with any third party that may create or suggest any conflict of interest (e.g., any relationship with or interest in the manufacturer or a competitor of any product you may be asked to review); and

G. Each contribution shall be free of faults, defects, viruses, worms and built-in time or use-driven destruct mechanisms and will not contain any injurious or damaging formulas, instructions or other material.

Boilerplate absolving our liability for plagiarism and such.

7. Use of Name and Likeness:

Filmcritic.com has the right to use your name and likeness and to publish and distribute information about you in connection with the publication, distribution and other exploitation of all or part of any of the contributions under this agreement and the advertising and promotion of the publications, products and services in which all or part of any of the contributions are included under this agreement.

8. Relationship of the Parties:

As a freelance contributor you are an independent contractor. You are not an employee of filmcritic.com and are not entitled to any employee benefits (such as social security, unemployment or health insurance). No amount will be withheld for purposes of FICA, FUTA or State or Federal tax withholding and you acknowledge that you are solely responsible for paying your estimated and self-employment taxes. We acknowledge that you will have clients other than filmcritic.com and that your services to filmcritic.com shall not take more than a portion of your business time.

The above two sections are more boilerplate, critical for making sure your writers don't file unemployment claims against you and such.

9. Term of Agreement:

This agreement shall commence as of _____ and shall continue in effect until terminated by either party on thirty (30) days notice in writing. Notwithstanding the termination of this agreement, any contribution which is submitted to and/or accepted or rejected by filmcritic.com during the period this agreement is in effect shall continue to be governed by the terms and conditions of this agreement.

Note that even if you fire a writer, you needn't terminate the contract; you can simply stop assigning him reviews and accepting his work.

10. Titles:

As between you and filmcritic.com, any titles/names including designs/logos under which the contributions shall be published, distributed and/or otherwise exploited pursuant to this agreement (the "Titles") are or shall be and shall remain the sole and exclusive property of filmcritic.com. As the owner, filmcritic.com may use the Titles in any form, manner and media, and in connection with any publication, product and service, now or hereafter known, including, without limitation, in connection with any other author's work. Except as specifically provided below, you shall not directly or indirectly use or permit the use of the Titles, or any confusingly similar titles/names, during or after the term of this agreement.

11. Materials and Equipment:

Any material or equipment sent to you as a contributor to filmcritic.com, including, without limitation, videotapes, DVDs, or CDs, remains the property of filmcritic.com or the manufacturer/supplier and may not be used for any purpose other than to assist you to prepare the contribution. You may not use any of the material or equipment for any party other than filmcritic.com. All such material supplied to you must be returned to filmcritic.com, or the manufacturer/supplier as designated by filmcritic.com, at the request of a filmcritic. com editor. Filmcritic.com may withhold your fee if you do not return any material previously furnished to you by or under authorization from filmcritic.com.

12. Miscellaneous:

This agreement is a complete statement of all arrangements between you and filmcritic.com with respect to its subject matter, supersedes all previous agreements between you and filmcritic.com with respect to its subject matter and cannot be changed or terminated orally. All waivers must be in writing. No contribution submitted to filmcritic.com during the term of this agreement may be excluded from the scope of this agreement, unless such exclusion is expressly agreed to in writing and signed by the Editor in Chief of filmcritic.com. In addition, if you confirm in a subsequent writing, whether at the request of filmcritic.com or otherwise, that any particular contribution is governed by the terms and conditions of this agreement, the absence of such a written confirmation with respect to any other contribution shall not be construed to mean that such other contribution, or contributions, is not governed by the terms and conditions of this agreement.

This agreement shall be governed by and construed in accordance with the laws of the State of California applicable to agreements to be made and performed in California. As used in this agreement, "filmcritic.com" shall be deemed to include filmcritic.com, Christopher Null, and its successors and assigns. As used in this agreement, "affiliate" shall mean any entity (including, without limitation, divisions) directly or indirectly controlled or owned by or under common control or ownership with filmcritic.com, or which directly or indirectly owns or controls filmcritic.com.

You'll want to use your state here.

Filmcritic.com may assign this agreement or its rights under this agreement, in full or in part, in connection with the sale or other transfer of trademarks and/or other intangible property or all or substantially all of the assets of filmcritic.com or any of its affiliates and may license or sublicense its rights under this agreement, in full or in part, at any time. As the copyright owner, filmcritic.com may freely assign the copyrights, and the rights composing the copyrights, in full or in part, in the contributions. Filmcritic.com may (but is not obligated to) file any and all documents necessary to register copyright (and otherwise protect its rights) in the contributions. You agree to sign such documents and take such further steps as may be reasonably requested by filmcritic.com to further the purposes of this agreement and hereby name and irrevocably constitute and appoint filmcritic.com, with the full power of substitution as your true and lawful attorney-in-fact during and after the term of this agreement, couple with an interest, with full irrevocable power and authority in you place and stead, and in your name or filmcritic.com's own name, from time to time to execute such documents, including, without limitation, any assignment documents, and take such steps.

If you sell your site to someone else, this gives you the right to transfer ownership of reviews and this contract to the buyer.

If any provision of this agreement is invalid or unenforceable, the balance of this agreement shall remain in effect. If any provision of this agreement is inapplicable to any person or circumstance, it shall nevertheless remain applicable to all other persons and circumstances. The headings in this agreement are solely for convenience of reference and shall not affect its interpretations. You agree that your rights and remedies in the event of a breach of this agreement shall be limited to your right to recover damages, if any, and in no event shall you be entitled to enjoin the publication, distribution or other exploitation of any edition or version of filmcritic.com or any other publication, product or service which includes all or part of any contribution.

Any provisions of this agreement which by their terms or sense are intended to survive the termination of this agreement, shall survive the termination of this agreement.

Any notice to filmcritic.com shall be addressed to the Editor in Chief of filmcritic.com, 123 Main Street, San Francisco, CA 94001, or such other address as is specified by filmcritic. com by notice to you. Copies of notices regarding the breach, interpretation or termination of this agreement shall also be sent to filmcritic.com's Legal Department at the same address. All notice shall be delivered personally or sent by registered mail, return receipt requested.

Please sign, date and return the duplicate copy of this letter to indicate your acceptance of this agreement.

Respectfully,

FILMCRITIC.COM

By: _____

Title: _____, filmcritic.com

Accepted and agreed to by:

Author: _____[your signature here]

Date: _____

SS#: _____

Address: _____

_____

_____

E-mail: _____

Phone: _____

Critics are not given any assignments until a signed copy of this contract is received and filed.

PAYMENT

Many film sites don't pay their writers simply because they can't afford it, but legally it's a good idea to offer some kind of compensation for your critics, even if it's minimal. Not only does cash compensation motivate writers to keep at it in the hopes of someday making more, it is also important to satisfy the idea of *consideration* to make your contract valid.

Consideration is essentially something you give the other person in return for them giving you something, in this case, a movie review. If you ever were to end up in court (and with a contract, that's unlikely), you need to prove that you were giving the writer something in return for his writing. If he isn't getting anything out of the deal (and "we'll publish your work on our website" rarely counts), chances are you're going to get burned.

How much to pay? That's up to you, but understand you're competing with people who pay nothing, so you needn't be extravagant. Most sites that do pay offer $20 or less per review, usually far less. You could also offer per-word rates of one or two cents per word written.

Another common tactic is to offer merchandise in exchange for a review. This is common with DVD reviews: You review a disc, we'll let you keep it for free. Many critics see this as the equivalent of earning $15 to $20 for a review, but because so much on DVD is not worth watching, many critics shy away from reviewing the bulk of the DVDs; they'll only want to review the movies they're interested in keeping.

In a pinch, you could also offer a t-shirt or other promo merchandise, but this gets into a tricky consideration issue, as most courts won't consider your t-shirts to be very valuable.

Finally, appropriate IRS recordkeeping is another concern when you pay your critics. Under the law, if you pay one of your freelance writers $600 or more during a calendar year, you must file a 1099 form with the IRS and send a copy to the critic (though you need not withhold or pay any taxes). If you find yourself paying each person $600 or more, it's best to consult with an accountant to make sure you're fulfilling the tax requirements in full.

WRITER'S GUIDELINES

Writer's guidelines are the companion piece to the contract. While a contract addresses the legal requirements of the site, you can use an informal writer's guidelines document to address common questions like how often and how much writers get paid, whether you italicize titles or put them in quotes, and other style questions.

Writer's guidelines can be a repository for just about any question you find yourself being asked, and you will likely find yourself updating and redistributing them frequently. Here is a small portion of filmcritic.com's writer's guidelines, which is currently a 10-page document:

A publicist wants to read the review (or interview) before we run it.

The answer is unequivocally *NO*. We do not offer any sort of approval system. This occasionally comes up regarding embargoes: So if you want to hint that a good review is a positive one so they'll let us run it early, that's fine. But in no circumstance should a publicist be allowed to see the actual review before it appears on the site. *Ever.*

I want to review *The Wizard of Oz* and *Citizen Kane.*
That's great. I encourage you to do so. We often put up non-current or archived releases, and are doing much more of this now as many oldies are being released on DVD. This happens more often than you'd think, so please ask me if you want to review something that I haven't asked for specifically. These are considered on a case by case basis. Of course, be sure you search the site to ensure the movie you've chosen hasn't already been reviewed. And also be aware that we don't simply put up a review for whatever you decide you want to write about.

I saw a test screening of an unfinished film, or a bootleg. Can I review that since I'll be the first one to see it?
No. We categorically do not review films at test screenings or via any other surreptitious method (one critic actually asked me if he could review a bootleg VCD). This is what the gossip sites do, and we are *not* a gossip site. Don't do it. Don't try to pass off one of these reviews as legit, either. Doing so will result in immediate dismissal.

I got approval from you and I just saw a new release, a new video, or a sneak preview of something. How long should I wait before turning in my review?
Don't wait! Once your review is in, it's going to run for sure. If you wait, someone could sneak in before you! Also if you take too long, I may not buy it.

But note that if you submit sloppy work, your review may be rejected and will neither appear on the site nor will you be paid for it. And then you'll get the boot.

You get the idea.

WHO SHOULD YOU ASSIGN A FILM TO?

Surprisingly, it's rare at filmcritic.com for more than one of our contributors to ask to review the same film. When it does happen, it's for very popular movies that everyone wants to see. How do you "break the tie" when multiple writers want to review the same movie? Here are a number of suggestions:

- **Seniority**. The longer a writer has been with the site, the more likely I am to let him review the movie over a more junior critic.
- **Expert insight**. Does the writer bring some special knowledge about the subject that might make his review more insightful and interesting? A degree or special training? If the movie is based on a book and the critic has already read it, that counts, too.
- **Predisposition**. I try not to give reviews of films like *The Passion of the Christ* to either die-hard atheists or born again Christians. Likewise, I look for political moderates to review Michael Moore screeds, and so on.
- **Fresh blood**. Is the writer someone who doesn't contribute much to the site but who I'd like to see more from? Fresh blood can be a good thing.
- **Timeliness**. Can one critic file a review earlier than another critic? This gives you more time to edit it and — if one critic isn't seeing the film in advance of release — can be a deal breaker.
- **First come, first served**. Finally, you can always default to this simple rule: Whoever asked for it first gets to write the review.

THE EDITING PROCESS

A library full of books has been written about the editing process, and novice editors are advised to check one or two of them out, as the full intricacies of editing are beyond the scope of this book.

Still, here are the most crucial things you should be looking for in the reviews you edit. By making sure each review you publish contains all of these elements, you will continue to develop your skills as an editor. Of course, by no means should you consider this list comprehensive.

- **Completeness of analysis**. Are all the standard elements of a review there? The plot summary, substantial analysis of acting, direction, story, and supporting elements? Does the review have a good lead and a solid conclusion? Most importantly: Are there big questions that audiences will be asking about this film that aren't answered in the review? You can't review a *Star Wars* sequel without drawing comparisons to the original.
- **Accuracy**. Does the writer have his facts straight? Are all the names spelled

correctly, and is he identifying the characters with the correct actors? Use IMDB to check, but remember that IMDB isn't always right, especially on obscure films.

- **Structure**. Does the review flow well, from lead to summary to analysis to conclusion? Or if the writer is utilizing a more complicated structure, is it working right? Editing for structure can be very time consuming, so try to hire writers who already have a good understanding of how structure works.
- **Grammar**. This is just good English. Are the sentences complete, not full of fragments and run-ons? Are the commas in the right places?
- **Tone**. Does the review match the tone of the site or the publication on the whole? And does the tone of the review fit the tone of the film? Not only does it not make sense to review a G-rated movie made for young girls and fill the writing with overblown language and expletives (unless you're making an elaborate joke), it's irresponsible and turns off the likely reader. Still, all reviews — whether the film is rated G or NC-17 — should fit the overall tone of the site.
- **Cadence**. Read the review out loud. Does it *sound* right? Cadence is the absolute toughest part of both writing and editing, and it can only be developed through years of practice. Keep at it.
- **Is the grade right?** This is actually the number one reason I return a review to a writer. He's written a positive review and given it a negative grade, or vice versa. Usually they change their mind and tweak the grade up or down when pressed for a more reasoned opinion. Remember: The final grade should always be supported by the text of the review.

In a nutshell, reread the first seven chapters of this book, and apply the lessons to the work you're editing as if it were your own.

COACHING JUNIOR WRITERS

New writers require help, and lots of it. If you're willing to take a chance on a newcomer, you should be commended, but realize that bringing in a green writer will result in long hours sitting in front of the computer.

To ease the pain of editing, it's critical to give feedback to the writer with every review. Use the "track changes" feature in Microsoft Word to show the writer exactly what you changed, and explain why in an e-mail or telephone call. Be supportive but firm. Over time, the writer should learn from the editing process and his work should improve measurably until it gets to the point where it requires only minimal editing to be ready to publish. If the work does not improve, perhaps that writer simply isn't cut out for the trade.

The downside is that grooming a writer can take years, and after you whip them into shape, they tend to quit for greener pastures (and better pay). I unfortunately don't have the time to give this kind of attention to a new writer any more and now recruit only writers who are fairly polished, but I genuinely commend those who do. Good luck!

CHAPTER 12:
FILM CRITIC ETIQUETTE

You want to be a film critic? Better be ready to act like one.

HOW TO BEHAVE IN THE PRESS ROW

Screenings of late have become run by paranoid studios convinced people are out to copy their movies. Bag searches, pat-downs, and metal detectors are common, so don't take anything to the movie that you won't need during the screening. (Some outlets even confiscate cell phones until the end of the film.)

This means no bags or backpacks, no computers, and definitely no cameras of any kind. Bringing a camera to a screening is probably the quickest way to get yourself banned from the press list and the theater for life — and possibly even arrested!

After you get in, find the press row and feel free to sit in it. I often sit outside the press row in the regular seats, mainly because if there is no publicist monitoring the seating, I don't want be the one who has to have to play policeman to keep the regular attendees out of the press row.

Be polite and cordial, and don't bring more than one guest unless you have cleared it beforehand. Don't talk during the movie, and, of course, *turn off your phone*!

When taking notes, be discreet. Some critics use a lighted pen or a handheld computer, but this is often a distraction to those around you. I have learned how to scribble notes in the dark — or I'll wait until there are "bright" scenes on the screen that illuminate my pad of paper.

HOW TO HANDLE OTHER CRITICS

It's a sad fact of life that many critics are blowhards you would be afraid of running into outside the safety of the movie theater. Don't be one of them. Here's how not to be despised by your peers.

- **Don't talk about movies before the movie**. Running through a list of films you've recently seen, expounding on what you liked and didn't like, inquiring about what other critics are going to see next: These are all topics that no one around you wants to discuss. There are other topics of conversation: If you must say something, keep it off the subject of movies, something that most critics already spend far too much time thinking about.

- **Don't spoil anything**. If you *must* talk about movies, whatever you do, don't give anything away to the other critics, who may not yet have seen the film that you want to blather about. I knew one critic that didn't want to hear anything — including opinions — about a film for fear of coloring her own thoughts on it. When one such opinion was offered, she would plug her ears and make loud noises like a child. Scary.
- **When in doubt, shut up**. God knows you don't want to make yourself look like an amateur next to seasoned professionals.

SCREENER ETIQUETTE

Screeners — DVDs provided by the studios as a courtesy — are a carefully controlled product. For obvious reasons, studios don't want copies of their movies being distributed online, and illegal duplication of screeners can make this all too easy.

Strictly speaking, you may not share screener DVDs with anyone, ever. Screeners can't be given away, sold, auctioned on eBay, or even disposed of. The legalese on a screener DVD almost always notes that it is the property of the studio and must be returned on request. While this rarely happens (the studio will tell you in advance if it wants the disc back), it's important to note that DVD screeners carry with them no legal rights. Don't think you can get away with copying a screener: These are encoded with serial numbers (sometimes they're invisible to the naked eye) and are coded back to the original person they were sent to. This has led to stiff penalties for people caught selling screeners or even giving them away to friends.

In practice, however, it's OK to give away a screener of a film after it has been out on DVD for several months. By then, any piracy taking place will occur with the shipping version of the DVD instead of the screeners, which carry warnings and don't have all the special features that many DVDs contain. Studios won't be actively looking for pirated screeners by this point, and pirates won't bother copying them.

The other exception to the no-selling-screeners rule is when you receive an actual retail copy of a DVD from a studio instead of an advance screener. (Screeners are clearly noted as "not for resale" and usually don't carry bar codes and have promotional or temporary packaging.) While this is sometimes debated among film critics groups and some studios discourage the practice, retail DVDs can be given away after the DVD has been released to the public. It's best to wait two or three months before doing this as a courtesy to the studio — and so you stay in their good graces.

TRACKING YOUR REVIEWS AND CONTACTS

In the beginning, you'll have no trouble keeping track of what movies you've reviewed and what you haven't, but after a couple of years and a few thousand reviews, you won't be able to remember whether you covered the 1998 film called *The Best Man* or the 1999 one — and what the difference between the two might be. Devising a system to track the films you've reviewed is critical for any large-scale operation. At filmcritic.com, I use the database for this purpose, but smaller operations might not have such technology at their disposal.

If you're building pages one at a time, consider a folder hierarchy that divides your films into logical groups so you can find the reviews easily. You might organize them alphabetically, dividing them into folders representing the first letter of each film's title. Or you could organize them into folders by year released. Whatever you come up with, do it early and stick with it. It will be an incredible pain to reorganize your reviews after you've got 1,000 of them festering in an incoherent mass.

You'll also need a system for keeping track of studio contacts. I use Microsoft Outlook, the same contact management program I use to keep track of screenings and release dates. Again, tracking one or two publicists is a snap, but now I have some 200 publicists listed as contacts, and those contacts tend to change once or twice a month as employees come and go from the various agencies.

The takeaway: You're going to forget stuff, so prepare for it up front.

BURNOUT

Walter Chaw of FilmFreakCentral.Net wrote eloquently on the subject of burnout in his review of the appallingly bad *Cold Creek Manor*:

> Conservatively speaking, I'm going to see something like four hundred films this year and write reviews for about three hundred of them. That's somewhere in the neighborhood of "too many" and "much too many," and it's fair to wonder at some point along the way if my point of view is becoming colored by fatigue, too many disappointments, too many deadlines, and the sort of imperious condescension to lackluster product that begins to feel a little bit like hate. You get into this business because you love movies, you love talking about movies, and you love criticism wielded with responsibility – and then sets in the sobering realization that maybe the experience of going

to movies might be permanently degraded by the experience of going to every movie and, worse, being forced to think about and contextualize all of them in a larger perspective.

It may sound funny and even a little sad, but burnout is a real problem with film critics.

No matter how much you love movies, eventually you will find yourself getting home from your tenth atrocious film screening in a row. You'll start putting it together in your head that, with travel time and writing, you've wasted two full days of your life on something that isn't even remotely paying the bills. In fact, you've hated every minute of your life during that time.

You wouldn't be the first critic who wanted to quit. Or who *did* quit. It happens all the time.

Fighting burnout is something that ultimately has to be addressed by the individual. There's no magic formula that will keep you interested in film during a particularly bad spell of junk movies. But I can offer some advice that has worked for me:

- **Take a break.** Take a week off. Or just skip the teen horror movie (or something else that just plain looks like it's going to be bad). Or go see it and write a one word review: "Crap!" Do something to throw a wrench into the usual routine. Your mind will thank you, and your real fans will understand.

- **Go part-time.** If you're running a one-man show where you're the sole critic, you probably won't last more than three years (unless you're getting paid well). Hire someone else to review all the junk movies you really aren't interested in. Chapters 8 and 9 explore how to do this more fully.

- **Review at home.** Ask for screeners, or review DVD releases for a while instead of theatrical releases, if your outlet permits it. Much of the headache of reviewing movies isn't sitting through a bad film, it's spending an hour in travel, another half hour waiting for the film to start, sitting with an obnoxious radio promo audience, paying for parking, and missing dinner, all while seeing a bad film. You can skip all of those except the bad film part if you can convince your local publicist to send you a DVD or VHS screener of a new release. (Never mind what they say, these almost always exist.)

- **Write shorter reviews.** If it's the writing that's getting you down, cut your word count. Going from 500 to 250 words can make a major difference in the time you spend writing up a review. Remember it's perfectly fair to let the length of the review fit the importance of the film. Does *Freddy vs. Jason* merit more than 250 words of "analysis" anyway? Why waste your time writing a long review that won't be read? If the hassle of actually polishing a write-up is a problem for you, this tactic can be invaluable.

- **Ask for a raise.** You won't get one, but it's fun to ask.

- **Have more fun with your writing.** You're seeing bad movies? Write nasty reviews! Writing a really biting review is one of the most fun and gratifying parts of film criticism. Remember that sarcasm and insults aren't just enjoyable for you: You're providing a service by helping moviegoers avoid spending money on rotten movies. So dish it up!

THE PERSONAL COST OF FILM CRITICISM

Film criticism sounds like the greatest job in the world, but it comes at a severe personal cost. Remember when you were a kid and couldn't wait to see the next *Star Wars* or James Bond movie? When the movies were a magical experience you couldn't help but love? Well, if you take film criticism seriously, watching movies will become *work*. Enjoyment will be second to your critical eye, and even if you aren't reviewing a movie, eventually you'll find it difficult to just sit back and take in the experience. You'll find yourself making mental notes about what you would have said, and the whole experience will be vaguely tainted.

It's hard to believe, but it's true. Time takes its toll on any serious critic; if you want to run a gossip or fawning fanboy website, you can avoid this effect, but it happens to most of us sooner or later.

This cost, of course, is mitigated by the substantial rewards of criticism (the free movies, the depth of experience, and more), but before you embark on a career in the movie review trade, it bears serious thought. If you can, talk to a few seasoned critics and ask them how they feel about their jobs. They'll always tell you it's the best in the world, but for some, the loss of "that feeling" is an incalculable cost.

CHAPTER 13:
HANDLING YOUR OWN CRITICISM

Nothing draws hate mail quite so much as a movie review with which someone disagrees. Film criticism requires a thick skin; here's how to get it.

DEALING WITH READER MAIL

I don't have to tell you how to respond to fan mail: Just eat it up and say thanks!

But it's a scientific fact that about seven out of 10 messages writers receive from readers are hate mail. So no matter how smart your reviews are, expect to get hate mail from those who read them. In fact, you should relish it: The more hate mail you get, the more people you know are reading your reviews and the more seriously they're taking your opinions. Note that nearly 100 percent of hate mail is from people who liked a movie that you did not; you'll receive very little mail about positive reviews (even from those who hated the film). I can't explain it, it's just something about human nature.

How do you deal with hate mail? The best and easiest thing you can do is this: *Nothing*. Don't respond, don't acknowledge the letter, don't start a debate. Ignore it completely and move on. Most hate mail (especially the really profane stuff) is meant to provoke you and nothing else. The writer typically has no goal of engaging you in a thoughtful debate, they simply want to tell you you're an idiot because you hated their favorite Pauly Shore movie. If you respond, that's great for them, because they can call you even more names the second time around.

If you get a letter that's not laced with profanities, you might elevate to a stock response. Here's one I often use when I've panned a movie that other critics have rated well (like *Spider-Man 2*):

> I know the world has embraced this movie, but frankly, I just didn't see it the same way. I'd like to think that readers would rather read an honest opinion than another writeup that simply falls in line with the conventional wisdom. Sorry we don't see eye to eye on this, and I hope you'll give us another shot in the future.

> Christopher Null
> filmcritic.com

The goal here is simple: Defuse the situation, try to explain that this is merely one man's honest opinion, and try to get the writer to come back for another stab at the site. A few letter-writers simply want their voices heard; they write letters to all manner of publications, and they patronize the ones that are listening, even if they disagree. I've had good luck turning dozens of these letter-writers into faithful regular readers of filmcritic.com, even though many of them seem to disagree with every word we write.

A few years back, Jeremiah Kipp and I digested the archetypes of our most common hate mail letters, then wrote how we typically respond. I'm including this story mainly for your amusement, but there's also a bit of practical knowledge contained here, as our stock responses can become the basis for your responses to angry readers.

> We get lots of mail from readers. Some of it is fan mail. Lots of it is incoherent. And tons of it is hate mail. "How can you give my favorite movie 2 stars!?!?!" "How can you disrespect some dead artist!?!?!" "You're stupid and I'm never coming back!"
>
> Well, okay. Thanks for sharing.
>
> So one day, New York Bureau Chief Jeremiah Kipp and I decided to provide our responses and commentary to some of the most common flaming hate mails we receive in response to negative reviews. Enjoy.

> **Why don't you try and make a better movie!?**

> **CN:** Oh this is my *favorite* type of hate mail! And I have a standing offer: Give me the same budget as the director got for whatever movie I panned and I will deliver you a superior product. But please, if you are going to send this kind of message, be sure to include a check.

> **How can you live with yourself saying such mean things about [insert actor/actress/director]? If they read your reviews, they'd be heartbroken! You crush the creative spirit! Do you know how much people risk emotionally to put their work out there?**

> **JK:** Honesty is the best policy, isn't it? If an artist came up to

me an asked what I thought of their film, I'd tell them point blank — and in my correspondences it has often opened up a much-needed dialogue between the artist and the critic.

I would hope critics don't go into things rubbing their hands together saying, "Whose creative spirit am I going to crush today?" Though, to be fair, someone has to tell Sylvester Stallone to cut the crap. He hasn't been making as many movies, so obviously he must have listened. You may have noticed that Robin Williams did a career rerouting, too.

Frankly, someone should be telling this stuff to the filmmaker *beforehand*, though I don't see anyone stepping up to the plate and questioning George Lucas's artistic vision. Money talks, doesn't it? Until they start changing their system around, I see no reason to stop criticizing their fallacies. To paraphrase a Sam Shepard play, we're looking for themes and all we're finding are theme parks!

CN: As Jeremiah alludes, believe it or not, filmmakers often do read our reviews and we've had some lively conversations with them. You get the occasional whiner, but by and large even if we pan a movie, the filmmaker is far more civil in his response than the moviegoer who thinks he's sticking up for his hero.

For mainstream movies: "Don't you ever just go to the movies for fun, you heartless ass!?" Paradoxical corollary for art movies: "You aren't supposed to enjoy this movie! You're just supposed to think about it! It's life-changing!"

CN: Sure we do, I just find it hard to have fun in the presence of cheeseball mediocrity like *Goldmember*. You see, jokes have to be *funny* or else we can't laugh. A fat suit and a couple of sex jokes just don't cut it.

JK: It's too bad most films have a limited idea of what "fun" is. I mean, "Wow, when the kid kicked that fat guy in the balls, that sure was *fun!*" Give me a break. Yes, not every movie has to be a grand philosophical achievement. But what folks need to remember is it takes a brain to be entertained! You're actively involved when you laugh. The idea that you have to shut your mind off to have fun is a popular, and stupid, fallacy. I had boatloads of fun with the *creative*, really audacious vulgarity of *Blazing Saddles* and *Kingpin*.

CN: As for the other side, some readers confuse a director's *desire* to make a life-changing movie with his *ability* to do so. Just because a movie aspires to be profound doesn't make it so. I humbly suggest that your closeness to subjects like the plight of the Kurds (*A Time for Drunken Horses*) and the Armenian holocaust (*Ararat*) might be coloring *your* opinion of the quality of the films.

Don't you know that Ebert and 100 other critics loved this movie? You're the only one who didn't give it five stars! You're stupid!

CN: Why are you here if you've read 100 other reviews? Are you just trolling for something to complain about because you need to have your voice heard?

That said, I'm saddened to inform you that many film critics are like cattle. They just go with the conventional wisdom, which is how pap like *Gladiator* ends up as Best Picture. We rarely follow the conventional wisdom at filmcritic.com, and we think that's what makes the site great. But just because we don't agree with a bunch of hacks doesn't make us wrong — it makes them wrong. Similarly, we don't respect the work of the ridiculous gossip sites, anonymous reviews, or "quote whores" like *The Movie Minute*, all of which praise everything as The Greatest Movie Ever!

JK: I've sometimes been accused of being contrary to the mainstream because I want to rack up my cool points, but that's not true. I really do believe *Black Hawk Down* is a nefarious, racist, and inaccurate piece of propaganda. *Monster's Ball* was a bland filmmaker's excuse to shoot an elaborate sex scene. *Requiem for a Dream* was all about its sleek surface, and never thought about what's under the skin. Those reviews pissed a lot of people off, because I didn't go with the herd in praising them. But I stand by everything I wrote. Who needs 100 party line opinions anyway? If anything, a different and unique review might shed some new light on a film. Even if you walk away still loving those horrible movies (you poor sucker), hopefully you have a clearer idea of why.

CN: The same argument goes for the "This movie made a bazillion dollars and you think it's bad? The people will prove you wrong!" Since when do "the people" know anything!? That's why we're here, to help them avoid making a terrible mistake in wasting their money on stuff like *Bad Boys II*, one of the top grossing films the year it was released. The sad truth is that most people will eat whatever is spoon-fed to them — in real life and in the world of cinema — but if we can keep *one person* from seeing *The Mummy Returns*, we're doing some good.

You can't review this movie unless you've been in the army/ are a woman/have one leg/etc.! You are ignorant on this subject matter and should not write about something unless you've read the book/done in-depth research on the subject/ lived for 10 years as a Bedouin/etc.

JK: Let's return to *Black Hawk Down* (there's no escape from it).
   A motion picture is not a historical treatise. If you want the non-fiction account of what happened, go read Mark Bowden's book. Once you translate that to film, it becomes something else. When I'm reviewing *Black Hawk Down*, I'm considering the cinematic aspects of it — and what those represent. Quite simply, *Black Hawk Down* fails as a story, as a visual experience, and even as a representation of history.
   I have not been in the army, but observing whether or not *Black Hawk Down* works in a dramatic medium doesn't necessitate my army experience any more than traveling to Mars affects my viewing of *Mission to Mars* or *Red Planet* or *Ghosts of Mars*. I wasn't aboard the Titanic, nor have I been in a shipwreck, but I can damned well tell you that *Titanic* was a disjointed narrative, the characters were pencil-thin sketches,

and the spectacle overwhelmed the sentimental pap humanity.

A foundation in movies and how they work is the tool for evaluating those films, not an expertise in the character's jobs or lives. Think about it.

CN: Let me also point out that we are film critics, not book critics or cultural commentators. I review 400 to 600 movies a year, and I work full time as the editor of another magazine. Suffice it to say that I don't have time to read the source material every movie is based on. Much along the lines with what Jer said, "reading the book" should not be a prerequisite for reviewing a movie. In a perfect world, that would be ideal, but ours, alas, is a world with Pauly Shore.

Who are *you* to say this movie stinks!? (i.e., What are your qualifications as a film critic?)

CN: Well, for starters, who are you to say it's good? Suddenly you're qualified to review a movie or critique a film critic just because you know how to send an e-mail? You can't have it both ways.

Personally, I believe that anyone with a basic understanding of cinema, a thorough history as a moviegoer, an ability to write well, and an intellect that's at least average can become a superior film critic. Hardly any film critics have been to film school. Most didn't go to journalism school, either. But few people agree on what "qualifies" anyone to be a critic. Case in point: In 1999, the venerable *New York Times* replaced retiring film critic Janet Maslin with its second-string critic, Elvis Mitchell, and a former *book critic*, A.O. Scott!

So what qualifies anyone to be a film critic? Depends on who you ask. Ebert lambasted the choice of Scott, asking "Has he seen six films by Bresson? Ozu?" Jesus, has *anyone* besides Ebert? How relevant is Ozu anyway when you're trying to say something coherent about *A Night at the Roxbury*? But I digress. I'll play that game: As for my qualifications, I've reviewed over 3,000 movies for countless outlets since 1995, and I've seen 16 films by Fassbinder and eight by Makavejev.

224

(As a side note, Ebert has since played kissy-make-up with Scott and counts him as a dear, dear friend. I guess that little outburst didn't look to good, huh?)

How *dare* you ridicule dwarfism, the holocaust, and the U.S. armed forces? What kind of sadistic, communist heathen are you?

JK: Yeah, we're such jerks. Maybe it's the movie that's being ridiculous, facetious, or simplistic. How about them apples?

CN: Or maybe we're being sarcastic. If you can't take a joke, you shouldn't come to our site.

Have you ever heard of the saying, "If you don't have something nice to say, don't say it?"

JK: Yeah. Have you ever heard of the saying, "Honesty is the best policy?" Besides, I'm not writing these reviews to coddle the artists (though, as I said before, a critic-artist dialogue can be useful whether you love or hate the movie). It's written for the audience that has to shell out the increasingly high prices for movie tickets. I would counter that statement with a smarter, more productive one: "If you don't have something *useful* to say, don't say it."

If you don't like this kind of movie, don't review it!

JK: What "kind of movie" is that? It can be just as valuable to trash something you know to be insidious or stupid as it is to praise something you cherish.

CN: This complaint usually comes up when a male critic trashes a "women's picture" like *Anywhere But Here* or that *Ya-Ya* movie. In general, we try to admit in the review when certain subject matters (the plight of the single mother is a typical one) fail to hook us due to cultural or genetic circumstances, but that alone doesn't let a movie off the hook. Some movies are just plain bad (like *Star Trek: Nemesis*), and they try to hide behind their devoted niche audiences — who will accept whatever pabulum they are served as if it's caviar — in a vain attempt to become critic-proof. And we are just not that dumb. You are, for buying into it.

(We also got the reverse complaint when an Asian female reviewed a Martin Lawrence movie. She was called out as a racist simply for quoting Lawrence's own dialogue!)

In the end, a movie needs to stand on its own merits regardless of who's reviewing it. If we only send to any given movie a critic who's sure to love it, what would be the point of that?

You didn't understand it!

CN: If I didn't understand it, then it's crap. But chances are I *did* understand it, and what I understood was that it was crap. If I *really* didn't understand it (*Lost Highway* comes to mind), then it's *really* crap.

JK: That movie is great. Chris, you obviously didn't understand it! *(laughs)*

CHAPTER 14:
REVIEWING DVDS AND VIDEOS

I covered how to get on DVD screener mailing lists in Chapter 10, but I wanted to add a few more words about the unique challenges of reviewing for the home video market.

WHY IT MAKES SENSE TO REVIEW DVDS

Reviewing DVDs, for starters, is much easier than reviewing theatrical releases. First, you can work in the comfort of your own home, so you don't face the drive, the parking, the long waits, and the thick crowds of the movie theater. I figure I save an hour and a half if I review a film on DVD instead of in the theater. That's substantial. You can watch an entire second film in the time wasted reviewing a movie in the theater. Assuming you are watching a screener DVD, it's also much cheaper, as you don't spend money on gas or parking.

Why not review all your movies on home video? Because the bulk of traffic you get will go to theatrical reviews. This makes sense: Most people will read a review when a movie comes out in the theater, even if they don't go to see it. They won't need another review when it comes out on DVD.

Still, there's a good market (about one-third of filmcritic.com's traffic) that heads for DVD reviews regularly. So it makes sense to serve that market.

The best news is that if you reviewed a film theatrically, you already have 99 percent of a DVD review. Some sites put a lot of effort into analyzing video and sound quality and detailing all the extra features on DVDs, but my experience hasn't shown that readers care much about that except in the case of a few highly anticipated films, like the *Lord of the Rings* movies or the original *Star Wars* trilogy. People just don't care if *Garfield: The Movie* has deleted scenes and a commentary track. Who can blame them?

Your approach to covering DVDs will depend on your outlet. If your site is focused exclusively on DVDs, you will want to spend more time analyzing extra features and bonus materials, in part because your competition will be doing so, too. If, like filmcritic.com, your primary focus is on theatrical reviews, you can get away with a sentence or two outlining the DVD features, or with saying nothing extra at all.

KEEPING UP ON NEW RELEASES

It's simple to keep track of theatrical release dates: Any number of internet sites will tell you what's coming up in the next few weeks, from IMDB.com to Yahoo Movies.

Keeping track of DVD release dates is tricky, as fewer sites keep tabs on them and because they are constantly changing. Here's what I use to plan DVD coverage:

- *Home Media Retailing* magazine. This is a weekly publication you can get for free at www.hive4media.com. It's a very helpful magazine that, each week, provides info on new VHS and DVD releases, re-prices, and other news about the industry. You'll also learn a lot about the video business by reading the publication.
- *IMDB at imdb.com/recommends/all.* This site goes into extreme detail regarding each week's DVD releases, including classic reissues and special TV edition releases. Unfortunately you only get the current week, the site doesn't have information on future releases.
- *Billboard at www.billboard.com/bb/charts/videos/dvd.jsp.* This page provides top DVD sales for the current week; we use this to update the top selling DVDs on the home page of the site. It doesn't provide any info on upcoming releases, however.

In a pinch, you can also use filmcritic.com as your source of upcoming DVD releases. Click the "New on Video/DVD" page, which contains releases covering the upcoming one or two weeks plus six weeks into the past.

REISSUES

One of the big tricks with DVD reviews is that, in their quest to squeeze every last penny out of each title, the studios keep reissuing the same DVDs. Some reissues are simple re-prices, but often a studio will put out a DVD multiple times, each one containing more special features than the previous one. *The Lord of the Rings* trilogy is famous for this: First the theatrical edition would be released, then six months later a director's cut would hit store shelves. I've seen three different versions of *Dr. Strangelove* on DVD over the years, each one with an extra featurette or retrospective piece.

The good news is that reissues give you the opportunity to reissue your reviews, too. Every time a new edition of a DVD comes out, we re-run our review of it on the home page of filmcritic.com. I don't do repost reviews for reissues when it's just a price change, but if the disc offers new extras, we always put up a fresh review. Make sure you update any merchandising links appropriately: If you're running a review of a DVD you need to make sure you're selling the new disc (in addition to any older versions, if you're so inclined).

THE PARADE OF MEDIOCRITY

Getting on DVD mailing lists creates one unfortunate by-product: Getting on straight-to-DVD mailing lists.

Believe it or not, soon you'll be receiving — unsolicited — more movies than you can dream of reviewing, and most of them will be awful. This is known as the parade of mediocrity, among less-flattering terms, in the filmcritic.com world.

What do you do about it? For starters, you have to be a little picky when you review a movie. If a studio sends you a direct-to-video disc that was released three months ago, starring Dolph Lundgren, what's the point? No one's interested in the movie, and no one's going to read your review. Why waste your time? Your stack of movies to review will help you determine where you draw the line, but use your best judgment: Remember that the bigger the film, the bigger the level of interest there is in it. Review the major releases and interesting smaller pictures, and then look at any oddities and question marks you have in your stack. Feel free to skip the dregs. Trust me, your brain will thank you.

CHAPTER 15:
CELEBRITY INTERVIEWS

One thing that inevitably comes along with writing movie reviews is the opportunity to interview the stars and directors involved with the movies. Interviews and profiles can be good traffic drivers to your website, but they do consume a lot of time and require a different set of skills to produce well. Here's what you need to know.

OUR PLACE OR YOUR PLACE?

Publicists set up interviews in two ways: They bring the stars to your town, or they bring you to their town.

For the new critic, seeing a movie star when they come to visit your city to promote their film is probably the only option you'll hear about. (Or you might get a telephone interview, which is functionally the same thing.)

When celebrities come to town, your publicist will let you know. Often interview opportunities will be noted on screening passes, or the publicist may simply call or e-mail you with an invitation. Typically interview timing is set several weeks in advance and usually takes place at a local hotel (either in a conference room or in a guest room; I've also done interviews in the lobby on numerous occasions). If you're interested in participating in the interview, just inform the publicist. If there's room to accommodate you (the bigger your outlet, the more likely you'll get the interview), she'll slot you in for a meeting, either a one-on-one interview or a roundtable seat, discussed below.

Interviews are usually 20 to 30 minutes long.

The other option, which you'll hear about as your outlet grows in size, is the *junket*. In a junket, the studio brings you to the talent instead of the other way around. Yes, this means they fly you to Hollywood or New York (usually), put you up in a hotel, and feed you, often for a whole weekend. During this time, you're at the mercy of the studio: You'll watch the film, then you'll be subjected to numerous interviews with the cast and crew. Junkets are a bit tricky, because they're designed to force you to like the movie and be predisposed to writing positive coverage. In a nutshell: You're being bought. As I've mentioned earlier, there's a small industry of critics who write nothing but good things about movies simply so they can go on one junket after another.

If you recognize the co-opting nature of junkets you can try to work around the subconscious effects they will have on you, but in such a claustrophobic environment it's difficult to do so. Many critics refuse to attend junkets on these grounds — not to mention that they're an enormous waste of time — so don't feel bad if you decline an invitation to go on one.

If you can sit through it, the film *America's Sweethearts* (2001) takes place during one such junket. It's an awful movie, but it does at least show you how the process works.

ROUNDTABLE VS. ONE-ON-ONE

Stars only have so many hours in the day — especially major ones that are heavily in demand — and with dozens of press outlets wanting to interview each star, they make do by lumping smaller press outlets together into one en masse interview called a roundtable.

A roundtable is exactly what it sounds like: You and eight other critics sit around a table with one movie star; each of you has time to ask one question, maybe two. The result is a disjointed bunch of questions that don't interrelate at all, and it can be difficult to craft a feature out of it. (See the Bob Zmuda interview below for an example.) I no longer attend roundtables, as I find they never lead to very good interviews, but for novice critics, they can be a good proving ground to help get your feet wet, not to mention the only option you may have.

NERVES

At your first few interviews, you'll probably find yourself quite nervous at the prospect of meeting a major celebrity.

This is normal, so simply find a way to deal with it.

First, recognize that movie stars are just people and they're just doing their job by talking to the press. After they talk to you, they're going to work out, take a shower, eat dinner, and go to sleep. They're anxious to get back home. They hate doing interviews because they get asked the same questions by everyone. In a nutshell: They are very bored.

Now, why would you be nervous talking to someone who's bored? Remember, it's *their* job to impress *you*. Convince yourself that you're just having a conversation with an old friend. It's best when an interview comes off sounding this way.

WHAT TO ASK

Ah, the tricky part. What you ask a celebrity depends entirely on who they are and what you want to know. Even if Kevin Bacon is promoting his latest film, you might want to explore his past work to find out how he reached the current point in his career. It's up to you, but here are some tips that can guide you along the way.

- **Do your research.** Figure out what you're going to ask well before the interview. Most publicists will require that you see the film the celeb is promoting before allowing you to talk to them. So take notes and write your review of the film before you go to the interview. Research the artist's past works and watch any of his older films if you can. How did the celeb get from point A to point B? Look for clues, then ask them if you're right.

- **Don't pry too far into private lives.** Most celebrities will turn cold if you start to sound like a stalker.

- **Don't ask too many questions about the current film.** Because really, no one is going to care that much about just one movie. There's only so much mileage you can get out of a single film, anyway. Interviews are much more interesting when they take into account the entire body of work of the artist and place the current film in context. Your interview will have more longevity, too, if it covers a broader range of topics.

- **Get the good quotes.** This is what it's all about: Dig the good quotes out of your subject. If they don't answer a question, or answer it in a boring way, ask it again but using a different wording. Juicy quotes sell stories.

- **Don't ask stupid questions.** "What kind of tree would you be?" Little chit-chat like this is fine for Barbara Walters, but it's painful for most of us.

- **Cut out the junk and the boring parts!** Even if you're doing a transcription in Q&A style, don't be afraid to cut out the boring bits. Chances are it's going to be too long anyway: Most readers don't want to read more than 1,500 words or so of celebrity schmoozing.

- **Edit at will.** Lead with something interesting, just like you would do with a review. Conclude with a good quote. Develop a flow along the way so you don't leave your reader so bored he quits reading.

- **Write down your questions in advance.** It's not cheating!

- **Use a tape recorder.** Common knowledge, but often forgotten. If you're doing a telephone interview, you can get an adapter that hooks up to your phone for about $10 from Radio Shack. Always ask if it's OK to use one before you turn on a tape recorder, whether in person or on the phone.

- **Don't forget a photo.** Your interview will look much better if you grab a quick picture.

- **Have fun!** This is the most important point: If you and your subject aren't enjoying yourselves, the interview won't be fun to read.

SAMPLE INTERVIEWS

Below you'll find three interviews I've done over the years, in a variety of formats. Different interviews lend themselves to different formats, namely Q&A vs. narrative style. Examples of each follow.

The following interview was the first celebrity interview I published on filmcritic.com. It's a little rocky in parts, but on the whole I still think it's a very interesting look into the life of one of cinema's most notorious characters, Russ Meyer. At the end of the interview, Meyer (who died in 2004) told me I did a great job, and I'll never forget those words. For format, I chose narrative because a Q&A didn't really work based on the line of questioning, as the interview was cut together from various sections of our discussion.

Russ Meyer, 1995, by Christopher Null

"It's just a lot of hard, sweaty work. And I love it."

Director Russ Meyer is blunt and vocal about what it's like on the set of his movies. The controversial visionary behind such films as *Mondo Topless, Supervixens,* and his classic *Beyond the Valley of the Dolls,* Meyer is just as straightforward when discussing the Hollywood power game, censorship, modern cinema, and even his love life. At the age of 73, the filmmaker makes no apologies for his past, embracing the success of his films as he basks in the fortunes they have earned him.

Quite proliferate in feature "skin flicks" from roughly 1959 to 1979, Meyer's 1966 film, *Faster, Pussycat! Kill! Kill!,* considered by many to be his best work, is now in theatrical re-release.

"I made a ton of money," he tells me. "I'm sitting here, looking out at the marvelous hills of Palm Desert, overlooking an azure blue pool that's heated to the temperature I want. I have my editing facilities here. Tall, tall ceilings.... I own a lot of water under Palm Desert... millions of gallons. So if people get mean to me, I can turn their water off."

Meyer started down the road to success while working in film and photography at the tender age of 12. Since then he has directed, written, produced, edited, and/or photographed over 20 motion pictures, often collaborating with long-time friend Roger Ebert, whom he likens to W.C. Fields. One of his first big successes was the film *Vixen*, made for $47,000 and grossing over $25 million. Meyer adds, "That's when tickets were only 80 cents.... And I got all the money."

Meyer may be a legend of a filmmaker, but he's an even better businessman. Not only does he have the ability to create a sharp-looking, pure-profit film on a shoestring, but he also has what he describes as "a kind-of shrine in Los Angeles," where he has three people hawking t-shirts, soundtracks, and videos.

Meyer himself considers his masterpiece to be the sex-and-violence-fest *Beyond the Valley of the Dolls*. Much of the world does, too. As Russ says, "It plays resoundingly, with loud noises and a big box office." Co-written with Ebert, Meyer describes the film as a labor of love. "We went to the mountain and made the film at [20th Century] Fox. It was a big success. That's the important thing: How many asses you get on the seats in theaters. That's it. Money talks. That's the acceptance of a film."

I may not be an expert on the films and philosophy of Russ Meyer. I don't think anyone really can be. But, the more Meyer flicks you watch, the more you start to believe that each film is part of a grand design — one hilarious running joke inside Russ's head. Every now and then you can catch a glimpse of the punch line: that Meyer's art is in giving people what they really want to see. Russ has the cash to prove that, by now, he *knows* what that is. In his own words: "Tits." Case in point:

Meyer recently completed a few videos of two of his "big girls ... hugely breasted women," Pandora Peaks and his fiancé Melissa Mounds. As he describes them, they're "videos to get you through the night." Not porn, mind you. "Documentaries." Girlfriend Melissa was apparently quite the rage at the Moscow Film Festival. After screening her films, Russ says, "I had to caution her all the time when she'd get up on stage, [telling her] you can't take any rags off because Siberia's not too far away." God bless America.

The mention of Siberia is something Meyer can relate to, having suffered through years of censorship and persecution from his critics in the Bible Belt. He says, "The Baptists and the sheriffs in the underbelly of the United States were getting on films that had nudity in them. So that's where I changed over and did *Motorpsycho* — no nudity whatsoever, just action — and it played in the drive-ins. And in fact, Texas was at the top of the heap of busting films." To this day, the city of Long, Texas, still has a copy of *Mudhoney* locked up in a depository. For Russ to get it back, the city insisted he declare it pornographic and obscene. He refused.

Faster, Pussycat! was the follow-up to *Motorpsycho*. Surprisingly, it was one of his few flops. Now, the film has been "discovered by the feminist ladies around the United States," as Russ says, and has a devout cult following. Obviously this was unplanned. Asked about his vision for the film, Meyer tells me, "I just figured I wanted to make a lot of bucks. I wasn't beating any drum. I made a movie with three bad boys [*Motorpsycho*]. It did real well. And I did one with three bad girls, and it thumped...." His explanation: "People didn't understand the lesbian aspect, as subtle as it is."

Right now, Russ is working on a new project, involving still photography of some 16 of his "big girls" in fashion magazine-style poses, wearing (as best they can) "the Godzilla sizes" of designer clothing. It's Russ's version of the fashion world, mocking its traditional use of women "built like hoe handles." The idea is to film the photo shoot and then intercut the action with scenes from his best films in a chaotic, *Pulp Fiction* style. The title? Well, today, he's calling it *Beyond the Valley of Pulp A Go-Go*, and Russ smells success all over it. "I think it might make a very good film... we've got about 90 pairs of tits."

And don't think Russ is just some callous exploiter of women.

All this is coming from a guy who can't stop talking about the most important woman in his life: his mother, Lydia. "I owe everything to her. She was a very special lady." Russ goes on to tell me that after her husband ran off, she was the one that took care of him and brought him up. He speaks of Melissa as if she's a jewel. It's very touching, and just when you think he has the sensitivity of a prison warden, you see that at heart, he just really, really loves women.

I asked Russ what he thinks about modern cinema. The answer: not much. He likes Clint Eastwood and Mel Gibson, but otherwise he's pretty non-plussed. He puts it simply and plainly, "I don't go to films. I just expect people to go to mine." You'd better. The way things are going, he may control *your* water supply next.

I've always had a crush on Alicia Witt, and as such, I think it led to my most engaging and fun interview. Witt is a natural interview subject, and Q&A format worked out well on this feature. Still, the interview lasted more than 30 minutes, so pieces of it had to be excised to keep it to a reasonable word count.

Alicia Witt, 2000, by Christopher Null

It's funny, but the very *last* thing you expect when you knock on the door of Alicia Witt's hotel room is that Alicia Witt will actually answer it.

Meeting the stunning 25-year-old star of TV's *Cybill*, *Urban Legend*, *Mr. Holland's Opus*, *Cecil B. DeMented*, and the new *Playing Mona Lisa*, a journalist couldn't ask for a more congenial subject than Alicia Witt. Patient with this reporter's star-struck sickness and candidly honest to a degree rarely seen in Hollywood, the talented Miss Witt reveals herself to be superbly charming, a little bit nuts, and every bit the brainiac she adamantly claims not to be.

In an old interview of yours you are quoted as saying, "I'm much more dirty minded and insane" than your character from *Urban Legend*. Explain.

That's true. I didn't have very much in common with that character. That movie... was basically a genre film. It turned out to be not that great of an experience. There was a lot that I wanted to do with the role... but that wasn't what the producers were interested in.

Yeah, but what do you mean by "dirty minded"?

I don't consider myself to be a quote-unquote good girl. I'm not prim and proper and polite. I'm very honest, and I love talking about sex, or people's deviances. I love psychology. I like listening to or talking about any personality traits that are unusual. That's what I like about acting.

My wife is a redhead and we have an ongoing discussion — a mutual agreement, really — that redheads are inherently crazy.

I think they are.

Why is that?

They seem to be much more bipolar. I don't know that I'm actually bipolar, but I definitely have huge mood swings, and I'm definitely passionate about the way I feel. I'm not really lukewarm one way or the other.

We see you in a lot of small and independent movies but also a lot of big ones. And you're always at the Hollywood premieres, dressed to the nines. What's you opinion of the big versus the small?

I like to play any character that allows me the freedom to explore it and teach the audience something they didn't know, and show them a journey they identify with ... or be inspired, or moved. Anything that touches someone's heart is important for me.

Do you think *Mr. Holland's Opus* is a good example of that, in a big-budget movie?

I do. Because I know people [like those in the movie], having been trained as a classic pianist. And my father was a junior high school teacher. I know that scenario happens. That people start out with dreams, they work hard towards them ... Mr. Holland is an aspiring composer and he ends up teaching at a high school for 30 years. He never leaves. And that story is so true.

I have to ask about one of my favorite movies of the 1990s and that's *Fun* [a semi-true story about a pair of murderous

teenage girls who kill an old woman "for fun"]. Why am I the only person who ever saw that movie?

I don't know! I'm very, very proud of it — my first sort-of lead role.

I looked at some stills from the movie last night and you look like a little kid.

I was a little kid!

How old were you?

Um ... I was 18 ... I would love for *Fun* to be more readily available. We shot it in eight days. It was such an intense experience, I didn't have time to get out of character at all. I felt like I was going crazy at night when I went to bed, because I *was* Bonnie. I couldn't leave Bonnie's skin.

Our dressing rooms were detention center cells. The prison scenes were all shot at the Los Angeles Detention Center for Youths in downtown L.A. — really horrible neighborhood — and I saw all the prisoners in their orange jumpsuits, which meant they had killed someone, and they were all looking at us pretending we were prisoners and they hated us for that. It just felt like we were making a documentary. It didn't feel like a real film.

I've read a lot about how you were a child genius and you were super-brilliant...

[Alicia shakes her head cynically. She's heard this one before.]

Hey, I've seen you on *Jeopardy!*

That's *Celebrity Jeopardy!* That doesn't really count. [Genuinely bitter.] It doesn't.

So where does the acting bug come from?

I think it comes from being fascinated with human nature, and I love performing. I love the social aspects of making a film. There's nothing like the bonds you make when you're working with someone that closely for a period of a few months.

Or eight days.

Or eight days. [Laughs.] I didn't make any bonds on that movie, in fact. I didn't have time.

There's just something amazing about [acting]. It's a great life! It gives you so much freedom. You can write and read and play the piano ... and pursue other things. And plus you get to be all these people. You get to explore psychoses without actually going nuts.

My favorite scene in your new film *Playing Mona Lisa* is when you show up in front of the guy's door with the "Yes!" signs all over yourself, a kind of desperate attempt to throw yourself at him. But to me it doesn't seem like something a woman such as yourself would need to do to "get a man." Do you really identify with the character?

I completely identify with her! Well, not any more. But it was very similar to what I was like when I was younger. The dichotomy between being very advanced in a professional sense ... but in my personal life, not knowing how to handle myself, not knowing how to be around guys. I used to get unbelievably goofy. I had that sort of jubilant excitement when I went out with a guy I liked a lot. I think I scared off some people because I seemed like such a nerd.

Do you go online at all?

Definitely. I play internet backgammon.

I play internet Scrabble.

I love Scrabble!

[A long conversation ensues about online games and what a colossal waste of time they are, which won't be reprinted here for the sake of keeping the reader from throwing up. Suffice it to say that if you keep tabs on the Yahoo! Literati tables, you might run into Ms. Witt someday. The Scrabble discussion eventually turns to the topic of vocabulary.]

...at least I'm learning new words.

That's good. I learned the other day what a doucet is.

What's a doucet?

It's a deer testicle.

How'd you learn that?

I found a site on the internet of unusual and sexual terms, and I found a bunch of interesting and bizarre words. One of them is nothosonomia. That's the act of calling someone a bastard.

Did you know you can download an Alicia Witt screensaver online?

I didn't know that. [Laughs.]

Does that creep you out?

Just the fact that it exists doesn't mean anyone actually downloaded it. I can't imagine anyone would actually want one.

My screensaver says, "I want gelato." [She makes a funny voice.] *I WANT GELATO!*

Some more rumors I read: That you enjoy watching porn for laughs?

It's funny.

What is your favorite porn movie?

I don't know any of the names of them. I've mostly seen porn in hotel rooms ... with the five-minute preview. I'll just keep watching, turning off, turning on ... There's one porno I saw in Toronto ... and it involves this really dorky guy, your stereotypical insurance salesman, with a big, pointy nose and big, horn-rimmed spectacles, bumbling his way up the stairs ... and of course, the door is opened by this gorgeous, double-D woman. And within five seconds she's all over him, and of course he has this giant penis. I mean, it's ridiculous. I mean ... those are *funny*. How could anyone get off on that?

[Nervous.] Um, well this is not an interview of me ... Er, so tell me about the gerbil scene in *Cecil B. DeMented*.

It was the most inventive porno scene probably ever filmed for a movie. It's vintage John Waters. I'm just happy that for the rest of my life, I will be able to say that I did a John Waters film and I played a porn star named Cherish who had a sex scene with a gerbil.

Do you think you'll ever work with John again?

I'd love to. He wrote on the inside of my wrap present [a book of Andy Warhol artwork], "You are a member of my gang for life."

John's such a nice guy.

Very nice.

Yet a dirty mind.

Very dirty. A very intelligent man. He's brilliant.

I've noticed a few TV appearances of yours lately, *The Sopranos* and *Ally McBeal*. Are you thinking about going back to television?

I'm not going back. I just did those two shows. I would do another guest-starring role if it was really good. I did *Ally*

McBeal because it was my favorite show. I felt completely star-struck being on the set. I know that sounds silly, but it was the only show I have watched since the beginning, and I call my girlfriends on the phone and we refer to everybody by character name. To be on the set for the first time ... I just felt like a little kid. It was a wild feeling.

Did working with David Lynch so early in your career on projects like *Dune* and *Twin Peaks* shape your expectations of Hollywood?

Well it certainly spoiled me. I expected the directors that I worked with in the future to be as wonderful as he was. I mean, my first movie had the biggest budget ever at its time — $75 million, unheard of in 1983. So, I didn't know any differently. I just thought, "This is the way movies are made."

This next one was of my least favorite interview experiences, and I think it shows in the final product. Bob Zmuda was Andy Kaufman's best friend, and during the release of the 1999 film *Man on the Moon*, Zmuda was offered as an interview subject to the press. This interview was the last time I participated in a roundtable: The questions were all over the map, many of them from the other members of the press were horribly stupid, and ultimately a Q&A format would never have worked for this story. In the end, it came out as a middling interview, which I include as an example of what you might have to piece together if you have iffy content.

Bob Zmuda, 1999, by Christopher Null

"Andy Kaufman asked me on his deathbed to do two things," says Bob Zmuda. "One was to write a book about him, the other was to produce a movie about him. He was scared of being remembered as Latka on *Taxi*. That scared him worse than death."

So Zmuda wrote the book (*Andy Kaufman Revealed! Best Friend Tells All*). Now prepare for Andy Kaufman: The Movie, also known as *Man on the Moon*, which opens December 22.

So who is Bob Zmuda? When you see the film, you'll understand. He was Andy Kaufman's best friend and writing partner (played expertly by Paul Giamatti in the film). He was

Employee #2 in a quiet partnership that got its jollies from playing tricks on an unsuspecting public. He was Tony Clifton (q.v.) from time to time. And after Kaufman's death, he was the creator of the Comic Relief specials, which have raised millions of dollars for the homeless.

On a recent press tour in San Francisco, Zmuda talked about the film, the book, and how Jim Carrey just about lost it trying to get inside the head of the most eccentric comedian the world has ever known.

Zmuda says, "Jim said he would never again approach a role like this. Jim Carrey is the biggest Andy Kaufman freak in the world. If he wasn't Jim Carrey, he could travel the country lecturing on Kaufmanism. He fought to get this role. He was born to play this role."

Zmuda continues, discussing Carrey's preparation to play Andy Kaufman. "Jim said, 'How would Andy Kaufman approach this role?' Jim approached the role just as Andy would have. We shot for 85 days. Jim was only there for 2. The rest of the time he was Andy or Tony."

Who's Tony? As the film explains, Tony Clifton was the anti-Andy. Kaufman, a die-hard Transcendental Meditation guru, health food nut, and all-around purist, had a dark side. That dark side was Tony Clifton, a rotten Vegas lounge singer that looked nothing like Kaufman and fooled people for years. Clifton would smoke, drink, and whore with the best of them, and that was just the beginning of the ruse. The only problem, of course, is that the guy didn't really exist. Says Zmuda, "Andy's contract with Paramount said that Tony Clifton had to have a parking space next to Kaufman's with his name on it, and he had to have his own dressing room."

As it turns out, Tony was quite the character, and the personality had a serious affect on Carrey, too. "One day we were shooting half Tony Clifton, half Andy. Next thing we knew, Andy showed up on the set with a bloody nose, saying he had passed Tony Clifton and Tony punched him out. I don't know if it was real blood, but a real medic was brought in."

It's hard to imagine anyone *but* Carrey in this role, but there was a time when Carrey didn't have it locked down. "*Everyone* wanted to play Kaufman. I was not a believer in the beginning. I thought Nicolas Cage looked more like Andy Kaufman. This was even before *The Truman Show*. Carrey calls me one day and says, 'Bob, will you come over and see my audition tape for Milos [Forman, the director]?' I said sure, thinking this is gonna suck eggs. The tape's not on a minute, and I'm crying like a baby. It was remarkable. He had the role. There was just something about him."

And what about the name of the film, *Man on the Moon*, which is taken from the R.E.M. song of the same name? I had heard rumors that one of Kaufman's hoaxes was that he thought the moon landing had been faked, but apparently that's not so. Zmuda explains the name, "R.E.M. were saddened when Andy died. But that whole thing, 'Is there a man on the moon?' means… is there a card up my sleeve?" Nothing more, apparently.

Still, Zmuda says, "The hoax and the practical joke are lost art forms." But did Andy Kaufman pull one last stunt on his deathbed at age 35? No, says Zmuda. "Andy Kaufman is dead. He's not in some truck stop with Elvis." While Kaufman tinkered with the idea, tells Zmuda, he never brought it up again. "The only thing that *is* odd is page 112 of *The Tony Clifton Story*, a screenplay that Andy and I wrote, that was never made. On page 112, Tony dies of lung cancer at Cedars-Sinai Hospital. Andy Kaufman would die of lung cancer at Cedars-Sinai eight years later. Pretty odd stuff."

But Zmuda does admit, "Had Andy Kaufman lived, he would have faked his death."

And what of that grand last scene, which hints at Kaufman's return? Zmuda describes an encounter with a woman who was begging to know. "'What does it mean? What does it mean?' Look, it's the monolith in *2001*. It's just there. We don't know. And if you have to ask, you really don't get it."

We got it, Bob.

APPENDIX:
300 MUST-SEE FILMS FOR THE ASPIRING CRITIC

The following pages offer a list of 300 "must-see" films, part of your ongoing homework assignment to better yourself as a student of film history. Do you absolutely have to see all 300 of these films before you can write an intelligent review from an informed perspective? Not at all. Will you write a better review if you do? Probably.

Keep in mind these lists are designed with the generalist, modern film critic in mind. In other words, if you intend to specialize in commentary on classic or foreign films or on a certain genre like horror movies, this list will leave you wanting — there's only so much from the last 100 years of cinema that I could jam into the list. In general, I've erred toward more modern releases, since they're more likely to be films you reference in your reviews. As well, I've kept hard-to-find obscurities off the list. Nearly all of these titles should be readily available on home video or DVD.

Still, the list does sample the entire history of film as well as many foreign titles, dating back to 1903 and stretching to Europe, India, and Japan. Altogether, the 300 movies comprise a good primer on some of the best movies ever made, the most iconic films in certain genres, plus a smattering of noteworthy oddities and box office disasters. The idea isn't to give you 300 five-star movies to work with, but to expose you to a base of films that is representative of the history of cinema up to the present day.

I've seen all of these films and, literally, thousands more, and more and more I find myself picking up in new releases little tidbits of homage, inspiration, and downright plagiarism from the films of the past. Lines are borrowed, shots are stolen, character names are referenced. Hollywood gets away with it because it's usually in good fun, but often it amounts to lazy filmmaking. George Lucas has acknowledged that he based the first *Star Wars* series on several films by Akira Kurosawa (among other works), but how many critics mention this in their reviews? Mentioning it doesn't make you write a better review, but it makes your review more authoritative and gives structure to your opinions. It's also food for thought for your readers, letting them take credit for your ideas by tossing off fun facts at parties and, in turn, elevating the level of conversation about film.

Enjoy your viewing time.

THE 300

1984 (1984)	The de facto go-to story for dystopian futures, a clear inspiration for *The Matrix* and other films.
2001: A Space Odyssey (1968)	Kubrick's space opera remains the thinking man's sci-fi film of choice.
The 400 Blows (1959)	One of the first pictures from the French New Wave.
8 1/2 (1963)	In my opinion, Fellini's finest hour, as he moved from Neo-Realism into pseudo-fantasy.
Adaptation (2002)	Self-referential films don't get more recursive and bizarre than this one, which also features a number of great performances.
The African Queen (1951)	A quintessential adventure screenplay; with *Chinatown*, it's one of the most studied scripts ever.
After Hours (1985)	The hysterical and bizarre template for "one awful night" movies.
Airplane! (1980)	The spoof that all modern parodies call back to.
Alien & Aliens	Two excellent sci-fi/monster movies, archetypes of the genre and proof of how sequels can be done well.
All About Eve (1950)	Big studio picture from the tail end of the Golden Age of Hollywood. It got five Oscar nominations for acting, alone.
Amadeus (1984)	Outstanding period drama with excellent performances.
Amelie (2001)	A worldwide sensation; romance and fantasy blend seamlessly.
American Beauty (1999)	Relaunched the suburban malaise mini-genre in 1999.
American Graffiti (1973)	George Lucas directed this solid coming-of-age movie early in his career.
Animal House (1978)	An iconic film that launched National Lampoon's films and the college movie.
Annie Hall (1977)	Woody Allen's best film, and one of the best romantic comedies ever.
The Apartment (1960)	An early template for romantic comedy.
Apocalypse Now (1979)	Coppola took an old story and updated it for modern viewers. Today it's the template for "descent into madness" road trips.
Assault on Precinct 13 (1976)	Scrappy John Carpenter film has heroes holed up in a police station who defend themselves for the entire movie.
Audition (1999)	Easily the best of the new wave of Japanese horror thrillers.
Back to the Future (1985)	You probably grew up on repeated viewings; watch it with a critical eye on the clever plot structure.
Barbarella (1968)	Notoriously shlocky sci-fi against which all bad space operas must be compared.
Batman (1989)	More than just a comic book movie. Tim Burton revived German Expressionism and gave it an American facelift.
Battleship Potemkin (1925)	Oft-referenced Russian classic, though its relevance is muted today beyond its single influential scene of a baby carriage rolling down the Odessa Steps.
Ben-Hur (1959)	The chariot race pioneered today's action sequences and car chases.
Beyond the Valley of the Dolls (1970)	Terrible Russ Meyer sexploitation film. Roger Ebert co-wrote the script.
The Bicycle Thief (1949)	The film that defines Italian Neo-Realism.

The Birds (1963)	Hitchcock turns the innocent into monsters with incredible style.
The Birth of a Nation (1915)	Historically important as one of the first major movies ever made.
Blade Runner (1982)	The high-water mark for science fiction.
The Blair Witch Project (1999)	Pioneered the internet as a viral medium for hyping your film. Fooled many into thinking it was a real documentary.
Blazing Saddles (1974)	One of cinema's best spoofs, featuring perhaps the most surprising ending since *Monty Python and the Holy Grail*.
Blood Simple (1984)	The Coen brothers' first picture and a classic thriller.
Blue Velvet (1986)	David Lynch's best and most accessible work.
The Bonfire of the Vanities (1990)	One of the most notorious disasters of the modern era, a cautionary tale of great books turning into awful films.
Bonnie and Clyde (1967)	Changed everything with its wild depictions of violence.
Brazil (1985)	Classic sci-fi/fantasy and one of the great movies of all time; film critics built up *Brazil*'s audience singlehandedly.
Breakfast at Tiffany's (1961)	Romantic comedy works best when the boy and girl are both losers at heart.
The Breakfast Club (1985)	Proves that teen comedies needn't be idiotic.
Breathless (1960)	One of the best films of the French New Wave.
Bride of Frankenstein (1935)	Probably the best "classic" monster movie, with the most notable hairdo ever.
Bullitt (1968)	Steve McQueen pilots his Mustang through one of cinema's most famous car chases, nearly 10 minutes long.
The Cabinet of Dr. Caligari (1920)	The first true horror movie.
Caddyshack (1980)	Juvenile comedy meets the uptight world of golf. Hilarity ensues.
Carrie (1976)	Gave the world Sissy Spacek and an icon of girls-gone-psychotic cinema.
Casablanca (1942)	Bogart and Bergman's highly influential masterpiece.
The Celebration (1998)	The finest example of Dogme 95 filmmaking to date; it also happens to be Dogme #1.
Chinatown (1974)	Deft thriller mixes thoughtful dialogue and intricate plot with outstanding performances. A screenwriting classic.
A Christmas Story (1983)	Both cult and Christmas film, some TV networks play this movie all day long during the holidays.
Citizen Kane (1941)	Often heralded as the greatest film ever made, and hard to argue with. Orson Welles never made a better film — and never came close.
Cleo from 5 to 7 (1962)	A classic experiment in near real-time storytelling; an interesting New Wave tangent.
Cleopatra (1963)	A bloated and not-great star vehicle that nearly ruined its studio. All big budget disasters owe a debt to *Cleopatra*.
Clerks (1994)	Another watershed indie flick, it launched the rollercoaster career of Kevin Smith.
A Clockwork Orange (1971)	Classic Kubrick, and not for the squeamish. Blends elements of future and present seamlessly.
Close Encounters of the Third Kind (1977)	Consistently underrated, it's one of Spielberg's most humble works.

Colossus: The Forbin Project (1970)	Little seen sci-fi gem is a predecessor to *WarGames*.
Cool Hand Luke (1967)	Paul Newman sears in this rebellious film, and he eats 50 eggs.
Coup de Torchon (1981)	Bernard Tavernier's period piece is universally lauded on many fronts.
Crouching Tiger, Hidden Dragon (2000)	Launched the wire-work kung fu styling that's become so popular (perhaps too much so) today.
Crumb (1994)	One of the great "profile" documentaries in recent years, this one is still a template for perfect structure.
The Crying Game (1992)	One of the great twists of modern cinema, it's a pop culture touchstone.
The Day the Earth Stood Still (1951)	Classic sci-fi, with its inimitable lines of alien language.
Days of Wine and Roses (1962)	The most famous of the small "drunks and druggies" drama genre.
Dead Poets Society (1989)	Robin Williams plays serious to excellent effect.
Deliverance (1972)	The classic road trip gone wrong. Very wrong.
Die Hard (1988)	"*Die Hard* in a_____" has become the shorthand way to describe the dozens of knockoffs this film generated.
Diner (1982)	Launched a number of careers, from Barry Levinson to Mickey Rourke.
Dirty Dancing (1987)	A pop culture reference; hard to sit through, but important nonetheless.
Dirty Harry (1971)	One of Clint Eastwood's most crucial roles.
Do the Right Thing (1989)	Still Spike Lee's best movie.
Dog Day Afternoon (1975)	Bank heist goes badly and turns into a circus; inspired dozens of follow-ups.
Double Indemnity (1944)	One of the most classic film noirs.
Dr. Strangelove (1964)	My personal #1 film of all time, this anti-war satire has stellar performances, expert writing, and spot-on direction.
Duck Soup (1933)	Essential Marx brothers.
Duel (1971)	Steven Spielberg's tense early battle between car and tractor trailer. Harrowing.
E.T. the Extra-Terrestrial (1982)	Impossible to put it all into one sentence. Sci-fi for the family, it doesn't get much better than this.
Easy Rider (1969)	The birth of acid trip as cinema.
Ed Wood (1994)	Probably better to watch this film than *Plan 9 From Outer Space* (see below).
El Mariachi (1992)	Robert Rodriguez's $7,000 action movie remains a record for cheap productions. Deeply instructive.
Election (1999)	Sets the stage for modern high school politics.
The Elephant Man (1980)	Tragic biography of John Merrick, directed tenderly by David Lynch.
The Endless Summer (1966)	Surfing documentaries are experiencing a huge revival; this one started the genre.
The English Patient (1996)	Epic filmmaking on the borderline of going over the top.

Enter the Dragon (1973)	Essential kung fu.
Eraserhead (1977)	Along with *Lost Highway*, one of the most inexplicable films ever made — both are by David Lynch.
The Evil Dead (1981)	A cult classic in the horror genre.
The Exorcist (1973)	An absolute horror classic, pioneered the "possessed kids" sub-genre.
Exotica (1994)	Canadian director Atom Egoyan's works are noted for their labyrinthine plot structures; here's his best film.
Fail-Safe (1964)	Stellar indie about the perils of the Cold War. Compare to *Dr. Strangelove.*
Fanny and Alexander (1982)	Ingmar Bergman's epic Scandi-family drama.
Fantasia (1940)	Disney's famous — and plotless — animated film.
Far From Heaven (2002)	Intriguing homage to the films of Douglas Sirk.
Fargo (1996)	One of the greatest modern noirs.
Fast Times at Ridgemont High (1982)	This coming of age film launched a dozen careers; it remains a classic today.
Ferris Bueller's Day Off (1986)	An extremely quotable guilty pleasure.
A Few Good Men (1992)	Jack Nicholson still gets quoted for this role, all the time.
Fight Club (1999)	Massive head trip meets masterful filmmaking.
Freaks (1932)	A very early scandalous picture, *Freaks* explores, well, circus freaks.
The French Connection (1971)	Widely considered the best cop thriller ever.
Fritz the Cat (1972)	Absolutely awful, this was the first X-rated cartoon and is an exercise in '70s juvenile excess.
Full Metal Jacket (1987)	Kubrick looks at Vietnam.
Fury (1936)	Fritz Lang's thoughtful piece on mob rule is an underseen gem.
Gandhi (1982)	Ben Kingsley's performance is almost too good here.
Gaslight (1944)	Ingrid Bergman gets her head messed with to incredible effect in this taut psycho-drama.
The General (1927)	A canonical Buster Keaton work.
Ghost in the Shell (1995)	If you see one anime film, see this one.
Glengarry Glen Ross (1992)	David Mamet's dialogue is unforgettable.
Glitter (2001)	With *Gigli*, the standard against which dismal failures of the modern age are measured.
The Godfather I & II	Considered to be two of the best films of the modern era, for obvious reasons.
The Gold Rush (1925)	Charlie Chaplin joins the gold rush; comedy ensues.
Gone with the Wind (1939)	Grandiose and lush, it is probably responsible for birthing the TV miniseries decades later.
The Good, the Bad, and the Ugly (1966)	The defining spaghetti western. You already can whistle the score.

GoodFellas (1990)	Revitalized the gangster genre. I think it's overrated.
The Graduate (1967)	Adolescent disillusionment embodied. Also note the soundtrack, which became as famous as the film did.
Grand Hotel (1930)	Greta Garbo is best known for this film.
Grand Illusion (1937)	Classic French anti-war film, often heralded as the best war movie and one of the best overall films ever made.
The Grapes of Wrath (1940)	Investigation into the American dust bowl era is heartfelt and instructive.
Grease (1978)	Spurred a small renaissance in musicals; now a cult classic.
The Great Train Robbery (1903)	12-minute short film represents a major early American film.
Groundhog Day (1993)	Unique structure, plus an excellent piece of character development.
Halloween (1978)	See Jamie Lee shriek.
Hannah and Her Sisters (1986)	Woody Allen's second best movie.
A Hard Day's Night (1964)	Come for the Beatles tunes, stay for the hijinks.
Heathers (1989)	A cult classic farce about teen angst; has inspired numerous imitators.
Heavenly Creatures (1994)	Peter Jackson's greatest movie isn't *Lord of the Rings*, it's this.
Heaven's Gate (1980)	One of cinema's most earnest and roundly despised disasters; original budget: $2 million; final budget: $40 million.
Heavy Metal (1981)	Animation for adults, it's still juvenile and titillating.
High Noon (1952)	An iconic western, with the tumbleweed showdown and everything.
The Highlander (1986)	A guilty pleasure and the standard for swordfight movies.
The Hours (2002)	Skillfully interweaves stories from three different eras, all interrelating.
House of Games (1987)	One of the most intricately plotted noirs of all time.
Howards End (1992)	Ismael Merchant and James Ivory — together "Merchant-Ivory" — specialize in lavish period pieces; their names are a reference point for all other period films.
The Hustler (1961)	The classic tale of billiards and braggarts.
I Spit on Your Grave (1978)	One of the most notorious horror sexploitation films ever; awful and difficult to watch, but critical for understanding the genre.
Imitation of Life (1959)	This version is more powerful than the 1934 original.
The Incredibles (2004)	For my money, it's the best animated film ever made.
The Indiana Jones trilogy	Indiana Jones is one of moviedom's great heroes. Action films have never been better.
Inherit the Wind (1960)	Fascinating fictionalization of the Scopes monkey trial.
It Happened One Night (1934)	Classic, early road trip movie. The first film to "sweep" the four biggest Oscar prizes (Picture, Director, Actor, Actress).
It's a Gift (1934)	W.C. Fields at his best.
It's a Mad, Mad, Mad, Mad World (1963)	The original madcap road trip. Watch for the cameos.

It's a Wonderful Life (1946)	More than Christmas kitsch. Understanding the feel-good picture starts here.
Jacob's Ladder (1990)	Amazingly underrated head trip.
Jailhouse Rock (1957)	Considered to be Elvis's best film.
Jaws (1975)	Birth of the event movie, rebirth of the monster movie, birth of Spielberg.
The Jazz Singer (1927)	The first talkie.
Jean de Florette (1986)	French classic, best experienced with its sequel, *Manon of the Spring*.
JFK (1991)	Best of Oliver Stone's conspiracy flicks.
Jules and Jim (1961)	Truffaut's best work, an epic triangle, and essential New Wave.
Jurassic Park (1993)	The arrival of computer-generated special effects. From here on out, computer effects become as good as reality.
The Karate Kid (1984)	Almost campy, it's a classic for the "crane" stance alone.
King Kong (1933)	The original monster movie is a tad dull, but nonetheless a classic.
Kissing Jessica Stein (2001)	Even though it's on the lame side, this film legitimized lesbian cinema.
L.A. Confidential (1997)	Give it three viewings and you'll pick up the intricacies of the plot.
La Cage aux Folles (1978)	The original *Birdcage*.
La Jetée (1962)	The most influential French sci-fi short film composed entirely of still images you'll ever see.
Lagaan (2001)	Probably the best Bollywood (Indian Hollywood) film ever made; this one's about a cricket match.
Last Tango in Paris (1972)	Brando's notorious sex romp through the City of Lights.
L'Avventura (1960)	Grim and hopeless, it's an indictment on modern society.
Lawrence of Arabia (1962)	Epics in the desert like *The English Patient* got their inspiration here.
Leaving Las Vegas (1995)	Watch how the grim and hopeless main story is balanced by Elisabeth Shue's redemption.
The Lion King (1994)	The modern standard for 2-D animation.
The Lord of the Rings trilogy	When a fantasy movie wins a Best Picture Oscar, it's time to rethink what you know about awards season.
Lost in Translation (2003)	Bill Murray's quiet performance was the standout of the year.
M (1931)	Classic German noir.
M*A*S*H (1970)	Find out why big movies lead to bigger TV shows: This was one of the biggest of them all.
Magnolia (1999)	Another story of interlocking lives — this one never flags through three hours.
The Maltese Falcon (1941)	Bogart's Sam Spade mystery is an icon of film noir.
Man Bites Dog (1992)	Early mockumentary (and well disguised as real) and a cult classic.
The Manchurian Candidate (1962)	The original paranoid conspiracy thriller. The 2004 remake is also great.
Marathon Man (1976)	"Is it safe?" has become one of cinema's epic quotes, it conjures one of the most terrifying torture scenes.

The Marriage of Maria Braun (1979)	Fassbinder's searing look at the end of WWII and how it affected Germany.
The Matrix (1999)	Proved that action films can be smart; spawned a veritable religion of followers. Advanced filmmaking technically by light years.
Medium Cool (1969)	One of cinema's greatest looks at urban tension in the 1960s.
Memento (2000)	Told its story in reverse. Compelling and unique.
Metropolis (1927)	The first true sci-fi film.
Metropolitan (1990)	Whit Stilman's indie look at the preppie scene is tragically underseen.
Midnight Cowboy (1969)	The only X-rated film to win an Oscar. (Alas, it's been re-rated as R.)
Minority Report (2002)	Best sci-fi in 20 years. Underrated and thought-provoking.
Misery (1990)	The best horror film to come from a Stephen King book.
Modern Times (1936)	Chaplin's finest; the scenes of him working an assembly line are classic.
Mommie Dearest (1981)	Rocky film, but an iconic biography. You won't understand "wire hangers!" jokes without seeing it.
Monty Python and the Holy Grail (1975)	One of the best spoofs ever.
Moulin Rouge! (2001)	The movie musical reborn.
My Man Godfrey (1936)	Classic pairing of William Powell and Carole Lombard.
Nanook of the North (1922)	Early Inuit documentary is also a lesson on how selective photography and manipulation can give you the film you want.
Natural Born Killers (1994)	Oliver Stone's violent road trip is one of the only movies to generate a lawsuit due to "copycat" murders. A critical film for understanding how movies affect society, and vice versa.
Network (1976)	Peter Finch's "mad as hell" TV anchorman has become a pop culture icon.
North by Northwest (1959)	Hitchcock directed many films featuring the wrongly accused. This is the best.
Nosferatu (1922)	Pioneering film on many technical fronts; subject of the 2000 film *Shadow of the Vampire*.
Ocean's Eleven (2001)	The remake to the Sinatra original is far, far superior; shows that vanity projects really can be good. *Ocean's Twelve* was a bust.
One Flew Over the Cuckoo's Nest (1975)	Jack Nicholson turns in one of his greatest roles in this unforgettable loony bin picture.
The Passion of Joan of Arc (1928)	Silent film, essential for understanding the era.
Pather Panchali (1955)	Best known work of Indian filmmaker Satyajit Ray.
Paths of Glory (1957)	Kubrick's masterful tale of war and cowardice.
The Philadelphia Story (1940)	Classic mix of Cary Grant, Katharine Hepburn, Jimmy Stewart, and romantic comedy.
The Piano (1993)	Holly Hunter won an Oscar, despite having no lines.
Pink Flamingos (1972)	John Waters' most reviled work, featuring a cross dresser who dines on dog feces.
Pink Floyd: The Wall (1982)	The only rock opera worth seeing.

Pinocchio (1940)	Early Disney feature film, this one has stronger lessons than most.
Plan 9 From Outer Space (1959)	The archetypal choice for "worst film of all time," it has to be seen to be believed.
Planet of the Apes (1968)	Borders on camp, but this monkey movie has become a minor classic.
The Player (1992)	You won't find a more instructive film about the realities of Hollywood.
The Poseidon Adventure (1972)	Another essential disaster movie, this one's got a sinking ship. The sets are fantastic. Shelley Winters, not so much.
Pretty Woman (1990)	This famous "hooker with the heart of gold" story earned a zillion dollars.
The Princess Bride (1987)	A cult classic, some people can quote the whole movie.
The Producers (1968)	Mel Brooks at the top of his game, it also became a smash hit on Broadway.
The Professional (Léon) (1994)	Luc Besson's hitman with a heart of gold is masterfully written and perfectly acted. Besson's best work.
Psycho (1960)	Widely influential horror movie. Killing off your heroine in the first act was unheard of.
Pulp Fiction (1994)	Quentin Tarantino's masterpiece launched a generation of imitators.
Raging Bull (1980)	De Niro's dramatic weight gain continues to be the reference point for actors undergoing major physical changes for their roles.
Rambo (1985)	The sequel to *First Blood* was responsible for launching the "let's go save 'em!" genre.
Rashomon (1951)	A landmark film that has probably inspired more plagiarism than any other. Kurosawa told one short story repeatedly from multiple points of view – in the context of a legal trial – and exposed the hidden agendas of all. "Rashomon-style" should be in the dictionary.
Real Genius (1985)	Stellar and underseen comedy.
Rear Window (1954)	Hitchcock showed you could make a movie without leaving a single room. His main character can't even walk. Much copied.
Reefer Madness (1936)	Designed to scare kids about the dangers of marijuana. A forerunner to today's "message movie."
Repulsion (1965)	Polanski's creepy, claustrophobic thriller — primarily consists of one character in one room.
Rio Bravo (1959)	Excellent John Wayne western, also featuring Dean Martin.
The Road to Utopia (1946)	Bing Crosby and Bob Hope's best "*Road*" movie (they made six).
Rocky (1976)	Pure Americana.
The Rocky Horror Picture Show (1975)	See it at a midnight showing with a live cast backing it up, then you'll understand what a cult movie really is.
Roger & Me (1989)	Michael Moore's best work, before politics got the best of him.
Roman Holiday (1953)	Audrey Hepburn enchants, this is the template for romance-on-the-road films.
Rope (1948)	Here Hitchcock didn't just tell his story in one room, he told it in real time and in one apparently continuous shot.
Rosemary's Baby (1968)	Along with *The Omen* and *Village of the Damned*, it's responsible for making people afraid of little kids.
The Royal Tenenbaums (2001)	Wes Anderson's finest film to date, a quirky look at an even quirkier family.

The Rules of the Game (1939)	A kick square in the pants of the French bourgeoisie.
Run Lola Run (1998)	Three 30-minute "what if?" versions of the same story, set to a blood-pumping pace.
Run Silent, Run Deep (1958)	Perhaps the best submarine movie to date.
Saturday Night Fever (1977)	Gave us Travolta, gave us disco, gave us a decade of bad fashion.
Saving Private Ryan (1998)	Heralded as one of the most realistic war films ever.
Scarface (1983)	A guilty, blood-soaked classic. Pacino chews enough scenery to fill his stomach for a week.
Schindler's List (1993)	Action directors can make heartfelt drama, too.
Scream (1996)	Revived the horror genre in the 1990s.
The Searchers (1956)	Considered by many to be the best western ever made.
Sense and Sensibility (1995)	Unquestionably the best adaptation of a Jane Austen novel.
Seven (1995)	Set a template for thrillers featuring serial killers with a bizarre agenda.
The Seven Samurai (1954)	Kurosawa's most classic samurai movie, its plot would later be stolen by westerns, sci-fi films, and more.
The Seventh Seal (1957)	If you see only one depressing Ingmar Bergman movie, see this one.
sex, lies, and videotape (1989)	Birthed the independent film movement that exploded in the 1990s.
Shadow of a Doubt (1943)	One of Hitchcock's quieter features, but extremely powerful.
Shaft (1971)	This famous blaxploitation film actually won an Oscar.
Shallow Grave (1994)	Friendships sour when a suitcase full of cash gets involved. A unique black comedy.
Shane (1953)	Classic western featuring the iconic white hat and black hat characters.
The Sheik (1921)	Rudolph Valentino was the Brad Pitt of his era.
Shine (1996)	It's magic when classical music and mental illness converge.
Shock Corridor (1963)	Samuel Fuller was a fiercely independent icon of gritty cinema; this is his best film.
The Silence of the Lambs (1991)	Another runaway Oscar success, this one was also a huge crowd-pleaser.
Singin' in the Rain (1952)	Probably the best pure musical of all time.
The Sixth Sense (1999)	Put M. Night Shyamalan on the map and revived the "big twist" mystery.
Slacker (1991)	Another independent classic, this one has no real plot, following some 70 characters for about a minute at a time.
Snow White and the Seven Dwarfs (1937)	A Disney masterpiece, though quite simplistic in animation by today's standards.
Some Like It Hot (1959)	Cross dressing never felt so good.
The Sound of Music (1965)	Much maligned by jaded fun-haters, it's still got some amazing songs.
Spider-Man (2002)	One of the best superhero movies ever.
Spirited Away (2001)	Hayao Miyazaki's animation is inimitable and accessible to both children and adults.

Stand by Me (1986)	One of the most popular and successful coming of age pictures.
Star Trek II: The Wrath of Khan (1982)	The only *Trek* movie you really need to see.
Star Wars (original trilogy)	You've already seen them, but see them again.
Straw Dogs (1971)	Difficult picture, with Dustin Hoffman and his wife attacked by local yokels.
A Streetcar Named Desire (1951)	The ultimate primer on method acting. Watch Brando closely.
Sullivan's Travels (1941)	Director learns about life by posing as a hobo and taking a road trip; swept the Oscars.
Sunset Boulevard (1950)	Possibly the best film noir ever.
Sweet Smell of Success (1957)	Dramatic portrayal of, oddly enough, PR professionals during the 1950s.
Swingers (1996)	Deeply funny independent, also generated dozens of knockoffs and the rebirth of the swing music scene.
Taxi Driver (1976)	Travis Bickle is one of cinema's most memorable psychos.
The Ten Commandments (1956)	Hollywood has had a long love affair with Biblical epics. This is the most famous of them all.
The Terminator (1984)	He said he'd be back, and he meant it.
The Texas Chainsaw Massacre (1974)	A pioneer of shock horror.
This Is Spinal Tap (1984)	Another must-see mockumentary, the Spinal Tap crew is still going strong today.
This Man Must Die (1969)	My favorite Chabrol picture, dark and brooding (if the title didn't give that away).
Titanic (1997)	Saccharine, but this highest-grossing film of all time says something about what audiences worldwide want to see.
To Kill a Mockingbird (1962)	Heartfelt and moving, this adaptation of the famous novel is top notch.
Tokyo Story (1953)	Yasujiro Ozu's most renowned film; you must witness his unique style in at least one movie.
Toy Story I & II	Set a new mark for animation by mingling unprecedented 3-D animation with a fun, clever story.
Traffic (2000)	Steven Soderbergh won the Oscar for this sprawling indictment of the drug war. Note the use of different film stocks for different stories.
Trainspotting (1996)	Best film ever made about the drug experience.
The Treasure of the Sierra Madre (1948)	Adventure, intrigue, tragedy — a fascinating character study on the range.
Triumph of the Will (1935)	Leni Riefenstahl's infamous Nazi propaganda film — does art trump politics? You decide.
Tron (1982)	Computer animation in the very, very early days. A slice of history.
Twelve Angry Men (1957)	The characters have no names as they debate the guilt of a defendant.
The Umbrellas of Cherbourg (1964)	This French musical has no spoken lines; it's all done in song. Vibrant.
Unforgiven (1992)	My personal favorite western, I hated it when I first saw it in 1992 and eventually grew to love the film.

The Usual Suspects (1995)	Launched a craze of whodunit pictures in the late '90s.
The Verdict (1982)	Paul Newman stars in one of the great courtroom dramas of cinema.
Vertigo (1957)	One of cinema's great thrillers, Hitchcock's greatest achievement. Check recent DVDs for their amazingly restored color.
Waking Life (2001)	The story's a non-starter, but Richard Linklater's rotoscoping animation technique is a revelation.
Wall Street (1987)	One of the best films about business you can find. Michael Douglas is a riot.
WarGames (1983)	Pioneered hacker cinema.
Wayne's World (1992)	One of the only good adaptations of a *Saturday Night Live* skit on film.
West Side Story (1961)	Heralded as one of cinema's great musicals, this is also a good example of how Shakespeare is being updated to the modern era.
Whatever Happened to Baby Jane? (1962)	Infamous thriller, with Bette Davis locked up in the attic.
When Harry Met Sally... (1989)	The standard for modern romantic comedy.
White Heat (1949)	Essential James Cagney.
Who's Afraid of Virginia Woolf? (1966)	Pioneered dysfunctional cinema, with two couples bickering their hearts out.
The Wicker Man (1973)	Horror film meets acid trip in this bizarre and underseen classic.
The Wild Bunch (1969)	Sam Peckinpah's notorious, blood-splattered masterpiece.
Willy Wonka & the Chocolate Factory (1971)	Good for kids, great for adults.
Witness (1985)	Another frequent example of masterful screenwriting.
The Wizard of Oz (1939)	Fantasy gets its start in this early color musical fantasy. There's no place like home!

ACKNOWLEDGEMENTS

This book would not have been possible without the contributions of the filmcritic.com staff, especially senior critic Sean O'Connell, who edited the manuscript. Many thanks, as well, to Chris Loesche, who has generously hosted the filmcritic.com website since its inception in 1995, and to Chris Imlay, for his layout and design work, including the stellar cover. Also, thanks to the Rotten Tomatoes website for providing some of the data used in the book, and for generally being great guys to work with.

I would also be remiss not to thank my family, who have suffered through some truly awful movies in the name of work. Finally, thanks to all the hundreds of thousands of regular readers of filmcritic.com, without whom the site — and this book — would never exist.

ABOUT THE AUTHOR

Christopher Null has been a professional film critic since 1992 and founded filmcritic.com in 1995. Since then, filmcritic.com has grown into one of the Internet's busiest and most read entertainment web sites, featuring more than 5,500 reviews and celebrity interviews. Null's analysis has been featured by dozens of media outlets, including CNN, *The New York Times*, *The Wall Street Journal*, and NPR's "All Things Considered."

Null also works as Editor in Chief of *Mobile*, a monthly high-tech magazine, and his 2002 novel, *Half Mast*, received rave reviews. He lives in San Francisco with his wife Ashley and daughter Zoe.